To Rosey.

With love and in
memory of our
'Valkyrie' days.

Christmas 1986.

Moon Boots and Dinner Suits

Moon Boots
and Dinner Suits

JON PERTWEE

ELM TREE BOOKS
LONDON

For Ingeborg Without Whom . . .

First published in Great Britain 1984
by Elm Tree Books/Hamish Hamilton Ltd
Garden House 57–59 Long Acre London WC2E 9JZ

Copyright © 1984 by Jon Pertwee

British Library Cataloguing in Publication Data

Pertwee, Jon
    Moon boots and dinner suits.
    1. Pertwee, Jon   2. Actors—Great Britain
    —Biography
    I. Title
    792′.028′0924   PN2598.P/

    ISBN 0-241-11337-7

Typeset by Rowland Phototypesetting Ltd,
Bury St Edmunds, Suffolk
Printed and bound in Great Britain by
Richard Clay (The Chaucer Press) Ltd, Bungay, Suffolk

My son Sean, who is dressed entirely by Oxfam and the Army Surplus Stores, has always regarded my penchant for elegant clothing as an embarrassing eccentricity.

When we were skiing in Andorra I said I would need to leave the slopes early, as Ingeborg and I were going to dinner with some friends and I would need to change. He raised his eyes to heaven and sighed, 'Moon boots and Dinner suits as usual I suppose.' I was about to administer an admonitory prod with my ski-stick when it occurred to me that this would be an excellent title for my book, so I stayed my hand.

I hope you will consider this merciful restraint to be justified.

I would like to thank George Evans for his help and for jogging my memory as it became necessary. I would also like to thank my friend Carl Hawkins. I don't quite know why except that he would never speak to me again if I didn't.

Introduction

I was told by my father about my first entrance as he was about to make his last exit.

Conceived on 11th November 1918, I'm the result of one joyful, victorious night. Yet I was the last thing my parents had expected or wanted!

Roland, my father, and Avice, my mother, had reached a sophisticated and amicable trial separation when they bumped into one another by chance, while celebrating V-Day amongst the jubilant crowds in Piccadilly Circus. I don't know if it was the heady atmosphere of victory, or some nostalgic, rekindled passion which drove them into that fateful connubial embrace, but nine months later it produced an unwanted, instantly demanding and very noisy consequence, one Jon Devon Roland Pertwee – me! Jon after the apostle and disciple, Devon after the county, and Roland after my father.

The Pertwee is of French Huguenot extraction. According to our family tree, researched by a French Priest, one Abbé Jean Perthuis de Laillevault and my cousin the late Captain Guy Pertwee RN, the original family of Perthuis de Laillevault were directly descended from the Emperor Charlemagne, who ruled France in 800 A.D., and the line continues unbroken through until the present day. The head of the family is Comte Bernard de Perthuis de Laillevault who fought with the RAF during the last war and is now a celebrated painter of murals.

After the Huguenot purge of 1685, the refugees fled to many countries including England where they settled mainly in Suffolk and Essex.

Norman Pertwee, the veteran tennis player and head of the Pertwee Flour and Flower Company in Frinton, is a direct descendant of the original Huguenot settlers, as am I.

Due to the inability of the English to pronounce the name Perthuis any other way than Pertwiss, it was subsequently changed to Pertwee. This proved a pointless exercise as over the years, even in England, I have been subjected to the following interpretations of my name, the veracity of which I will swear to, having avidly filed them away over the years:–

Tom Peetweet
Jon Peterwee
Jon Peartree
Mr Twee
Saniel Pertwee (A strange amalgam of my son and daughter, Sean and Dariel)
Mr Pardney
Mr Bert Wee
John Peewee (School, of course)
Newton Pertwee (Scientist?)
Mr Pickwick
Miss Jane Partwee
Master J. Peewit
Mr Pertweek
Joan Pestwick
J Pertinee
John Between
Mr and Mrs Jon Perkee

And the most recent addition, from a gentleman in Zimbabwe, assuming presumably that I am a "Brother" . . .
J. Parpertwuwe

In the United States of America, however, I found that if you have a complicated, almost unpronounceable name of Lithuanian, German, Bulgarian, Russian, Czech, Japanese, Polish or Hungarian descent – a name like Pztyltz for example – they will get it in one! But, if you happen to have a simple, honest-to-God name like Pertwee, they are utterly confounded!

I was playing on Broadway in *There's a Girl in my Soup* when our ancient name received its final indignity. The stage door keeper of The Music-Box Theatre was sitting, cigar in face, guarding the keys, when I entered the stage-door.

"Hey Jan!"

As my Christian name is Jon, and as I was being proudly reminded of that fact by the regular sight of it emblazoned in letters of light on the Marquee above the theatre, it was a natural assumption that the cigar-chewing voice was addressing somebody else!

The summons came again this time *molto forte*.

"Hey! *Jan*"

With puzzled expression and finger pointing at my chest, I turned, asking, "*Who? – Me?*

"Yes! *You*! Jan Putrid! There's a letter for you!"

Chapter One

All the world's a stage,
And all the men and women merely players:
They have their exits and their entrances;
And one man in his time plays many parts,
His acts being seven ages. As, first the infant,
Mewling and puking in the nurse's arms.
And then the whining schoolboy, with his satchel
And shining morning face, creeping like a snail
Unwillingly to school. And then the lover,
Sighing like a furnace, with a woeful ballad
Made to his mistress' eyebrow. Then the soldier,
Full of strange oaths, and bearded like the pard,
Jealous in honour, sudden and quick in quarrel,
Seeking the bubble reputation
Even in the canon's mouth. And then the justice,
In fair round belly with good capon lined,
With eyes severe and beard of formal cut,
Full of wise saws and modern instances;
And so he plays his part. The sixth age shifts
Into the lean and slippered pantaloon,
With spectacles on nose and pouch on side;
His youthful hose, well sav'd, a world too wide
For his shrunk shank; and his big, manly voice,
Turning again towards childish treble, pipes
And whistles in his sound. Last scene of all
That ends this strange, eventful history,
Is second childishness and mere oblivion,
Sans teeth, sans eyes, sans everything.

Jacques: *As You Like It*

Very few members of my profession can reach maturity in their careers without acknowledging the Bard in some way and so I've used Jacques' speech 'The Seven Ages of Man' as a peg on which to hang the various hats I've worn throughout my life. The baby's bonnet; the school cap; the velour snap-brim trilby with feathers – which I wore to woo my first love, the delicious Patricia of Caterham-on-the-Hill; the two naval hats which the government kindly gave me to put on during World War Two; and the 'funny' hat which I put on when I entered the theatre. Two of the pegs are still empty because I'm sure that none of my readers would be rude enough even to hint that I might be in my second childhood and, although my profession makes me something of a pantaloon, I *am* fairly lean – apart from a slight inclination to bulge around the midriff – and I'm not quite slippered yet.

First the infant, mewling and puking in his nurse's arms! Well, I dare say I mewled a good deal and probably did my fair share of puking, though I hope I had the good taste not to do it actually in Nanny Hankins' arms.

For some months after my birth, I led a happy, useful and productive life, lying in the nude on an astrakhan rug eating coal, preferring, I am told, the nutritious Welsh seam to the de-vitaminised anthracite nut! This will show that even at *that* tender age I was an infant of taste and discernment!

My mother, however, having taken a good look at me and presumably not liking what she saw, divorced my father for his best friend, a romantic Frenchman named Louis de la Garde, and albeit temporarily, left the lives of my brother Michael and me.

Michael is three years older than me and very different, both in character and looks. He was a much better looking child with round, blue eyes, and for a Pertwee an uncharacteristically short nose, slightly turning up at the end; his looks when he was older were often compared to the golden blond glamour of the then Prince of Wales.

With he and I now being left 'motherless', it was decided that we should go to live with my Granny and my Uncle Guy at their house in Caterham-on-the-Hill, Surrey.

At Caterham, having been successfully weaned from coal and waxed fat on to a combination diet of Glaxo, Robolene and Bengers, with the odd teaspoonful of Gregory Powder when the occasion demanded, I became so stout and sturdy that my poor Grandmother Emily, who used to take me on her knee to read me stories, swayed perilously when she subsequently tried to stand, my excessive weight having cut off the blood supply to her legs. In the event, she wisely decided that it would be better to wait until I had been put to bed, and sing me lullabies instead, a blissful experience, as having once been a concert singer of repute she could still tip a pretty stave.

My grandmother was a dear, plump, Victorian lady, whose husband Ernest, an architect and fey compiler and reader of verse, had died many years earlier. She was of medium stature, with a proud, jutting bosom whose cleavage was ever modestly covered by a piece of lace, and whose neck was always circled by a black velvet band, studded at the throat with intricate beadwork by day, and sparkling paste diamanté at night.

She lived with her bachelor son Guy, spending winters in the town house in Campden Grove, Kensington that my father had bought her, and summers in the country house in Caterham. Uncle Guy was a dear, kind, six foot celibate, with the hereditary nose of the Pertwees, referred to in the family as a 'beezer'. His was original, in that it was built on a bias and had a curious kink to it, with, in winter, a permanent dewdrop hanging from its end.

He would start, stop, re-start, hiccup and backfire his way through a sentence, with an 'I say, what? – now look here – er – can't ever you do it? – no question! – do what you did – er – Mother, this was delicious, don't you know!'

By profession, he was a teacher of elocution!

Frequently he travelled the country adjudicating at Eisteddfods and Girls' High Schools, and subsequently had myriads of young ladies falling madly in love with him – a circumstance that afforded neither him nor the young ladies any satisfaction whatsoever!

Both he and my father were blessed with almost total recall. Ask 'Uncky' what he was doing on Thursday 23rd October 1923, at 8.30 in the morning, and he would promptly recount, in exact and true detail, his breakfast, the headlines of his newspaper and the quality of his bowel movements!

This gift I sadly do not possess. If I did, it would have made the writing of this book a far easier task.

My earliest recollection of Caterham is one of complete and utter frustration on the lawn in front of the house. The sun was shining splendidly, and to get its full benefit I was imprisoned in my playpen, hot and fuming! After rattling all the rattles out of my rattle, hurling my stuffed bear at Mr Green, the gardener, and making many unsuccessful attempts at escape, there was only one thing left to do.

3

Calling my elder – and therefore 'free-ranging' – brother to my penside, I sweetly requested the loan of his finger.

Ever trusting, the gullible Michael did what was expected of him, and dutifully pushed it through the bars, whereupon I promptly grabbed it and bit it to the bone. Michael understandably did not enjoy this experience, but I did – *enormously*! It more than made up for my infuriating incarceration!

My father Roland used to visit us regularly at Caterham. He was the younger brother of my Uncle Guy, and another typical Pertwee – a tall, rangy man with bat ears, sharp features, that 'beezer' again, and a very ready wit to match! Although the background of his life was the theatre, he had started his career as a painter, but despite his considerable talent he seemed to lack the absolute dedication necessary for such a demanding profession.

As a very young man, he joined the Westminster School of Art, then moved on to Cope's School of Art in South Kensington where he was granted a three-year scholarship at the Royal Academy School. In 1909, aged twenty-four, he went to Paris and studied at the famous Atelier Julien, which improved his work to such a marked degree that on returning to London, some of his portraits were accepted by the Royal Academy and were hung on exhibition.

After much heart-searching, he came to realise that painting was not a very lucrative profession and he decided to go on the stage instead. Sir Henry Irving's son, H. B. Irving, gave him his first walk-on, but his big chance came when Violet Vanbrugh wanted a partner to appear with her in a duologue at the Coliseum. She chose my father and they appeared together on stage all over England for a year.

By then, my father had fallen in love and married my mother, Avice, and perhaps it was a combination of financial need and creative aspiration that made him start writing one-act plays, which were, at that time, regularly presented as curtain raisers to the featured play.

After the First World War, which he spent fighting in France, he was hospitalised for three months, during which time he wrote his first novel *Our Wonderful Selves*.

The next few years were eventful. He was divorced from my mother, he wrote, produced and was the leading man in his first full-length play *I Serve*, which gave Edith Evans her first star part in London, and swiftly followed it with *Interference*, directed by Gerald du Maurier, and starring Herbert Marshall and Edna Best. Writing then claimed his time until he was eventually tempted to return to the stage by his old friend Gerald du Maurier in a play called *S.O.S.* His

4

wife in the play was Gracie Fields, making, I believe, her only appearance on the 'legitimate' stage. She 'died' in the first act, and by the time my father came on, she was doing a Music Hall turn at the Alhambra, and by the time he was back in bed, she was singing at the Café de Paris!

Inevitably, Hollywood called, and he joined Warner Brothers as one of their principal scenario writers for several years.

I don't remember my father ever showing me an over-abundance of affection – not that it was really expected in those days when parental love seemed to manifest itself in merely providing for one's children according to one's financial means and status. I shall always remember him as a somewhat remote figure who stepped in and out of my childhood shrouded with a vague indifference. When he married 'D' (of whom more anon) and we lived together as a family, he decided that his loyalty had to be with his new wife, who demanded a very different kind of respect and obedience from us than we had been used to when living with Granny. 'D' had little patience with my childish problems and tantrums, and my father's apparent unwillingness to give me any moral support when 'D' seemed so obviously in the wrong offended my immature sense of rightfulness and justice.

Later, when I was working in Brighton Rep, he maintained this remoteness, in a most classic way. We were doing his successful murder mystery *Interference* and to the anticipatory delight of the Company, he agreed to come down and see the play. That night I peered through the front tabs until I found him sitting by himself in the Dress Circle, and duly told the anxious cast that he was indeed in front. Imagine my dismay when, after the show, he failed to come round backstage and I was left tearfully yet angrily alone in my dressing room, the rest of the Company, doubtful of the truth of his actual presence, having left.

The next day I plucked up courage and rang him.

'Dad?'

'Yes?'

'Why didn't you come round after the show and say hello to me last night?'

'What show? Where?' he said with feigned surprise.

'*Interference*, on the West Pier Brighton, remember?'

'Ah, yes, of course, so sorry old chap I couldn't make it, too busy, you understand?'

Of course I didn't understand and never will, but I suppose in his own strange way he had shown me more than a little concern and interest in my abilities as an actor by going down to Brighton at all. The recollection of him sitting there alone, and his denial of it, will remain with me always.

My first recollection of him was also from my playpen at Caterham. I can only assume that it happened on the same day that I bit Michael's finger. Either that, or I spent more time locked *in* my pen than *out*!

He arrived at the garden gate with a wave of his hat and a loud 'Huzzah!' Michael ran up over the rockery to receive a hug, a kiss and a 'chuck-in-the-air', whilst I was left to hurl myself around my cage in yet another agony of frustration. After what seemed an eternity, he strolled across the lawn towards me with a beaming smile across his face, Michael under one arm, and an enormous tin of Sharp's Toffees under the other. Michael always claims that it was a tin of Mackintosh's, but it was inaccuracies like this that probably made me bite him! What headway my father imagined that a two-year-old boy with baby teeth would make on a treacle toffee I've never ascertained. Perhaps he reasoned that if I could bite through a finger, I would make short work of a 'Sharps'.

Granny was a cuddly soul, and I spent a lot of time with her in my early years being rocked, read to, sung to, or just plain loved! Perhaps my own tactility is a legacy of that love. Every morning when I awoke, now in the toddling stage, I clambered up the steep stairs to Granny's bedroom where I hurled myself into her brass bed and waited for my morning 'buppers'. Delicious! Granny used to have a tray of tea brought up and a plate of fresh French bread, sliced and buttered. These came to be known as 'buppers', for it was easier for me to say 'Can I have another bupper, please Gran?' than 'Can I have another slice of bread and butter, please Gran?'

After my morning 'buppers' with Granny, it was always into Uncky's bed to watch him dress and do about twenty things at once. His morning routine was always the same. He had his breakfast, read the paper, talked to us, was attentive to his mother and habitually finished with a last minute rush out of the front door to start his mile walk to the station. This he did twice daily at great speed, which probably accounted for his never having a day's illness in his life! I only once knew him to take an aspirin, and this nearly did him in, for he promptly changed colour, perspired and panted to such a degree that we thought he was having a coronary! Although Uncle Guy commuted daily by train to his position as Professor of Elocution and Verse at the Guildhall School of Music and Drama, he had an immaculate old Morris open tourer stashed away in the garage. This

6

machine was only allowed out at weekends and holidays and was lovingly washed, brushed, polished and talked to by my uncle who looked upon it almost as a member of the family. We used to go for 'spins', but the preparation for these events was considerable. First, as the roof was seldom up, we had to put on very warm clothes and woolly over-ears hats. Granny had a special motoring hat with a veil over it, tied under the chin, a rug around her legs and her feet pushed into a fur-lined foot warmer, for no cars had heaters in those 1920s days. Then came the awkward rigmarole of assembling and adjusting Granny's glass windscreen and waterproof skirt (not hers – the windscreen's!) The apparatus comprised a series of hinged chrome rods supporting a main screen, and required constant reference to the instruction book every time it was put up. This unenviable task would have been quite superfluous if only Granny had taken notice of Uncle Guy's request to sit in the front, like anybody else of her years, but no, she was adamant – in the back, like the Queen, or she wasn't going!

Once started, the trip was always immensely enjoyable. There were jolly songs, interesting information on flora and fauna, and stops for tea. There was also the endless fascination of watching and listening to Uncle Guy, with felt homburg hat's brim blown up flat against the wind, whispering, coaxing and cajoling the car up anything but the smallest gradient.

'Come on, old girl, you'll make it.'

'Easy now, easy.'

'There she goes, up and over.'

All this while swaying back and forth in his driving seat as if the additional momentum of his shifting weight would aid and assist the ancient motor more easily up the hill. In retrospect I am of the opinion that the occasional change of gear might have helped.

My other favourite mode of transport at that time was with 'Mick-the-milkman' in his 'Chariot', for that was what it looked like when I was little. It was a brightly painted, two wheeled, iron shod cart drawn by Pogo, a perky little horse bedecked with beautiful leather tack and burnished horse-brasses. It had a polished iron reins-rail up front and an open back for leaping in and out of, just like a real chariot, and up under the reins-rail two enormous steel, brass-bound milk churns with dippers of various sizes clanking from their handles. 'Come on, Ben-Hur,' Mick would shout as soon as he had delivered our milk, 'the race is about to start.' I'd bid farewell to Granny, leap into the back, preferably with Mick on the move, and away we'd go. At full trot. At each stop a maid or cook would come out with a large jug covered with a glass-beaded net to collect their milk. I would manfully heave off the heavy top of the churn, while Mick sank his dipper into the now – thanks to the bumpy ride – frothy and creamy milk.

'One pint or two, Sarah?'

'Two please, Mick.'

'With a 'There you are love,' back would go the dipper, on would bang the lid and after a 'Thank you Mick' and a 'Thank you Ben' we'd be off on yet another lap of that furious race.

As I grew older, we could only rarely be inveigled down from our 'Tarzan' tree-house. We constructed a platform to lie down on, a pulley to haul our meals up with, and a rope to swing from branch to branch. This caused Granny intense worry and alarm, but 'Uncky' managed to dissuade her from going on at us too much, as 'boys will be boys, you know, Mother! Although on closer inspection they look more like monkeys the way they're swinging about! And why should you worry about a damned monkey!!'

One day, after performing one of my most spectacular 'monkey' tricks, a 'left-in-charge' – and therefore 'demented-with-worry' – Nanny pleaded,

'Master Jon, Master Michael, come down from that tree at once! You're behaving very *childishly*!'

We were, severally, six and eight years old at the time . . .

★

Granny was such a stalwart soul. She was invincible, unsinkable, a vanquisher, a triumpher. In command, she was like a captain on the bridge, the leader of an orchestra, a cavalry officer heading a charge. At the dinner table when we were allowed to sit with the grown-ups, she was the undisputed mistress of the house. After each course, she followed a strange ceremony, by bowing slowly over the table three times. This was done in complete silence and with grave dignity. Seeing the solemn ritual performed many times, I became convinced that out of respect I too should participate. So when I next saw Granny 'genuflecting', I copied her exactly and gave three respectful bows, so deep as to bang my forehead with a slight thump on the table top.

'What on earth are you up to, young fella me lad?' asked Uncle Guy.

'Ssh, I'm doing Gran's prayer,' I whispered.

'Prayer, what prayer, old son?'

'This one,' I said, demonstrating once again my most reverend bow.

He rocked back in his chair choking with laughter.

'Granny's not praying, old boy,' said Uncle Guy, mopping his eyes with his napkin, 'she's pressing the bell button under the carpet, to summon Edie to collect the dishes.'

For those interested, here is Granny's bell-code –

One ring   'Edie, come in at once, something's not right.'
Two rings 'Send *Cook* in at once. Something's *definitely* not right.'
Three rings   'All's well, come in and remove the plates.'

★

There was hardly any reason for our going further afield than that wonderful Caterham hillside to play. It was approached over a stile, and after continuing along the narrow path, afforded a never-ending series of visual delights. The flowers were there then, the primroses, the violets and the most delicate of all wild flowers, the cowslip. Oh! Where have all the cowslips gone? I have seen nary a one in many years of searching, except recently, a few clumps in Le Lot, France.

As well as cowslips, snakes and swinging trees, there could be found flint, spear and arrowheads in abundance. There must have been a Flint Age encampment up there once and why not? Why shouldn't Flint Age people enjoy a beautiful view like anyone else? It did not take much of a scout along its top-soil before, with a cry of excitement, another souvenir of centuries was kicked into the sunlight. Apart from the spear and arrowheads, there were the daggers, the cutting knives and the flint tools themselves that were used for the chipping and shaping. What a way for a small boy to be transported back through time! During these quests we transformed ourselves into grunting cavemen, and 'Woe betide any passing female,' we threatened. She would've been *grabbed* by her long hair, *dragged* into our cave, and as our imagination could go no further on matters sexual, would've been hit over the head with a bone.

Further along - just before one came to 'View Point' (one of the most famous views in England) – was to us the most exciting place of all. Clambering over a locked gate and struggling through a dense forest of ancient yew trees, we came across our chalk-pit. It rose up from the edge of a 'jungle', like the temples in King Solomon's Mines. At its height was a barbed-wire fence. A part of the First World War's defence against invasion, we were told. From the top, this fence protected our chalk-pit from further invasion, and there was no man, it seemed, prepared to risk his life, fighting through that impenetrable 'jungle' at the bottom. So the cliff lay before us to be explored. In the first minute Michael had cried, 'Hey! look at this.' Five feet up the cliff-face for all to see was the large and perfect fossil of an ammonite at least six inches across. From that day on with the aid of hammers and picks we collected dozens of near perfect specimens: a small chest of drawers was allotted by Granny to put all our best finds in. At one time it was bursting with every kind of flint weapon and a fossil collection that was the envy of any young collector in Caterham lucky enough to get a peek at it. What became of that museum I shall never know. Maybe it was thrown out by an ignorant cleaning lady who decided that it was nothing but 'a load of old rubbish'!

Along the hillside was the 'swinging tree', so-called for its near-horizontal branch of some twenty feet, with small, dipped 'saddle' for sitting in at its end. Being only a few feet from the ground, the 'swing*er*' – with hands on a lower branch – could control the ups and downs of the 'swing*ee*'! The idea, as in all small boy sports, was to flip the 'rider' off his 'bronco', causing him as much grief as possible. Michael and I became virtually unseatable, but the havoc we wrought amongst the local lads was legion.

In the 60s, when I came to live in the area again, my children and I rediscovered and 'rode' the 'swinging tree', but of the flints and fossils there was no sign. Had we taken them all, or had they shrunk back into hiding to await later discovery by a band of deserving lads who would really appreciate the finding?

The cows grazed right across our hillside, kindly depositing many a cowpat for our delight. Why, you may well ask, should cowpats so delight us? The answer lay not in the cowpat itself, but in what lay beneath. We discovered that a sun-warmed pat made the perfect refuge for many varieties of snakes. With a quick flip of a forked stick the pat was overturned to reveal the sleeping serpent; a lunge with the forked stick behind the head and the pinned viper was grabbed with safety and whipped into a bucket, as quick as nine-pence. Luckily we rarely caught anything more dangerous than slow worms and grass snakes, but the latter were so beautifully marked that we were often able to convince apprehensive onlookers that what they saw before them was a bucketful of adders. One day another intrepid serpent-hunter of less tender years tripped before us and fell, literally spraying us with snakes. This time, however, the catch really *was* a bucketful of adders, causing the junior hunters to take to the hills with all speed and a mutual agreement that we should retire from such sport forthwith.

Naturally, something new had to be found, something of 'derring-do', but what? Suddenly it came to me! Finding a crushed cowboy hat, chaps and gunbelt in a corner of the toy cupboard, I realised that as yet I hadn't tried 'the hold up'. So, donning the cowboy outfit, six-gun loaded with new roll of caps, and frightening burnt cork moustache (by courtesy of cook) I advanced boldly and bandy-legged, with all the confidence of my seven-and-a-half years, to the cross roads to await my prospective victims.

The first was a young lady taking her dolly for a walk in her pram – 'Thstop,' I yelled in my best baddie voice, 'hand over your money, or you're dead.'

My 'prey' was not to be so easily fazed, however, for without pause or any consideration for the dastardly end that might befall her, she sniffed, 'Go away, you silly little boy, and play your silly game somewhere else! You'll wake up my dolly!'

And she was off up the hill with a toss of her curly head.

So much for victim number one. I must, I decided, do better with number two.

Hiding behind a wooden paling, contemplating the vagaries of my new profession, I heard footsteps crunching up the gravel road. Unable to see my quarry I lay with madly beating heart until he or she was level with my ambush, then with a loud bloodcurdling yell of 'your money or your life', I leapt out into the road with gun blazing, to find my adversary towering over me – a veritable giant of a man of at least five foot three. He went quite white, teetered for a moment, then thrust his hand into his trouser pocket. Pulling forth a handful of coins, he threw them on the road before me, saying with quavering voice, 'Here take this, it's all I've got!' and with that he hot-footed it up to the crossroads and was away. I was staggered to find that on counting the haul, it amounted to the grand sum of three shillings and elevenpence halfpenny, truly a king's ransom. I could retire from banditry, and did so at once! Some years ago I met an old man who said, 'Pertwee, I know you. You once robbed me of practically everything I had in the world.' To this day I'm ashamed to admit I believe he spoke the truth.

★

Nearby in a pretty little cottage lived a family of husband, wife and daughters, and it was through my close friendship with them that I had my first two sexual encounters. The first, when I was small, only just five, but nonetheless 'curious', was with the daughters. Here I had a double advantage, in that when we were playing 'doctors', my 'patients' happened to be identical twins, and naturally wanted to do everything together. But the venues that I chose for our mutual examinations were not always of the most private, so that one day during 'morning surgery', we were observed in mid-inspection by their indignant and irate mother, with the result that my practice was promptly closed down. Strange to relate, when I was in my early teens, my second foray into matters female happened with my previous 'patients'' mother.

Enjoying a cup of tea and a ginger-snap in her cottage one day, I was softly summoned from above, with 'Jon, can you pop upstairs for a minute?'

Me: 'What for?'
Her: 'I've got something for you.'
Me: *'What?'*
Her: 'Come upstairs and you'll find out!'

Testily putting down my tea, my ginger-snap slipping into the overspill, thus ruining its snap, I reluctantly climbed the stairs to find my hostess sitting on her bed with a very funny look in her eye.

Her (coquettishly):   'Come here.'
Me: 'I am here.'
Her: 'No, over here, close to me.'

Tentatively taking the necessary number of paces to close the gap, I was promptly grabbed by the hips as she fell backwards on to the bed pulling me with her, at the same time emitting a strangled cry of 'Come on, do something, quickly.' Utterly ignorant of what I was expected to do and flushing furiously, I struggled to get off her, missing the whole point of the exercise. It was not until long afterwards that I came to realise, *far* too late, the full purpose of that lady's cunning machinations. Unaware as I was at the time of the appealing and desirable qualities of the Fair Sex, however, I was not to remain forever in that blissful state of limbo – only until the age of fourteen, in fact, when I fell in love – 'sighing like a furnace, but with no woeful ballad made to his mistress's eyebrow.'

It was on a memorable June evening, when my Uncle Guy and I were returning from one of our walks round Caterham Hill that he proposed a drink at the Hare and Hounds, a pleasant old pub to which he paid many a visit. This seemed a manly thing to do, so I readily agreed. 'Bag a couple of seats in the garden,' he said when we arrived, 'and I'll go in and order. Ginger beer all right for you?' I would have preferred to try a more adult beverage but, as I clearly wasn't going to be given any choice in the matter, I thanked him and sat on a wooden bench on the lawn.

'Patricia's bringing them to us,' he said, joining me, 'and here she comes.' I looked up and my heart leapt, for, floating across the garden bearing a tray, was the most beautiful girl I had ever seen. Corn-coloured hair, rosebud mouth, gently rounded figure – an angel in a print frock.

'Here we are, Mr Pertwee,' she said. 'Bitter for you, and a nice ginger beer for – er . . . ?'

'My nephew Jon,' said my uncle.

'And very nice too,' said Patricia, dimpling delightfully. 'You must bring him again. It's nice to serve a good-looking customer for a change.' I tried to thank her as she gave me my ginger beer but was too full of emotion to speak. The Cupid's dart which had pierced my breast had also affected my vocal chords. She sashayed away and my uncle, taking a deep draught of bitter said, 'You've made quite a hit there, my boy.'

I was ecstatic. I had made a hit with Patricia. She had specifically asked my uncle to bring me again. My love was reciprocated.

I went home on a cloud of euphoria. That night I dreamed only of Patricia. Of rescuing her from an assortment of serious dangers, of beguiling her with songs at the piano (my fevered imagination endowing me with not only invincible courage but also musical skills which I did not possess). When I awoke I pondered the matter and realised that my next visit to the Hare and Hounds would only be at my uncle's whim and, in any event, it would not be very easy for me to declare my love properly over a glass of ginger beer with him sitting next to me. I therefore determined to grasp the nettle and ask her out for a walk, thus getting her to myself without putting any strain on my meagre finances.

I bicycled to the Post Office, bought a postcard with a tasteful photograph of a haystack on it and, addressing it to Patricia? c/o the Hare and Hounds, Caterham, wrote: 'Dear Patricia, I am Mr Guy Pertwee's nephew Jon who you met last Thursday in the garden. I was wondering if you would care to come for a walk with me one day. Yours truly, Jon D. R. Pertwee.'

I posted it and bicycled home, confident of an early acceptance. A week elapsed and none came. Nor, in spite of much prompting, did my uncle suggest another visit to the Hare and Hounds; although I had a sneaking suspicion that he had gone there several times without me. I was desperate. I couldn't sleep, I scarcely ate – well, not as voraciously as usual – and life began to lose its meaning. It was then that I suddenly realised I had not put my home address on the postcard. That Patricia, not knowing how to get in touch with me, would be in a similar state of agonised frustration. So I bought another card with a delightful view of Old Coulsdon on it and, writing my address in block capitals at the top, wrote 'Dear Patricia, It was all my fault that you couldn't reply to my invitation as I didn't send my address. To make sure you get this I shall push it in your box. Yours very sincerely, Jon D. R. Pertwee.'

I bicycled smartly to the Hare and Hounds, popped it through the letter box in the front door and went home to await her early and enthusiastic response.

Again nothing. Zilch! Perhaps my postcard had got stuck under the mat or been chewed up by the dog. I was about to cycle to the Hare and Hounds to investigate when my uncle sent for me. 'I say look here Jon old boy,' he said, crossly, 'I've got a letter here from the landlord of the Hare and Hounds. He tells me that you've been sending his wife postcards.'

His wife? Jumping Jehosophat! Patricia was another's! My head reeled, as Uncle Guy went on: 'The first postcard I gather, invited her to take a walk, which I would *like* to think was for the sole purpose of enjoying the sights and sounds of the country. The second, and here I quote, states that "to make sure she gets it, you will push it in her box." An unhappy choice of phrase wouldn't you say?'

I couldn't say anything, I was in no condition.

'If,' said my uncle, 'it is your intention to make a career of adultery, I can do little to prevent it, other than earnestly request you *not* to start it with the wife of the landlord of my favourite pub!'

I hardly heard. My life was in ruins and my world crumbled round my feet. I saw no way out of the tunnel. This black despair lasted all day and well into the next morning. Just before noon, however, I managed to rise above it like a lark and went out, as suggested, to muse on the beauty of Nature, having reconciled myself to a life of total celibacy.

*

A few miles from our house was a famous World War One fighter station, Kenley Aerodrome, which had many wartime flying aces stationed there flying Bristol Fighters and Siskins. Mike and I used to cycle up to the airfield to spend the day lying in the grass and watching 'the intrepid aviators' demonstrating their skills. They climbed straight up from a steep dive, literally hanging on their propellers before peeling off into another dive that took them at full speed right over the trees above our heads. Many a time an under-carriage would hit a small top branch, leaving it to sway to and fro in the stillness of the summer's day. Another favourite heart-stopper was the 'falling leaf', in which the aeroplane at the top of its climb would, on reaching stalling speed, suddenly fall from the skies, spinning round and round like, as the name of the manoeuvre implies, a 'falling leaf'. Then at the last second the pilot would pull out and roar across the field towards us; performing what was later to be known in the Second World War as the Victory Roll. Afterwards, struck dumb by their fearless audacity, we would cycle home without a word spoken.

I think the reason we stopped plane watching was that one day one of our favourite 'aces' powered himself at full bore right into the ground above a chalkpit in Warlingham. Cycling full tilt towards the plume of tell-tale smoke, we became more and more apprehensive and fearful. We had started the mad dash to the scene of the crash with the usual callous excitement of all small boys for disasters, but finished staring tearfully, with gigantic lumps in our throats, at the sight of that burning, smoking wreck with its pitiful charred contents.

Nevertheless, it didn't stop me from going to see Sir Alan Cobham, the celebrated flying ace, with Granny and 'Uncky'.

Sir Alan was an especial hero of ours, and later ran an exciting Air Circus where we saw for the first time wing-walking, dog-fights, hanging upside-down from the under-carriage and clambering from one plane to another in mid-flight. However, in This Year of Grace 1926, he had just broken the World Air Speed Record from England to Australia and back, in his open, single-seater De Havilland DH50, with specially adapted floats for landing in the water, so we simply had to be part of the crowds gathered on the banks of the Thames to welcome him when he arrived.

It was an epic and historical moment. Granny, 'Uncky' and I, suitably provided against hunger and thirst by a bag of Bovril sandwiches and a thermos of sweet tea, took our places on Waterloo Bridge, right opposite the House of Commons, to await his arrival.

He arrived on the dot . . . some five hours later . . . flying right under the bridge beneath us and landing to the roars of thousands, right before the assembled Government sitting waiting on the terrace. For this he received, quite correctly, his knighthood.

★

Although bicycles were our main form of personal transport, just riding a bicycle was not much cop in itself. It needed that additional fillip – something that would amaze and impress the passer-by! So when free-wheeling down the long Stanstead Road, we decided 'running repairs' were the answer. This necessitated turning your caps back to front, leaning forward over the handlebars, legs outstretched behind and balancing without hands. This, because both hands were busily occupied, twiddling and tightening invisible knobs and nuts, adjusting non-existent brakes and oiling wheel-hubs with an imaginary oil-can.

The expressions on the faces of the passing pedestrians were read by us to denote nothing less than unstinted admiration. 'Will you just look at those boys, Herbert! They are actually repairing their bikes while on the move!'

'Well I'm damned, Lottie! Whatever next, I wonder?'

When Michael perfected the equivalent of the pursued cowboy crouched at full gallop on one side of his steed with both feet in one stirrup, the question was answered. Danger was the order of the day! Even *off* the bicycle! To prove he was the bravest of us all, Michael made up his mind to re-enact the tale of William Tell, standing with his back to Granny's sunhouse, with a cox's orange pippin balanced precariously on his head. His chosen archer, one Wally Wall, drew his long-bow and before the assembled multitude of six assorted scruffs, shot Mr Tell Junior in the eye. Well when I say *in* it, close alongside it, enough to cause a lot of blood to flow and various members of the multitude to have the vapours. It also brought sharp criticism of Master Wall's bowmanship from those still able to speak. Wally took great umbrage at this and claimed that *he'd* been under the impression that we'd been playing King Harold at the Battle of Hastings.

★

And so, sadly, we say farewell to baby Pertwee sinking slowly in his cot, hang up the bonnet, put on the school cap and move, with considerable reluctance on my part, to becoming a 'young gentleman' in 'Miss Maxwell's Junior School for Young Ladies and Gentlemen . . .'

Chapter Two

When we first attended Junior School, we lived in Campden Grove, Granny's London retreat. It was a lovely little house, and I have many nostalgic memories of the area. I suppose that, coming from such a theatrically-orientated family, it was natural that the desire to show off in public would appear at a very early age, and I must have been all of four years old for my first performance in a small hall between High Street Kensington and the Earl's Court Road.

It was all Granny's idea, for she was already convinced that as far as I was concerned Laurence Olivier had better look to his laurels. I waited nervously in the wings for my big moment, and then, due to over excitement, unfortunately had one, necessitating a quick change of underpants and white shorts, and a hurried rush back to the stage. Came my cue and with a firm push I was slid out on to the stage. 'Round the corner out of thight,' I squeaked. 'Luckily all of uth armed to fight. "Who go'th there?" cried little Jack, and a thmall voice answered "Quack, Quack, Quack."' 'Bravo! Bravo!' roared the tumultuous throng. 'More, more!' I'd done it. A star was born. Gran was ecstatic and allowed her 'I told you so' look to wreath her proud and smiling face. Naturally, I was invited the following year to repeat my sensational success. Uncle Guy came up with a spanking new verse in which for no apparent reason I wished I were a sausage. I can only tell you that after the shrieks of silence that followed my splendid rendition of the piece, I sincerely wished that I was.

My uncle Guy had a great love and knowledge of classical music in all its forms, and would daily play to us on his gramophone various examples to be read, marked, learned and inwardly digested. This early influence gave me the catholic appreciation that I have for music today. There being no television, the radio and gramophone were the principal sources of sedentary entertainment. I thus grew to have a good basic knowledge of opera, chansons and the popular classics.

I tried to imbue this self-same influence on my own two children but with resounding failure. They took one look at each other after only a few minutes of the chosen 'piece' and collapsed into uncontrollable giggles. A pity really.

Amongst my most treasured memories of life in Campden Grove are the varied cries of the street vendors. The 'Muffin Man' regularly strolled up our road wearing a flat black cap, hard, padded ring atop to facilitate the balancing of a large tray of muffins and crumpets, and his Muffin Man's brass bell ringing to tell us there would be hot buttered crumpets for tea. The muffins and crumpets were covered by a bright green-baize cloth, which, though highly decorative, was hardly hygienic, as I doubt if it made many visits to the washtub!

The Muffin Man rang the brass bell in his right hand without fervour, cling-clang-cling-clang, at the same time crying out, 'Muffins, come get yer fresh muffins!'

When approached by a customer he would whip the tray off his head and bang it down on the pavement. A tower of crumpets was quickly purchased and rushed away to a sitting room to be toasted on toasting forks before a blazing fire.

Another favourite cry was the coster-monger's, so when the first strains of 'the Lavender family's' songs floated down the Grove, I was up straightaway to the window, to enjoy the sights and sounds they brought. The father, pushing an intricately painted coster-barrow with handles to the front as was a coster's wont, led the traditional chant. Grey-tophatted he sang in fine baritone 'Who will buy my sweet-scented lavender' and his family dotted all around him, in long skirts and braided hair in colourful kerchiefs, would hold before them bunches of ribboned lavender as they picked up the chant in perfect modal harmony. These harmonies were of the primitive kind, but oh what a glorious sound they made against the rumbling of the solid-tyred London traffic.

Of our Junior School I remember very little and recently found that some of *that* was wrong! Called 'Miss Maxwell's Junior School for Young Ladies and Gentlemen', it was just around the corner from us, and was ruled with strictness, yet kindness by Miss Maxwell, a lady of not a little authority. That much is correct.

However, to my childlike mind, the school was a big, imposing building with numerous large classrooms on each of many floors. Imagine my amazement, therefore, at passing by some twenty years later to discover it to be nothing but a small terraced house of some two floors only, with a dingy basement. So much for the accuracy of a child's memory.

One day I was summoned from my class by a white-faced Michael, who told me that we were to go home at once as Gran was desperately ill. We ran hand in hand down the stairs and, filled with trepidation, turned the corner of our street to find that it had been covered from one end to the other with straw. This was to deaden the noise of the wheels of the passing traffic. Standing before our house stood a diabolical monster with long elephantine trunk stretching upwards. It was huffing, puffing and blowing its dreadful breath with great show and noise into our Granny's bedroom window. Hurtling up to her room we were caught and calmed by Uncle Guy and a lady in a white coat.

'There's no need to worry,' Uncle Guy said. 'Granny's got a touch of pneumonia and has to be kept very quiet. You can go in for a moment – she's been asking for you.'

We crept into the room like frightened mice to see our beloved Gran lying in bed, completely surrounded by an airtight house of a strange see-throughable material. The monster's trunk intruded through a hole in the side and was still puffing its terrible breath at its victim. It was carefully explained to a near-hysterical me, that this was no monster but an 'oxygen' machine that was helping my Gran to breath and therefore to live. I have since had the deepest respect for all machines medical, for I remember so well *that* one, the one which enabled me to receive so many more years of my Granny's unselfish love.

*

Things were to change drastically. Our father Roland had a friend, Geoffrey Colbourne of Hove, who was dying. Geoffrey and his young wife Dorothy, known as 'D', had a son, and when Geoffrey knew that he hadn't long to live he said, 'Bussie [Dad's nickname], you, "D" and the boy seem to be very fond of each other, and as you are alone with two sons and "D" will very soon be alone with one, when I'm gone, why don't you marry and amalgamate?'

And amalgamate they did in 1927 – where I don't know, as we weren't invited to the wedding. A large London house was bought in South Kensington – 'Red Lodge', 86 Drayton Gardens. Staff was obtained – Kate Cafferty, cook, and Ada Smith, house parlourmaid. We boys were ensconced on the top floor out of the way. 'D's' son became our new brother. As his name was also Michael, we abbreviated his surname Colbourne to Coby to avoid confusion and 'Coby' he became from that day. He was an original and possessed a dry sense of humour that was remarkable in one so young. Dad, who turned a pretty phrase himself, was Coby's principal sparring partner and to the amusement of all held great verbal jousts with him around the dining table.

Coby looked then much as he does now (though a trifle younger), with his hair parted neatly on the right and swept across his head to the left, and a permanent coxcomb sticking up on the crown. He wore spectacles that gave him a 'professorial' look that he never lost – and which stands him in good stead now that he actually is a professor! Sartorially speaking, he was not out of the top drawer and still isn't – managing to look then, as now, like an unmade bed. He was nearer to me in age, being only two years older, and I had perhaps a closer rapport with him than with Michael, who is three years older than me. Although in my experience three was an unlucky number. With three, boys or girls, there are always factions. Two will generally break away, leaving the third to play more by himself. It's a natural thing to do and no-one is to blame. In my case, it was Michael and Coby who were to become the splinter group.

Coby and I shared a bedroom on the top floor, with Mike, as the eldest, being given a room of his own. There was a bathroom with Edwardian bath on legs, and in an emergency, the close proximity of the ever helpful Kate and Ada.

Next floor down, Dad's study where his writing was done, his dressing room, bathroom and bedroom with a big bed for him, 'D' and the dogs.

Ground floor, sitting room with niche, dining room, hall and magnificent mahogany-seated loo with pull-up flush and highly polished lid of same material. It was here that Dad took his daily paper and cut himself off from all outside contact until it was read from cover to cover. How he avoided the legacy of all long-time loo-lingerers, haemorrhoids, is to me a complete mystery!

The sitting room 'niche' was a deep bay window of considerable size, with small, padded seats around it, and enough height and width to rig up some front tabs. With curtains drawn across the windows at the back and lit by electric light bulbs in big jam tins, a perfect little stage was set.

Every Christmas, we performed a playlet in this niche; Roland and our friend Denise Robins, the prolific romantic novelist, were the regular authors and parts were always written for us boys and 'guest stars'.

The first 'naughty' line I ever heard was in one of these plays, involving Roland and Denise. They were secret lovers, about to elope, and in unison delivered these two immortal curtain lines:

'And now for life, life passionate and gay
(*aside*) we'll stop the car at "Hepple's" on the way.'

Hepple's being one of the only chemists at the time where condoms could be obtained over the counter.

The most extraordinary coincidence happened some forty years later. My wife and I were living in Chelsea and heard of a splendid new kindergarten opening in South Kensington. We went to inspect it, as we were looking for a school for our daughter. I found to my amazement, that it was in none other than our old house, Number 86!

That Christmas, on going to see Dariel appearing as a Christmas angel in a Nativity play, I was not unduly surprised to find that she performed the play in the self-same niche in which I had made my first appearance, so many years before.

The basement consisted of the 'kitchen-cum-staff-room', scullery, larder, butler's pantry, toy cupboard and playroom. Here, all hell could break loose. Dad said, 'My floors are to be looked upon as Heaven, and treated as such, but if you want to make a Hell of yours that's your concern.'

Every Christmas Eve 'Santa Daddy Claus' in full regalia of red dressing gown, red Arab head-dress (from a previous sortie into Egypt) and cotton-wool beard, would tip-toe into our rooms to fill our much prized stockings, which, alas, I don't get any longer, but I miss them. Trembling from excitement, we feigned sleep to avoid upsetting 'Santa-Dad'. But as soon as he had left, we felt the contours of the 'woolly-wonders', and tried to establish the exact nature of their contents, before drifting off back to sleep.

In the morning at first light, all three of us gathered in my and Coby's big room and ripped into them. By dint of tradition on the top of each stocking was a wind-up tin racing car. These were pulled out and wound up before you could say 'Merry Christmas' and the annual 'Mo-Mo Races' began. Rugs pulled to one side, the floor being lino covered made a perfect track. A 'book' was opened on the result of each race and stocking presents put up as stakes. In all the years of 'Mo-Mo Racing' I never remember winning a single race. Even after committing in the dead of night, the heinous crime of switching Coby's 'Mo-Mo' for mine, he still won. Being an extremely bad sport, I kicked up such a shindig that my two racing rivals were forced to return their ill-gotten gains to their rightful and tearful owner, on pain of missing out on the 'Biggies' under the tree.

Life was full and varied. There were shopping expeditions by number 11 bus to Hamleys, Harrods and Gamages, our favourite emporiums, as the latter two not only had wonderful sports and toy departments but also zoos with exotic inhabitants. There were honey bears, bush babies, foxes and assorted species of lizard and snake. I determined to own a honey bear *and* a lizard just as soon as my money box was sufficiently full. We travelled on these jaunts quite unaccompanied, for although still young, we were considered sufficiently responsible to roam London at will.

Usually these trips cost us little more than the tuppenny bus fare, as serious shopping purchases were rare. Our zealously guarded pocket money was in the main saved for visits to the 'Kinema'. For threepence we could enjoy a double–feature, newsreel, 'mighty-Wurlitzer' organ recital, with the audience participating in the singing, under the guidance of that splendid 'bouncing ball' that bounced about on top of the words on the screen to give us the necessary tempo and rhythm. If one went to the Paramount in Tottenham Court Road, the organ would be replaced by Big Show Bands like Anton and his Orchestra or Troise and his Mandoliers. This gave me my first taste of the vaudeville side of show business, for those showbands had dancers, singers, soloists and comedians as an integral part of their entertainment. Years later I myself was to appear with Anton on that very stage in 'Cine-Variety' as it was then called, when, in between each big feature, five times a day, I performed my very raw twelve minute Variety Act, gaining little or no benefit except the experience of learning how to 'die' gracefully.

There were times when 'flush' that we actually managed to see four different shows in one day. And on one epic occasion Michael and Coby beat the all time record by making it five. But at a cost of one shilling and threepence for tickets, plus a penny lolly at each venue, what foolhardy extravagance!!

Each Christmas the entire family would foregather at Number 86 for the celebration. There would be Dad and 'D', Uncle Guy, Granny and all her living widowed sisters, including Aunt Decima ('Lady Moore-Guggisberg, and don't you ever forget it') an ex-Savoyard and a great favourite of W. S. Gilbert. She was one of the original 'Three Little Maids' in *The Mikado*, and later married the much loved then Governor of the Gold Coast, Sir Gordon Guggisberg. When Coby later joined the Medical Service in Ghana in 1947 he casually mentioned that he was 'sort of related' to Sir Gordon, and was immediately fêted and taken without more ado to see all the streets and hospitals named after that worthy gent.

We had by now an addition to the staff (by dint of Dad's success as a scenarist in Hollywood) – a butler named Henry. Henry, for some reason known only to himself, would always wear a white tie with his tail suit at Christmas, instead of the traditional black of the correct Major-Domo. It was because of this idiosyncrasy that Aunt Decima annually kissed Henry foundly on both cheeks, being firmly under the impression that he was a smartly dressed member of the family. It was not until Granny had hissed, 'Decima, for the twentieth time, *will* you stop kissing the butler' that Henry was able to break free from her fervent embrace and mutter, 'Good evening milady, can I take your coat?'

Aunt Decima once gave 'D' as her Christmas gift a hideous pink powder-puff on a long tortoiseshell handle. It was immediately put in the drawer labelled 'unwanted gifts to give away'. This was in fact done, on many occasions, for various birthdays and highdays of friends and relatives, resulting in the same 'grateful', 'Thank you so much! How useful!' Useful or not it was *always* left behind and once more relegated to the 'unwanted-gift' drawer. The day came however, when the 'puff' was once more up for grabs and 'D', forgetting the identity of the original donor, gave it to – yes, you've guessed! – Aunt Decima. A hushed silence fell on the room as we awaited the inevitable 'I have never been so insulted in all my life etc. etc.' but no! Pulling the dreadful article from its newly gift-wrapped box Aunt Decima cried, 'A tortoiseshell powder-puff!! How useful! *Just* what I've *always* wanted!!' A fine old lady was Aunt Decima, with tremendous verve and guts. When asked what she would like to do on her eightieth birthday, she announced, after a full second's deliberation, 'Shoot a tiger, dear.'

Next in the pecking order was Aunt Eva Moore, the eminent actress. She had been married to the great actor-manager H. V. Esmond. Her daughter Jill Esmond, also a renowned actress, was often present with her startlingly good-looking husband Laurence Olivier. He was at that time enjoying enormous success in the West End and was destined to become in my opinion the world's greatest actor – as the following example will indicate. Larry doesn't like big parties very much, and equally does not like to be touched, particularly by a stranger, and from behind. He was at a friend's party sitting quietly in a chair having a relaxing drink when an elderly lady crept up behind him, clapped her hands over his eyes and said, 'Guess who?' Larry leaped up, knocking the poor lady backwards to fall A.O.T. over a sofa, with legs waggling pathetically in the air.

Paying no heed to the lady's predicament, he strode outraged straight up to his host and with eyes flashing and finger pointing demanded, '*Who* is that old woman?' The surprised host after a quick glance at the now upright old lady – replied, 'My mother-in-law – why?' At which Larry, proving my point that he is the greatest actor in the world, smoothly changed gear and without pause said, 'Isn't she *marvellous*!!'

Larry and Jill were very good to me when I was young. I used to visit them with Granny at their beautiful period house that was then situated next to Chelsea Old Church. Sadly it was destroyed by bombs in 1941, but happily a little green park for pensioners now exists on the site. Larry had a rascally ring-tailed lemur called Tony as a pet, who skulked in his 'hide' until Granny had entered the sitting-room before pouncing on her hat. Granny's hats were usually of the 'flora' and 'fruit' variety, and so realistic as to be irresistible to the vegetarian Tony. On discovering to his chagrin, however, that fruit *and* flowers alike had the same flavour – wax – he hurled them willy-nilly round the room at friend or foe alike. Larry, Tony, Jill and I became friends, and later when I was a prospective drama student Larry gave me unstinted encouragement and advice. I was to see him perform his famous 'double' – at the then 'New' Theatre, St Martin's Lane. He starred in *Oedipus Rex*, a translation from Sophocles, and played 'Mr Puff' in Sheridan's *The Critic*. After the gouging out of his eyes with the accompanying blood-flow in *Oedipus* during the first half, the audience sat stunned and silent. Few moved from their seats, so overwhelmed were they by his talent. Yet in the second half, within minutes I was wracked with pain from the laughter he evoked with his performance as Mr Puff. He was whipped up into the flies whilst stepping over a roll-cloth, slid down lines, tripped, fell and continually prattled his way through the piece, never stopping for breath. But it was his endless diatribe whilst pinning his tiny tricorn hat to the top of his periwig that finished the audience off completely, and sent them out of the theatre overcome by his greatness!

Aunt Bertha, another fulsome lady of tremendous charm and dignity was next. A splendid pianist, and accompanist to Joseph Joachim and Alfredo Piatti, the international violin and viola vir-tuosos, on their concert tours, she had been marred to Frank Huth, a Jewish gentleman of 'unknown profession'. Their son, Harold, also my godfather, rejoiced in the nick-name of 'Uncle Choo-Choo'. 'Uncle Choo-Choo, brave and fair, I'll make a mattress of your hair', the sonnet went. He, being a star of the silent screen, always took part in the specially-written playlets that were to be performed for the family's delectation.

Aunt Bertha also ran a school for Young Debutantes, to put them through their paces before being presented at Court. By the time I was a manly fourteen, we three, Michael, Coby and I, were much in demand as escorts (bribed!). Suitably spruced up in dinner jackets and black ties, we accompanied the young fillies to Aunt Bertha's soirées and social functions. The term 'filly' was in the main appropriate, for I remember few that did not resemble horses!

Uncle Choo-Choo's much maligned sister, Marjorie, a tall lantern-jawed ex-actress, was an irregular member of this select company of players. 'She is such a ham,' commented my father, 'as she will argue the toss all the time.'

'Ham! Look who's talking,' I thought, for Roland, my Dad, was the biggest 'ham' imaginable. None of the modern techniques of Gerald du Maurier's interpretation of the 'Method' School of Acting had rubbed off on *him*, even after *many* years of working together. Thank God he retired from the boards when he did, and became such a successful writer, otherwise I fancy we would have had a somewhat *deprived* childhood.

I was fond of Auntie Margy, for all the things she'd done and said. She was always kind to me and listened attentively when I was having a trauma over something or other. She could also tell a pretty tale so what more could you ask of an aunt? Married to a British Colonial Officer called Major Angus Duncan Johnstone, she dutifully followed him to Africa to be at his side. It is a good thing she did as being more than a little fond of the grain and the grape he regularly needed her broad shoulder to lean on.

'Tom-Tom' talk being rife in Africa, he soon became known throughout that part of the continent as 'Drunken Johnstone'. 'A most unwarranted reputation,' complained Auntie Margy vehemently, 'he rarely touched a drop!' It was a surfeit of sausages that caused him to stagger – or another attack of beriberi – malaria – breakbone fever – or whatever disease was rife at the time – but never, she reiterated, *never* had he overstepped the mark, and then in an almost inaudible aside she plaintively added, 'I only wish he would.' At the time I failed to understand the wistfulness of her remark . . .

But the tales she told! Once when about to cross a river, going up country for a 'pow-wow' or whatever, her husband was approached by the headman of a nearby village and told that there was an infestation of man-eating crocodiles at the very spot they were about to cross.

'Then what's to be done?' asked the perplexed District Commissioner.

'Call upon the services of my personal witch doctor,' suggested the chief.

'And what will that cost me, as if I didn't know . . .?'

'Only one hundred shillings, Bwana,' grunted the Chief, impassively.

'And so my dear,' said Auntie Margy, 'the bargain was struck and the Chief's personal witch-doctor was sent for. Laying out his sticks, his feathers and his stones, he awesomely invoked the gods, with unearthly cry and mumbo jumbo, to strike the crocodiles with stillness, until such time as the Bwana and I, the "Missie", had safely crossed.

'The water frothed and churned from the thrashing of the tails of a thousand crocs, as the witch-doctor, letting out a blood-curdling scream, threw a sacred chicken into the water amongst them. My dear, may I be struck dumb if I tell you one word of a lie! In a second, there was not a movement! Those crocs lay there side by side, absolutely motionless, as if frozen in a block of ice! "You are safe to cross now, Missie – the gods have so decreed," the headman said, and with that, the Major, I and all our bearers walked over the backs of the once ferocious beasts as if walking over Chelsea Bridge.'

The most surprising part of this story is that I have seen a photograph taken by the Major of this extraordinary happening. With Auntie Margy in the foreground, you can plainly see that the river *is* full up with crocodiles and there *is* a native standing with one foot on a croc and the other on the far river bank. A case of 'You go first, Bwana, Missie and I will follow.'

So *that's* where James Bond got that idea from for *Live and Let Die*.

I remember little of my Aunt Ada other than on one occasion she physically forced me to eat a cold brussels sprout – to this day, the smell alone causes me to retch and vomit. My son Sean seems to have the same aversion, for he once, having assured us that a proffered sprout had been properly swallowed, slept the entire night with the offending vegetable tucked into his cheek like a hamster.

Aunt Ada was once giving a very smart supper party, when in walked my great-grandfather, a rough diamond of a man with gypsy blood in his veins, being born with a Lee for a mother and a Moore for a father.

Permanently concerned for the regularity of his bowels, he carried a rubber hot water bottle into the very room where Aunt Ada was entertaining and taking his coat off, asked a startled guest to drop it down the back of his trousers. Once down, he sloshed his way back out of the room without so much as a nod of gratitude!

Aunt Ada, mortified with embarrassment, went to the piano and, indifferent concert singer that she was, sang a song in which she wished she were a tiny bird.

As my father said in his autobiography, 'had this unlikeliest of wishes been realised, I imagine that she would have flown away, in all probability as far as the Pyramids!'

As well as the family at Christmas, there were friends: Denise Robins and her three daughters, Eve, Pat and Ann (destined, if Denise had her way, to marry *us* three), followed by barristers, judges, lawyers, painters, writers, musicians and actors.

At dinner we ate ourselves to a standstill with Kate the cook being continually summoned from the kitchen to settle 'society' arguments such as one between Aunt Decima and a sparring partner as to which daughter of the Duke of Chatsby had married that South African 'hobbledehoy's' son? Kate, whose knowledge of society was encyclopaedic, pondered for a second, then in her soft Highland lilt rattled off the whole of the discussed Duke's family tree in a twinkling finishing with 'and will that be all madam?' On receiving an affirmative, she gave a quick bob and was away to her own domain to send up more 'cuckoo-spit' pudding and other such delights.

I remember with nostalgia the sight of my father with nervous paper hat from a cracker jammed splitting on his head, involved in a heated political discussion with a guest wearing an equally stupid hat. There are few things more ludicrous than the sight of two grown men locked in verbal combat, completely unaware that they are sporting silly paper hats!

★

Sometimes in the evening, Dad asked, 'Who'd like to see some "All-In" Wrestling?'

'We would!' we cried enthusiastically, and as one man piled into our gangster-like Chrysler and headed for 'The Ring', Blackfriars. This was a very unsalubrious area in those days and young villainy was rife.

Pity the poor motorist unwise enough to leave his car unattended in *that* part of London! As soon as one arrived there, small boys would appear out of every dark alleyway. 'Guard yer car fer yer, Guvnor?' they asked, threateningly, implying that if you were stupid enough to reject their kind offer, your car would not be operable by the time you returned. Flat tyres, scratched paintwork, sugar in the petrol tank. You name it – for persuasiveness, they had it. 'How much?' Dad would ask.

'Half-a-crown,' replied urchin-in-chief. 'But could yer see me now, Guv, I might not be 'ere by the time yer get back.'

On the face of it, this seemed an utterly pointless arrangement, for as soon as the half-a-crown changed hands, the recipient would be off to the nearest 'chippy' for a 'nosh-up'.

But the surprising thing was, that in all the years we visited 'The Ring' once a 'guarding bargain' has been struck, not so much as a fingermark was to be found upon the car under contract and ever since those days I've become a believer, albeit reluctantly, that there *is* a certain honour amongst thieves.

Once inside 'The Ring' itself, it was hard to see your hand before your face, so great was the smoke fog. The noise was cacophonous and unceasing, until the Master of Ceremonies, Mr Frankie Blake, (later my brother Michael's Sergeant in the Field Security Police, and later still my 'Schlapper' during our Vaudeville days), would hop up into the arena, with a 'My Lords, Ladeeees and Gentlemen!' (A bit of wishful thinking here, as most 'Lords, Ladies and Gentlemen' would have thought twice before gracing 'The Ring', Blackfriars with their elegant presence). To a scratchy fanfare of recorded trumpets, the two contestants jumped into the ring, heads covered by grubby towels. At the very sight of the infamous wrestler, Jack Pye, the crowd went berserk, spitting and screaming obscenities at him. The MC would then bellow over the tumult, '*This*, is a five round heavyweight contest between the undisputed champion of the North, Jack Pye, and . . .'

Shouts, boos and catcalls greeted the very mention of his name. Not that Mr Pye was cowed by this in any way, for he would without hesitation give the Nazi salute, lean over the ropes, raise two fingers in a most unseemly gesture and scream to the now hysterical crowd, 'Ah, get fucked.' That *really* got them going.

'Gentlemen, *please!*' yelled the MC. There was a temporary lull. 'Jack's opponent tonight is your favourite – Black "Butcher" Johnson – a Cockney from the Congo!'

This introduction of the 'hero' was followed by loud cheers and the stamping of a thousand feet.

'Butcher' had a 'special' called the 'Back-kick', a blow much favoured by Thai boxers or those skilled in La Savatte. When he seemed at the end of his tether, was when he was at his most dangerous. He would lie gasping over the ropes, eyes rolling like the 30s screen actor 'Stepin Fetchit', but if you watched those eyes carefully you could see a twinkle and a glint in them that told you that Butcher was a crafty bastard and was about to deliver up his 'special'. The eager Mr Pye, sensing that victory was nigh, advanced upon the luckless Butcher snarling and gnashing his gums. He only had two top teeth, the rest having fallen by the ringside many years before. Butcher, carefully watching his opponent from the corner of an eye, shifted his weight almost imperceptibly to his left leg. That was the moment the crowd was waiting for. 'In the tomatoes, Butcher,' they implored. Like a bolt from the blue the right leg shot backwards, catching the unsuspecting Mr Pye right in the 'goolies'. Going completely crosseyed and cupping both hands over his privates, he staggered around the ring, crying copious crocodile tears and appealing to the ref (affectionately known as 'The Spider'), for an immediate disqualification.

The bell for the end of the round rang and Jack's seconds, rushing into the ring, escorted him crosslegged and wailing, back to his stool.

'Serves you bloody right, you bleedin' Nazi,' opined a 'lady' sitting in the front row, shaking her umbrella at the stricken Mr Pye. Jack took a secretive swig of water from his bottle, leaned over the ropes opposite his critic, and, with deadly accuracy, spat a jet of blood-tinged water right into the astonished lady's face. Her gentleman friend, leaping to her defence, attempted to climb into the ring and admonish Mr Pye for his singular lack of manners. Luckily for the gentleman friend, he was held firmly back by accompanying followers of the 'fancy'. At this impending onslaught upon his person Jack Pye took extreme umbrage. Picking up his wooden stool, he advanced threateningly upon the lady's defender. But by now 'The Spider' was angrily ordering Jack back to his corner, and he, finding no-one else in proximity to assault, hit the startled referee smartly over the head with the stool. Bedlam again broke loose, to be quelled eventually by a beseeching Mr Blake. There was then a short respite, during which time 'vendors' walked up and down the aisles calling out their unique sales pitches.

'*Wants* a nice apple?'

(How succinct can you get? No extraneous words here.)

'*Wants* a nice apple, *then*?'

(Note the subtle change of phraseology to prevent boring repetition.)

From the opposite side of the arena came another fascinating exhortation.

'Any minerals wanted 'ere?'

Swigging my mineral, and munching my apple, I felt a disturbance under my feet. Looking down I saw to my intense surprise a ruddy bibulous face peering up at me from between my legs. It was covered in ash, melted ice cream and gunge of every description, the result of his long inexplicable crawl under the seats. Breathing the breath of a buzzard, he asked, 'Oo's winnin'?'

'Black Butcher Johnson,' I replied tentatively.

'Good ole Butcher,' he belched, and crawled back under the seats whence he had come.

There was one bout where a certain Mr 'Tiger' de Lisle was fighting 'Gentleman' Cliff Warner, a British Admiral's son who was later to become a great personal friend. De Lisle was a muscular villain who revelled in his reputation of being the best-hung wrestler on the circuit. That night Douglas Fairbanks Jnr and Joan Crawford, with whom he was then having a tempestuous love-affair, were present. Seated in the front circle in a specially roped off area, they were enjoying the evening enormously, until the Tiger, down on points to Gentleman Cliff and feeling that the reputation of his virility and manliness was in jeopardy, decided that he would give Miss Crawford a treat, by exposing his splendid genitalia. I have rarely seen anything so ludicrous as Gentleman Cliff living up to his prenomen by repeatedly pulling *up* the wrestling tights that the Tiger was equally determined to pull *down*. The MC, Frankie Blake, realising de Lisle's intentions, rushed headlong to the circle, calling upon the services of a fat usher to place himself between Miss Crawford's line of sight and 'Tiger' de Lisle's flashing privates. Doug Fairbanks, quite unaware of the reason for this corpulent barrier, kept yelling at the two overweight dodgers to 'Get out of the bloody way, we can't see a thing.'

Sad to relate neither did we, as Gentleman Cliff had done a sterling job of safeguarding Miss Crawford's moral susceptibilities, by tossing the unprincipled Tiger out of the ring on to the time keeper's table and bell, which, ringing inadvertently, brought the evening to an uproarious conclusion.

I wish 'The Ring', like 'The Windmill', had never closed: for there indeed lay the heart of London at its best.

★

Dad was enjoying considerable success at this time, as his play *Interference* was packing them in in the West End, and he was writing film scenarios for the British and Americans, as well as short stories for *The Strand Magazine* and *Blackwoods* in England, and for *Colliers* and *The Saturday Evening Post* in America.

Being an enthusiastic sportsman, he had always hankered after his own place in the country to go with a number 86, his town house, a place where he could shoot, hunt and best of all, fish, and with the considerable income now coming in from his writing, he was able, in 1929, to buy a new home in Devon, and indulge himself in his hobbies. Rejoicing in the romantic name of Highleigh St Mary, it was also a haven of new delights for us boys and we were able to indulge them by spending much of our holidays, both summer and winter, there.

If you have ever, for the amusement of your children, taken an old shoe-box, cut out the windows and front door with a pen-knife, and put it on the coals of a fire to watch 'the house burn down', then you will know what our four-up, four-down cottage in Devon looked like. Highleigh was perched on the top of a steep hill overlooking a lush valley and could be approached three ways. *One*, by car along the bottom of the meadow, and then up in a broad sweep through the newly planted pine wood to the car port, and its terrifying 'turn-around', with only a horizontal tree trunk of pitiful circumference between you and a 'back somersaulting' death.

Two, along the meadow again, and a sharp turn right up a hill so steep, that only a tank could make it with any degree of certainty.

And *three*, up the long steep path and across the meadow. This journey, undertaken as it was several times a day, caused the blood to course invigoratingly through our young veins.

At the bottom of the hill, and through the valley ran the river Exe, one of the West Country's most renowned trout and salmon rivers. Our property ran a mile or two from Exebridge, along the valley to Oakford Bridge and afforded excellent sport in the pools, mill-leats, shallows and weirs, for the residents. There was a fishing hut with old rods, gaffs, creels, tackle, tins of mummified worms and all the assorted bric-à-brac of those men and women who thought and dreamed of little else than the 'big-one' and its subsequent visit to Mr Tout, the unlikely, but nevertheless true name of the local fish taxidermist, for stuffing, mounting and glass-casing. This corrugated iron hut sat rusting away by the edge of Highleigh pool, the best spot for salmon and also the best spot for swimming, not always a popular combination. It was situated just above a wide, fast-flowing weir, which, with plenty of water running about, could have swept us over the lip and drowned us, but as ever danger was of the essence in our games. So, under Michael's orders – Michael was always our leader, despite his unaggressive temperament; he was much more restrained than me, and only occasionally bordered on the bossy – we built a raft of oil drums and timber, roped it together and sailed it over weir and rapid, on the way to Tiverton. This, without a single loss of life, and only the occasional 'Man overboard!' A fig for Captain Bligh!

At Highleigh St Mary – BC (that is, before conversion) there was no running water, so in our shared attic we had to make do with a china jug and basin. Having no lavatory up there, we had to use 'pos'. 'But only,' threatened Dad, '*only* in extreme emergencies.'

So the pos rested, virtually unused, under our beds until that dreadful day when the minuscule 'caca' was found nestling in the bottom of *my* po! The attack came from all sides . . .

'You little pig!'

'Have you *no* self-control?'

'Don't you ever consider poor Elsie?' (The pretty '£18 a year and all-found' 'tweeny' and a sure favourite in Dad's book!)

What could I say? I was completely innocent of the dirty deed.

'If it was me, it would've been bigger than that,' I protested.

'Well, don't let it ever happen again,' said Dad, 'or you'll really catch it.' I was afraid he meant it literally.

That night I hardly slept a wink. If the 'Phantom Crapper' struck again, he would not go uncaught.

In the early hours of the morning I heard a movement under my bed. Shaking Coby awake and snapping on my torch we peered underneath. There sitting right inside the pot was Tinker, our cat, not only making another little offering, but this time really putting the thumb-screws on by adding a quarter of a pint of pee. Throwing the offending animal out of the window and on to the roof, I marched downstairs and held out the malodorous contents before Dad and his assembled guests.

'There, see! It happened again! But it wasn't me, was it, Coby?'

Coby gravely shook his head. 'It was that stinker Tinker all the time!' The annoying thing was that I really don't think they believed me – even then!

Below the house on the banks of the river stood Highleigh Farm, excellently run for Dad by one Farmer Broomfield and his kin. There were fascinating new areas to be explored which until then were unique in our experience. There were the pig-sties for example, where we watched pop-eyed as the boar was 'introduced' to the sow, and the fact that the pig's 'winky' resembled a corkscrew left us speechless. Ditto the cow-sheds and the subsequent serving of the cows by the bull. 'Gosh! Look, Mr Broomfield actually touches the beastly thing *and* he puts it in! Can't the old bull do it for himself?'

'Course not silly, he might miss and break it off,' said Coby, already showing off his pre-medical-school superiority.

Mr Broomfield actually gave me a dried bull's 'twizzle' as a walking stick once but a rude boy stole it.

After all this, the sex life of chickens and ducks was just plain laughable, and no longer to be considered seriously as a spectator sport. There was a morbid hypnotic fascination, however, for the horrific sight of the farmer's way of killing chickens for the table. To ensure that the meat should be as white as possible, the poor bird would be bled by having its feet tied together with a handy thong, hung upside down from a convenient hook, then with the sharp hooked blade of a penknife have the roof of its mouth sliced open. I was assured by both Mr and Mrs Broomfield that once this was done the bird was off into 'limbo' in no time at all. But by the way it was flapping and thrashing about flinging its life-blood all over its executioners, I was inclined to doubt them. Thank God the RSPCA have since banned such cruel practices.

Parallel to the river ran the mill-leat which slowly turned the mill's huge wooden water-wheel. This, when engaged and set in motion, started the crushing wheel of the cider press on its endless circular journey. Every summer when the day came for the annual cider apple pressing, Mr Broomfield went into the barn where the press lay and removed various things that had been thrown on to it during the winter months, such as an old pram, a boot, several dried up mangel-wurzels, a child's headless doll, last year's Christmas tree and a quantity of straw that Janet, the Broomfield's tabby cat, had had her bi-yearly litter of fourteen kittens on. A couple of buckets of water, quickly sloshed across the crushing area and the press was once more 'clean and ready for them apples'! When queried on the question of hygiene and taste Mr Broomfield would reply, 'You'm mazed me dear!! It's all the gubbins that gives it the flavour.'

In the stable was Dad's big hunter Polly, 'D's' broad-beamed chestnut, Tommy, and our 'hunter', a minuscule fat black Shetland pony called Shadow. It was an extraordinary little beast in that it never seemed to tire. It took itself off to the 'meet' with one of us up, at full trot; rested before the 'off' by going round and round in ever decreasing circles; went flat out during the chase; did its circling routine again throughout the 'kill' and when it was finally time to hack the many miles home at what one hoped would be a leisurely pace to lessen the pain of a red, rubbed-raw posterior, it would be off again at a 'double-time trot' as if there was a rocket up its bottom. This most unenviable experience could best be likened to sitting on top of a red hot vibrator.

From our bedroom through a low bolted door was the water tank room. It was dark, dusty, covered in cobwebs and after a fruitless search for a 'sea-chest with treasure map therein' made the perfect 'lair'. One day while scrabbling about I found a loose floorboard. 'Aha! Maybe *that's* were the treasure is buried,' I whispered. How right I was, for on prising up the plank there before our eyes lay the greatest treasure we had ever seen – a *completely* naked lady. Below the attic floor was Dad's bathroom ceiling and directly above the bath was a wrought-iron 'flower petal' ventilator. Through this ventilator we closely observed the supine soapy body of a beautifully constructed famous authoress who was Dad's guest at the time. Her splendid attributes were all there for us to feast our eyes upon and we, being in the dark with little chance of discovery, hurried not at all our detailed examination. The only intrusion to the whole exciting episode was a continuous verbal discourse by Coby on the finer points of the female anatomy.

'But how do you know all this?' I breathed.

'Because, you ass,' he answered grandly, 'I've read a medical book and I'm going to be a doctor.'

There were daily chores to be carried out at Highleigh which, if done satisfactorily, were rewarded by a few coins of the realm.

They were as follows:–

1) If a boy wound up the gas weight (a Heath Robinson contraption that, raised to the top of a 'gibbet', was party to the making of gas for lighting the house) he received one penny.

2) If a boy went down to the farm and collected the milk he received

one penny, *plus* the additional perk of a sip of the rich cream that floated invitingly on the surface; and

3) If the three boys *didn't* wake up Minnie Hooper with their 'early morning caterwauling', they would receive one penny a-piece.

Minnie Hooper was a widow-woman from Hove with a whiny, wingeing voice that always brought a smile to the lips of those who heard it. She was a funny and highly original lady who seemed to derive great pleasure from being joshed. The most memorable part of Hoopie however was an *accoutrement*, i.e. her spectacles. She had a different pair for every mode – red dress, red specs; blue dress, blue specs; red and blue dress, red and blue specs. They turned up at the corners, or down; they were round, square or oblong; they were plain or covered in sparkling bijouterie; but *all* were held round the back of the head from ear piece to ear piece by a gold link safety chain. 'If I once put them down and mislay them, I'm too blind to find where I put them – if they are chained to me, that eventually won't arise.'

When Dad decided the time had come for 'Hoopie' to be properly summoned from her leaden stupor he would lead us into the garden under the slumbering lady's window and at a given signal, the cry in French of 'Arsh-Dooble-O-Pay-Eh-Air-OO-Pair!!' would rend the air and ricochet down the valley. After a moment's pause allowing the echo to fade into nothingness, the sight of a reluctant Minnie Hooper would be framed in the window. Hair in curlers, covered by a mob-cap, glasses on the end of her nose, and shoulders covered by a hastily-grabbed eiderdown, she would moan, 'Bussie, you really are the bottom! Can't you and your beastly boys go and yodel somewhere else? I was just getting to sleep!'

And this at ten o'clock in the morning!

★

When Highleigh was being converted, Dad rented 'Stag Cottage' in Oakford Bridge as a temporary home. This consisted of two simple Victorian cottages knocked into one. There were therefore two front doors, and two staircases leading up to the bedrooms. Dad and 'D' would say goodnight to us before going out to dinner, and on occasion one of them would return to see if we were all right, opening one front door, mounting the staircase, coming into our bedroom in the dark, passing through it to Michael's room, down the other staircase and finally out through the other door to wherever they were spending the evening. To us, who were perfectly all right, it seemed a pointless exercise, and we told Dad so – that he need not bother to come all the way home just to check-up on our welfare. He looked at us as if we were quite mad.

'What on earth are you waffling on about?' he asked. 'I've never been back to the house to check on you once, you must've been dreaming.'

That, we weren't. Three people don't dream exactly the same thing, at exactly the same time. I'll never forget the cold tingle that passed through my body when he said this, but I *can't* remember if the experience was ever repeated, before we returned once more to the unspooky Highleigh.

★

Sex is not a matter to be organised. I don't know how it started, but around 1929 young lust was certainly churning away in our loins for a flowering young lady called Peggy Burnell. I think it was Roland who put into our three heads the idea that the search for perfect bliss ended at Peggy's gate. So assignments were sought and rendezvous in secret bowers made, in the vain hope that the 'trysts' would be held in perfect privacy. But no, somehow the location of the assignations always leaked out and the longed for twosome inevitably turned out to be a hated foursome. So 'la grande passion' died away and was quickly replaced by competition as to who was to be regarded as the nicest and best-mannered of her three stalwart suitors. Michael, being the eldest, was odds on favourite, Coby next in seniority was evens and I, the youngest in age and experience of life, was 50 to 1 against. But despite dawn rises, when Coby and I would walk silently and without addressing a word to each other, to the 'half-way-rock' rendezvous situated on the road equidistant between our house and Peggy's, the romance came to naught and the whole affair was declared a non-event. On thinking about this for the first time in fifty-five years, I am of the opinion that the probable cause of the romance's failure was the fact that I was eleven and Peggy was twenty-three.

★

We had two local postmen down at Highleigh, one from Exebridge, a Mr Huxtable who delivered on foot, and another, 'Pa' Curtis from Oakford Bridge who delivered by bike. 'Pa' Curtis rode with immense pride a 'Hercules Racer', with bent handlebars. A most impractical machine for the job, but one he swore by: ''Ead down, arse up, that's the way to get up those 'ills, me dear.' 'Pa' possessed the longest eyebrows I've ever seen on a man, which, when he was at speed, flapped around his eyes alarmingly, making vision extremely difficult. He wore an ancient fore-and-aft postman's hard hat and really looked the part. One day he took a terrible toss and landed up in hospital.

'What on earth happened?' we asked.

'Well,' opined a local, 'It seems "Pa" was goin' up Stoodleigh 'ill with 'ed down against the wind, when 'is foot slipped off 'is pedal, down further went 'is 'ed and as luck would 'ave it, 'is eyebrows caught in the front spokes of 'is bike, flippin' 'im over the 'andlebars.'

A folk tale no doubt – but it's always left me with a wonderfully funny mental picture. 'Pa' lived to a very old age and I was glad to have been able to visit him before be cycled off to that 'great Post Office in the Sky'.

Mr Huxtable, *our* postman, was a man of astonishing stamina, his daily deliveries on foot covering many many miles. It was once calculated by a local 'schoolie' that in fifty years he had walked the equivalent of two and a half times round the world, and this in gum boots. 'You can just imagine,' said the schoolie, 'the condition of his feet!!' Mr Huxtable was, however, fortified somewhat by regular 'stop offs' at 'locals' along his route. Here, he would be invited inside to partake of a little refreshment, like a glass of scrumpy cider or two. Now this scrumpy was a killer and, bearing in mind the number of stop offs, and the subsequent intake, his resilience was startling. However, after tippling a few tastes and coming to the end of his round, there was one thing he simply would *not* do, and that was climb up our hill. He would stand by the gate at the bottom of the meadow rocking gently on his feet and look up, fighting for focus.

Then with a heartfelt 'Cor 'ell, I bain't goin' up there this time a' day, let them young buggers collect 'em!' he would hurl the letters over the gate into the mud and the sometimes mint-fresh cowpats. So there was yet *another* penny to be earned by the boy who collected these letters, and couldn't care less about the cows' stinking effluence upon them.

★

When we had grown out of Shadow, or rather when Shadow had grown out of us, Dad bought us an Exmoor pony. 'The perfect mount for this kind of country,' he assured us.

If you went to Bampton Fair in the early 30s, the pick of a bunch of wild Exmoor ponies could be bought for the sum of five shillings.

'But how do you get it home?' one would ask.

'Now you'm bought'er I doan't give a bugger' *ow* ye gets 'er 'ome,' would be the reply. '. . . Er – 'ang on though, young maister – 'ave ye got a car or a cart wi' ye?'

'Yes, sir, a car.'

'Well you could try puttin' an 'alter round 'er neck and towin' 'er 'ome.'

And so back home one would have to go, at nought speed, in low gear, with a wild, prancing, kicking, 'bucking-bronco' zig-zagging its way through the narrow lanes. Once there, it would have to be broken – before its new owner was, that is, for Exmoors are the most cussed and independent of all ponies.

Trained, however, they are the most marvellous ride. Maggie, for that was her name, had tremendous stamina and always finished well up front when we went hunting, much to the annoyance of the principal huntsman, Percy Yandle, who, with his farmer brothers Ernest and Jack ran 'The Devon and Somerset Staghounds'. Percy must have been the only huntsman in the world who would gallop full tilt right through the middle of his pack, shouting fit to bust, 'Out the way you buggers, get out my fuckin' way.' Maggie was usually in his way too, causing many a tongue-lashed encounter. She also caught a few from me, as she delighted in the habit of galloping full speed down any precipitous gradient, and only coming to a halt when a few inches from the oncoming hedge or wall. This despite my lying right back on the beast's rump, feet and stirrups up parallel, sawing her bit frantically from side to side, and emitting vain cries of 'Whoa! Whoa back! there you ruddy idiot.' If only *my* four letter word vocabulary had existed then.

Among many notable members of the Hunt was the Master of Hounds himself, a retired Colonel who, having lost an arm during the war, permitted his groom, Toskett, to strap him permanently into the saddle, thus making the whole outing somewhat foolhardy!

Throughout the Hunt, the most difficult undertaking was the passing of the Colonel's water. Rather than be unstrapped and have to dismount, he allowed the faithful Toskett to unbutton his fly, take out his Private, and point it to whichever side afforded the most concealment. This chore the Colonel could not do himself, as being one-armed, he chose to control his horse, rather than the stream of his urine. One day in full cry, the Colonel was taken short for the second time, so veering off into a convenient clump, he bade Toskett do the necessary. Fly-flap unbuttoned, the willing groom plunged his hand into the dark recess to grasp his master's person, but this time something was wrong. His hand went first this side of the trouser, and then that, until the by now bursting Colonel cried out, 'Come on, man! What are you fiddlin' about down there for? Get on with it for God's sake!'

The wretched Toskett, looking apprehensively up into his master's suffused face, stammered, 'I'm very sorry, Colonel, but I can't find it!'

'Can't find it?' roared the Colonel, 'can't *find* it? Good God, man! *You* had it last!'

Those who have read my brother Michael's autobiography *Name Dropping* might remember that he included this very same story. He also said that he had just read the identical anecdote in *Out of My Mind*, written by his good friend Monja Danischewsky, who attributed it to General Carton De Wiart VC, who also had one eye and one arm.

Humorously, Michael says that from this, the reader can draw one of two conclusions.

1. That one of them is a liar.
2. That both of them are liars.

My own drawn conclusions, having heard the story personally attributed locally from my father over the dinner table, are *three*!

1. That one of them is a liar.
2. That both of them are liars.
3. That all three of them are liars!

★

Life at Highleigh was not over happy for me, as being the youngest brother I was the odd man out. For example, Mike and Coby were old enough and responsible enough to be gun owners and were the proud possessors of 'Diana' air rifles. Armed with their weapons they would go 'pinging' for rabbits. Under sufferance I would be allowed to go with them, not as a hunter but as a 'watcher-man'. This was as boring a bit of casting as my son Sean's best friend's sister Hjordis who was always cast as a lorry.

I hated being the 'watcher-man' almost as much as I hated being 'Stinkers' the butler, another of my regular roles. So for a few years I swallowed my pride and steadfastly saved up for my 'Diana' fowling piece.

The great day came when, proudly armed, I presented myself to the two senior sportsmen. Waving my gun above my head I informed them that I had at last obtained the required permission from Dad, and that I was now ready for the 'beat' of Ramsbottom Wood. Imagine my disappointment, therefore, when they said '"Pinging"? but we don't go "pinging" any more.' Shooting rhinos and bears on one's own turned out to be a rather lonely sport.

There was a time in my life when I would shoot and kill any creature that moved, like the pot-valiant Spanish huntsmen who go out with hounds, shot guns, shooting bags and all the paraphernalia of the chase, to blast into oblivion anything the size of a sparrow. Served at table the consumer of one would be presented with more lead than flesh.

It was very much in this frame of mind, that one lonely day I was sitting, my back to a tree, contemplating nothing, when a young bird, just now fallen from its nest, hopped unsuspectingly towards me. To alleviate boredom, I had been aimlessly thrashing at the grass with a long thin switch. Imagining I was a hooded inquisitor perhaps? A charioteer? So when the poor bird came within striking distance, without hesitation I brought the stick down. I caught it only a glancing blow and it hobbled off, with myself in full cry slashing and cutting at the wretched fledgling until, with a final twitch of its tiny body, it lay dead. For what reason I had done this dreadful thing was, and still is, a complete mystery. I sat squatting on my haunches and stared at the now lifeless little bird, stirring it anxiously with my stick in the vain hope that it was not dead. When the realisation that it was indeed no longer living hit me, I emitted a low keening moan, and with a gasping and heaving of my chest, burst into uncontrollable sobs. I do not remember how long I stayed and wept, but some considerable time elapsed before I had got sufficient control of myself to stir from that place. When I did, it was to make a small grave, with a headstone, on which I scratched 'Here lies a killed bird. RIP.' I have never before told anyone of this episode for it has always filled me with a fearful sense of shame. Perhaps this confession will act as a palliative. We learn. But at what cost!

*

As a chronic sufferer from vertigo, it always surprises me that as a boy I spent so much time up trees and cliffs, so when 'Whymper' Coby observed that the local 'Matterhorn' quarry had not as yet been scaled, the challenge did not long remain uncontested.

The day of the attempt on the north face soon arrived, and after a cursory hand shake and wishes of good luck, the ascent commenced. Up and up the stone quarry we went, hand and toe, until eventually, after some forty-five minutes of hard nerve-jangling climbing, I managed to reach the lip of the summit. Coby was some twelve feet behind me when he started to slip very slowly backwards. The angle at the top was less vertical and he was lying on the loose shale at about fifty degrees. But no matter how hard he tried to stop his inexorable fall by digging fingers and boots into the pebbly earth, his gradual slide down was not to be averted and if I did not think of something quickly he would almost certainly plunge to his death. Rope? None. A belt? Too short – what could I find that would take his weight? An urgent forage produced a broken bough. This proved to be useless as on bending, it snapped in two. Meanwhile, Coby was slipping further and further towards the drop.

A branch from a dead tree was the only thing left of the required length, so lying face down, I gingerly handed Coby the end of the rotten limb, and telling him to hang on tight, started to draw him slowly upwards. Anything more than a gentle continuous pull and it would have disintegrated . . . Inch by inch he wriggled his way up those last few feet, never looking back but just keeping his eyes fixed on mine as we silently entreated each other to make no mistakes. Thank God we didn't, and in a few minutes he was over the top and looking down at the two hundred foot drop that would have made his a very short life.

Moral:– in an emergency, don't bend dead branches – just pull on them, v-e-r-y g-i-n-g-e-r-l-y.

★

My father, being an inveterate gambler, decided when I was about ten that during the summer holidays we should return to the land of our forefathers, and whilst he was playing chemin de fer in the casino, we should try to pick up our grass roots.

So we lived in various houses in Dieppe, Veules-les-Roses and best of all, the Auberge du Clôs Normande at Martin Eglise. There we learnt to speak reasonable French and enjoy good food and wine because Madame Démarquais, la Patronne, was above all else a cook of quality. I went back to the Auberge two years ago with my family and the half-century had passed it by without even rippling its surface. The bedrooms smelling of beeswax were still uncarpeted, the plumbing complained but still didn't function, the mattresses sagged, the beds creaked and there in the corner behind a tattered curtain was the chipped enamel bidet on its portable stand. Evidently Madame had no intention of allowing it to go anywhere. In the yard on the wall outside the dining room there was fixed the same old china water tank, with its cemented-in basin beneath, and a hand towel hanging on its original nail. Time certainly stood still in Martin Eglise, but Madame was prompted to observe that in her considered opinion, I had changed a little. It was here in 1929 that Dad started playing 'Pooh-Sticks'. For the uninitiated, the players had to find a stick, leaf, cork, tin or whatever, mark it with a mast of colour for identification, and drop it, at a given signal, over the edge of a bridge into the fast flowing stream beneath. Rushing to the opposite side of the bridge to ascertain their positions, the contestants would then run along the banks of the river that coursed through the village, shouting gleefully at successful navigation and cat-calling disasters, such as sinking, going aground, or being caught up in whirling eddies. At the end of the village was another little bridge, where participants jostled and shoved each other for the best position to see the finish and acclaim the winner. Dad, being an artist, would have none of the tin and twig type of boat. It was beautifully carved corks with orange-stick masts and lavatory-paper sails for him, and for perfect balance a fifty-centime copper keel was slotted into the bottom of the hull.

'There, you see how true she runs, me hearties?' cried Dad, RN.

We had to agree, for he was right. So from that moment on it was 'all hands to make and mend'. You've never seen such a collection of well designed and original craft that were entered for the next big race. (My wife Ingeborg when playing 'Pooh-Sticks' last year produced a tin with both ends cut out. 'It will go much faster, because the water will rush in and out so quickly,' she explained excitedly. She was bitterly disappointed when her beautiful shiny boat sank like a stone.)

'Monsieur Pertwee?' It was the Mayor Fernand Deglas who had approached. 'Regarding the question of your boat races.'

'Oh, I do hope we haven't been disturbing you,' said my father. 'My friends and children are inclined to be a little over-boisterous and noisy.'

'Au contraire, mon cher Monsieur Pertwee, the Committee have approached me, to approach you, to issue a 'Challenge des Bateaux', le village de Martin Eglise contre la famille Pertwee. You will accept?'

We accepted all right, and throughout that summer holiday the Pertwees and the villagers of Martin Eglise were locked in battle at the weekly Sunday regattas. The time and skill that went into the making of those minuscule craft was astonishing and the 'needle' atmosphere intense.

I shall never forget the sight of all those wildly gesticulating figures, charging down the river banks, shouting their instructions to unmanned toy boats in English and French patois. The French exhortations frequently bordering on the hysterical, but that was understandable for being gamblers by nature, it was imperative to have a little flutter of a few francs on the results of each race, 'just to make it interesting'.

When I was strolling along the river bank on my last visit, in 1975, two small *gamin* boys came leaping and shouting along the path towards us. A quick look into the stream soon found what I had expected, two cork boats were rushing in and out of the eddies on their way to the finishing posts by the lower bridge.

'Qu'est-ce que vous faites?' I cried. 'Qu'est-ce que c'est le nom de votre jeu?'

'Le boat-race anglais, le boat-race anglais,' they replied breathlessly as they tore by.

Fifty years jumped in one second as my returning shout of 'Vive le Pooh-Sticks' echoed joyfully through the summer's eve.

★

A certain morning at Highleigh in 1935 when I was fifteen, pushing sixteen, is forever engraved on my mind. I was sitting on the terrace when the post arrived, and there was actually a parcel for me. Excitedly tearing it open I revealed a cardboard Easter Egg containing a very handsome wrist watch.

'Cripes!' I said, looking at it admiringly. 'Will you look at that! I wonder who it's from? There's no card *or* letter with it.'

'From your mother, I expect,' said my father.

I stood stock still.

'You mean "D"?'

'No, I mean your mother.'

'But, I haven't got a mother,' I protested. All my life I had believed that my mother was dead.

'Well, you have, and she must've sent you that watch. I suppose that it's time you and she met.'

'B-b-but, who is she, I mean where does she live and all that?' I stammered.

'You can find that out for yourself, I've no wish to get involved.'

And with this unexpected bombshell duly dropped, my father turned and walked back into the house.

I sat staring at the watch, as it zoomed in and out of focus, trying to make some sense out of this shattering piece of information. It was too much for me to take in. I have no recollection of discussing the matter with either Michael or Coby, so I can only assume that they were not there, and this was a subject that I certainly could not discuss with 'D' I thought, probably quite mistakenly!

After all, a child's estimation of an adult is fundamental. It is a black and white opinion without any of the concessions we make in later years. Basic feelings like love and hate are still undisguised, for the young child has not yet learned to reason with the habit of mind.

When my father married Dorothy and she became my stepmother, I hated her from the bottom of my childish heart. I missed Granny, her warmth and her love, and I resented 'D's' efforts to discipline me, to bring her own blend of order into my life, which up until then had been such a happy one. And when committing that classic boner of taking my father's side in an argument with 'D' I found myself in no-man's land!

Like most adults, my father strongly resented my immature but loyal interference. It is hard for me to say whether 'D' tried to replace the mother I didn't have because I never got to know her well enough.

Later, after her divorce from Roland, when I was a young man and living on my own, I saw her from time to time. She appeared to be an assertive, strong-willed woman who vigorously believed in her own convictions. If it hadn't been for the memory of those bleak childhood days, I feel that given time, I might have got to like her very much.

In the circumstances, all my tangled and confused brain could come up with, was to get to Granny as soon as possible and ask her. This I did, and as usual she was wonderfully tender and understanding. It seems that she had been in touch with Avice, my mother, ever since the divorce. This was remarkable when you consider my grandmother's Victorian upbringing and her strict adherence to the moral code. One would have thought that following the dreadful scandal the case had caused in the press, she would have 'cut' my mother completely out of her life, as she expected her son Roland to do. But possessing the character she had, she swallowed her pride and with great humanity, kept in touch with my mother, informing her regularly of her two small sons' progress. Granny was most patient in her explanation of the break-up and even opened up her deed box to get out all the press-clippings for me to read.

However, my father being a private man, preferred to leave his private past undisturbed, and my only real knowledge of my parents' divorce stems from my father's autobiography, *Master of None*. With great sensitivity he described his return from the war and the vague intuition that all was not well, followed by the stark realisation of his wife's affair with one of his best friends . . .

Avice was still asleep when I woke next morning. It was my habit to shave in L's room [La Garde's] which adjoined ours. As I opened his door, a folded page of a Walker's Loose-Leaf Diary, at the instance of a draught, fluttered past my feet. I thought it was the page on which I had scribbled the list of snapshots we were going to take. So I stooped and put it in my dressing-gown pocket. L, too, was asleep, and I stropped my razor and soaped my chin without waking him. In those days I used to shave with a knife, and a knife has to be wiped on something. The little packet of papers which hung by the washstand had been exhausted the day before, so I took the Walker's Loose-Leaf from my pocket to wipe the razor on. The leaf was folded down the centre, and when I opened it I found that it contained a few words in Avice's handwriting. Except that they told L she loved him, I do not remember them.

I have often tried to reconstruct what went on in my head at that moment of discovery. I am very sure, however, that anger had no part in it. I remember standing looking at him with an open razor in my hand. But I had no thoughts of doing him an injury. In some indescribable way he had become a new person – a stranger about whom there was an extraordinary interest. Something which I had believed to be wholly mine had passed into his keeping. Or hadn't it? I don't think I even bothered to reach out after that straw. Avice was much too serious to stumble into a trivial love affair. I knew beyond hope that she now felt for him what once she had felt for me.

Granny and I talked it over until the early hours, and I could see how bitterly she felt that anybody could have walked out on her handsome, talented son and his two little boys. It was something incomprehensible to her and would forever remain so. Louis de la Garde was a viper in her bosom, and should have been stamped under foot, but, she grudgingly admitted, he did seem to make my mother happy, 'and that was something, not much, but something.'

My brother Michael had evidently already made contact and was seeing our mother fairly regularly, but Granny thought it better not to involve him in my first meeting. At least I *thought* that this was to be our first meeting but I was wrong.

Over the years a mysterious Mrs Guard, introduced to us by Dad as an 'old friend', had periodically come to Number 86 for tea. Usually 'tea' for Dad was nothing but a cuppa, and a digestive biscuit, to be enjoyed privately in his study during a fifteen minute respite from work. But when Mrs Guard came, Michael and I were invited down to join them. Then tea was an occasion remembered principally for its fare, rather than its guest, for there were sandwiches, biscuits and pastries on these visits. Not knowing that this pretty, fine looking lady was our mother, we couldn't understand the reason for being summoned to the presence, and spent most of the time stuffing ourselves rather than talking and answering the poor woman's agonised questions. Things that she desperately wanted to know seemed to us 'boring' and 'typical of grown-ups' and not worthy of much consideration when answering.

Questions like 'How are you enjoying school?' 'Do you two get on well?' 'My goodness aren't you tall?' and 'Aren't you like your father?' were too stupid and obvious to be worth our attention. The first question worth answering was 'What do you want to be when you grow up?' 'An actor, of course.'

It did occur to me that Mrs Guard's attention was focused more on us than on her 'friend' Roland, but that didn't cause me any suspicion, and never for a second did I think that the lady anxiously and nervously sitting before me was my mother. Once tea had been consumed, the beano was over as far as we were concerned and we couldn't wait to leave and return to the fascination of a caught mouse or some such divertissement.

But now the moment had come for a confrontation and, armed with the address of my mother's house in the country, I set off to find her.

She was an elegant, attractive woman, slim, with gently greying hair and sharply chiselled features. She walked like a dancer, but wasn't. She was more than a little startled to find me standing before her, but after the initial shock had worn off, welcomed me with joy, loving hugs and promises of great future happiness. Sadly, this happiness never quite materialised, as I found it hard to accept that she had not made sufficient effort to enter my life earlier and although she proceeded to spoil me rotten, I could somehow never think of her as my real mother, only as a rather friendly aunt.

She lived in a beautiful Elizabethan manor house in Holtye near East Grinstead. There was a wirehaired terrier of great sagacity and character called Jim, and a friendly duck called Quacker, who left permanent cards on the Persian rugs.

My mother's brother Keith Schöltz was a dapper disaster. His life had been fraught with failure from the outset, but it never seemed to get him down.

With very little money, he managed to effect the appearance of an affluent member of society. His grey flannel trousers, of which he had two pairs, were always immaculately ironed and pressed; his tweed jacket, of which he had one, never showed a crease, and his dinner jacket was frequently rubbed with sandpaper to keep down the shine. To top off the 'Born in the Purple,' effect, he sported a monocle on a string, and liked to be addressed as 'Captain', a slightly upgraded legacy of World War One.

Uncle Keith was a charmer and in his day considered something of a masher with the ladies, but somehow, no matter how hard they tried, none of them managed to get him to the altar. This was probably just as well, as he was a man very set in his ways and would've driven his wife to distraction.

He used to regale me with wonderful stories of his life with my mother in South Africa, where my grandfather, Doctor Scholtz, had I believe been Cecil Rhodes' personal physician. The doctor had been a secret emissary between Lord Roberts and President Kruger during the Boer War, and I still possess a fascinating collection of letters that they wrote to each other. Reading between the lines, the good doctor seemed to be walking a very thin line between being an emissary and a spy!

Uncle Keith said that when he died, he would leave me not money (for his position as a cinema manager was not the best paid of professions), but his one good lung, which he said should be worth a fortune from all the gold dust he had sucked into it, while working down the mines.

As he liked to tell it, his other lung had been removed years before to pay off a long-standing debt. In truth, he had stayed down the mines too long, and had developed chronic silicosis.

His one great claim to fame was that he had been a member of the Magic Circle. There was nothing he liked to do better, than to stupefy me and my friends with his close-up magic, including one trick which I've never seen done before or since.

As I remember it, I took a new, sealed pack of cards, thrust a table knife through its paper wrapping, and separated the pack into two piles, face down on the table. The Captain would then name the two cards on the bottom of each pile. Now that *was* magic! As to me, my Uncle Keith was a magical, lovable, useless old rogue, and I loved him!

I thought I would hate my mother's husband, the infamous Louis who had appropriated her when I was a baby; on the contrary, I liked him enormously, and could see straight away what had attracted my mother to him. He was then the Managing Director of the big Lex Garage chain and extremely well set-up financially. With this beautiful house, a large staff and a flat off St James Square sw1., Mother and he led a very comfortable existence.

Louis, who, when in a reverie, unconsciously twiddled his hair into a long, 'narwhal-like' spike at the top of his head, was of French birth and liked to live like a Frenchman. Tall, slim and elegant with iron grey hair, he and Mother were a pigeon pair. Remarkably, despite the disparity in our ages, we were of identical build, so Mother, noting the indifference of my garb, took me to their London flat and searched through Louis' cupboards like a dog after a buried bone for my new wardrobe. There were suits from Hawes and Curtis and Huntsman, shirts and ties from Turnbull and Asser, shoes (hand made) from Lobbs and hats from Scotts. I was the best dressed young blade in Britain and it did my stock in the eyes of the young ladies a power of good. Louis seemed quite unconcerned that this stranger in his midst was stripping his cupboard bare; if it gave Avice pleasure, that was all right by him.

The sweetness and light was not to last however, for one day when we were out shopping I noticed something in a window and called out, 'Mother, *Mother*, look at this.' She stopped dead in her tracks, fixed me with an icy glare, and hissed, 'Never, but *never*, call me Mother in the street.'

That night I lay in bed, trying to see her point of view. I was probably expecting too much. After all, two near adult sons had suddenly come into a life that until then had been without any encumbrances. After those initial introductions of 'Jack, Phyllis, this is my youngest son, Jon,' and the ensuing platitudes of 'No really? He can't be, you're *far* too young to have such a big boy', she realised that the admission of our existence aged her in the eyes of her social circle.

For my part I had desperately wanted a mother to love, and be loved by, all my life. To find her and be rejected by her (for it was a form of rejection) was irreconcilable. From that day forward our relationship trod a rocky path, culminating in her refusal some years later, to allow me to sleep on a sofa in her little cottage. (Louis' death had left her in much reduced circumstances.) I was in the lower-deck of the Navy at the time and my cousins and some other relations were staying in Mother's cottage for Christmas. On asking where I was to sleep, Mother said, 'In the pub in the village.'

'I'd rather sleep on the sofa, so we can all be together,' I said sentimentally.

48

'No, dear, in the pub and you're to have your breakfast there as well.'

I was pretty miffed. After all, I thought, I am her son, and I wouldn't even mind sleeping on the floor! In the Navy I was used to that. But she would have none of it. The next morning, arriving with gifts, I banged on the cottage door and loudly demanded that the portal be opened to admit Santa Claus himself.

'Is that you, Jon dear?'

'No, it's Santa, bearing gifts,' I replied rapidly losing confidence in my assumed identity.

'Yes, well it's a bit too early, go back to the pub, have your breakfast, and come back again in a couple of hours.'

From then on our affiliation deteriorated to one of little else but 'keeping in touch' and the very occasional visit.

I was in Australia in 1948 when I received a telegram saying that she had died aged sixty of a heart attack. She was much missed by many friends who loved her dearly, but I would be hard put to it to say that I genuinely felt as a son *should* feel when his mother had died.

Chapter 3

'The whining schoolboy with his satchel
And shining morning face, creeping like a snail
Unwillingly to school.'

I must now go back over the years, and fill in the gaps between
holidays. My childhood was not entirely filled with wrestling matches
and Devon hunts, alas. Let me tell you that I was the most unwilling
creeper on whom you could ever clap an eye! Not that I *disliked* school
– I *loathed* it! Passionately! It would be lovely to tell you stirring tales of
prefect Pertwee the Pride of the Prep, or Pertwee minimus, the Hero
of the House. But I did *not* win through. In fact the only achievement
in the four schools I attended, was to have been beaten more often and
more thoroughly than any of my fellow pupils, simply because I
firmly, if painfully, refused to conform to the norm, and in my day,
conformity was the rule. If you broke that rule, you were beaten. Like
a carpet. 'We shall make you, or break you,' they cried. Well they
never succeeded in breaking me, but they did make me even more
determined to oppose what I considered to be injustice.

On leaving Miss Maxwell's 'Academy', I followed Michael to
'Aldro', a boarding school in Eastbourne. I was about seven and a half
and not at all happy at the idea of being so far from home. There was a
kind old master there called Mr Craft, who closely resembled
Rudyard Kipling; well, he seemed old, but as I received Christmas
cards from him for twenty years afterwards, he was probably only
about thirty-five at the time. To me he represented kindness. Mr Hill,
the Headmaster, on the other hand represented unkindness, for I was
often to be caned by him. 'Go and change into gym shorts and wait for
me in the gymnasium,' he would order. That wait was more terrible
than the thrashing. Even at seven and a half, I could take the beating,
but the waiting made me sick with apprehension.

At Aldro, I received several beatings for several misdemeanours but
the final straw came when I broke a lavatory chain.

The school lavatories were (presumably to discourage the young

50

from taking themselves in hand) without partitions, and set out in a nice friendly line. Having just seen the latest Tarzan film, I thought I would try to emulate my hero by performing his swinging-from-vine-to-vine trick.

Grasping firmly the flushing chain of lav number one and letting out a mighty 'Ah-oo-ah-oo-ah-oo aaah!!' I swung successfully to the chain of lav number two, then on to chain number three, which unfortunately, in mid-swing, broke, dropping 'Tarzan' neatly into the bowl, one leg in and the other leg out. There I was forced to remain, 'man trapped', until assistance was called and 'Tarzan' was freed.

This was altogether too much for Mr Hill.

'Monstrous behaviour! An incorrigible young man!' he said.

I was beaten again for good measure and – after a phone call to my father – expelled.

Between schools, I had a salutory respite, and it was during this that A. A. Milne, a mucker of my father's, invited us to his house in the country to tea.

There we met his son, Christopher Robin Milne, who was dressed from head to foot in a suit of shining and glittering armour. Whether this was because he expected to fall victim to violent assault from my brothers and me, or to withstand onslaughts from neighbouring enemy hordes I really can't say. Anyway, he must have looked at me through his visor and considered I was friendly, because he was good enough to introduce me to his toy animal friends, Piglet, Owl, Kanga, Kanga's son Roo, and best of all, his teddy bear, Winnie the Pooh. He also, as a great concession, let me ride his donkey which lived in a field by the house. His name, of course, was Eeyore.

And there aren't *many* people who have *met* personally, and actually *talked* to, such illustrious animals as these!

★

My second boarding-school was Wellington House preparatory in Westgate-on-Sea, Kent. The Isle of Thanet nearly sank under the weight of 'good schools' in Westgate, Wellington House, Hawtrey's and Stone House being the top three. There was such a plethora of Marquis's, Viscounts, Lords, Sirs and Hons at W.H. that without a handle of some sort you really felt out of it. The head was the very reverend Percy Underhill, an ex-rowing blue with crossed oars over his fireplace to prove it. He was a man who demanded strict obedience at all times, and got it, for a quick look at the size and bulk of this monolith was all that was necessary for him to receive instant acquiescence.

The tool of *his* chastisement trade was a fives bat, a wooden instrument used instead of gloves in the game of fives. Two inches thick and about eighteen inches long it was a frightening deterrent. A blow from the fives bat when wielded by the Rev not only had a paralysing effect on the behind, it also shot the offender forward at such velocity that he was in danger of having his head rammed through the opposite wall. The bruises left by the bat were of a variety of hue that would've put Turner to shame, and were the source of endless discussion and debate on the merits or otherwise of corporal punishment, and the visual results of the tools used therein.

But Percy Underhill, although of alarming demeanour, was always a fair man, and I grew to have a great respect and fondness for him. His dear wife was the complete opposite of her husband, a desperately thin, permanently hatted, jaundiced lady both in spirit and in the colour of her skin.

I remember Mrs Underhill mostly for her beautiful flower arrangements in the chapel, and her 'much-looked-forward-to-invitation-teas' in her sitting room. There, chosen boys could stuff themselves solid with unlimited sandwiches (cucumber), buns (Chelsea), and cake (Dundee), at the same time as ogling Rosemary, the Underhills' lovely daughter – the mental image of whose beauteous body would be neatly stored away until bedtime. In the privacy of his cubicle, many a small boy would happily fall asleep with Rosemary as the subject of his erotic dream.

Each cubicle was about eight foot square and sparsely furnished with an iron cot bed, a small mat on the bare floorboards, a washstand with the familiar jug, basin and tooth mug and a small locker for one's 'things'. The six foot high walls were wooden so forbidden holes were easily bored to facilitate communication with one's neighbours, both written and visual. If a rift developed between stable companions, a quickly made spitball of blotting paper would bung-up the orifice, and one's privacy was once more absolute.

Each night before lights out, 'Moon', as the Head was tagged, went on his rounds. Being so tall, he could peer easily over the top of each monklike cell. 'Goodnight Frederick' – 'Goodnight Sir' – 'Goodnight Willoughby' – 'Goodnight Sir' – 'Goodnight Jon, sleep well!' – 'Goodnight Sir.'

It was always Christian names for the 'sleep well' exhortations, but, amicable as he tried to sound, you could often tell from an inflection in his voice as to whether or not you were likely to be called forth for sentence at 'Readover' the next morning. A 'Good*night* Jon' guaranteed Jon a *bad* night, and a bad night guaranteed a bad morning, for 'Readover' was like sitting in on Judgement Day. All the school gathered in the 'New Hall' (built circa 1900) and silently awaited his Lordship and accompanying jury. On the dot of nine, in swept the Reverend Underhill, enveloped in a vast black gown, like the 'Great Avenger'. Under his arm he carried 'The Doomsday Book' which he placed with great veneration on an Eagle lectern before him. The staff, similarly gowned and padding along behind him, paled into insignificance with the sheer force of his personality, and seated themselves in a straight line to his right and left.

The trial commenced – and after a prayer, a hymn, some fascinating directives about the care and cleanliness of urinals et al, came the dreaded opening of the 'Book of Doom'. You could've heard half a pin drop as the Reverend, placing his half-moon glasses on the end of his nose, announced, 'Here is today's "Readover" list.'

The guiltless, the goody-goodies, the swots, grinned with self-satisfaction, knowing that the only time *their* names would be mentioned was when paeans of praise would ring out for their excellent marks, or their prowess on the sports field.

It was quite the reverse, however, for the likes of Freddie Gibson, Robin Lucas, Laurence Jolivet and me. We were *always* on the black list. What did we do? Well, *you* name it and evidently *we* did it.

Those fearful quakes would start again, the blood rushing to my feet, and the only thing holding me upright was the close proximity of my adjoining misdemeanants. My friend 'Jolly' Jolivet once said that on the frequent occasions when my name was read out, I looked like 'a dead cat, before rigor mortis had set in'.

'Pertwee,' boomed 'The Moon', peering over the top of his glasses, 'will I *ever* be honoured by someone saying something good and encouraging about you? Today, for tripping up Matron, you have received your third "stripe" in a week, and you know what *that* means!' I knew all right! A fives ball was once again to be replaced by my behind. 'See me in my study after Readover,' he commanded. The simping eggheads and rugger-buggers hugged themselves in anticipatory glee. 'Botfield Senior,' went on the Head, 'receives two stars for the second time this week. The first for courage on the rugger field and the second for obtaining full marks for his biology exam.'

'Dirty devil,' I thought, 'I know why he's good at biology!' – and as for courage in the field, anyone would think he had had a leg amputated without anaesthetic, instead of having a knocked-loose tooth pulled out.

Nevertheless, despite all these rebellious thoughts, as requested, I dutifully reported myself in the Headmaster's study after Readover, awaiting my punishment.

P.C.U. gazed at me with intense disapproval for what seemed like several minutes, then with the care of a golfer selecting the right club for a particularly tricky shot, he chose a fives bat from the assortment he kept in his umbrella stand.

'Pertwee,' he said, testing it for durability by administering a quick whack on the arm of his leather sofa, 'you are a wretched mumchancer. That is not mere opinion but an indisputable fact. Left to pursue the path of idleness and profligacy upon which you have set your feet, I have no doubt that you would probably end on the gallows as an example to others of your ilk and kidney. Happily, vile Pertwee, I intend to divert you from this unhappy course for, as Carlyle reminds us, it is the indisputable right of the ignorant that they may be guided by the wiser, either gently or forcibly. In your case it will be *very* forcibly, to impress both upon your person and what for want of a better word I shall call your mind, that ignorance is not necessarily bliss!'

And the extremely one-sided battle commenced!

That is what I shall term the 'heavier' side of Wellington House, but it also had its 'lighter' sides, and one of these occasions was 'Parental Visits'. Following these, small boys who went to bed early were allowed a short 'look-in' from their loved ones, but I am ashamed to admit that I dreaded the visits from Granny. Being of shortish stature, she could not see over the cubicle walls, so that on one previous occasion she had had to hazard a guess as to which cubicle her 'Jonny-Boys' was sleeping in. Inevitably, she chose the wrong ones and several embarrassed small boys were caught knickerless, or 'pointing at the porcelain'. 'Whoops,' she said in feigned horror. 'I'm *so* sorry, I must've got the wrong room.' Her plaintive cry of 'Jonny-Boys, where are you?' echoed down the dorm – closely followed by an unseen chorus of giggling schoolboys chanting, 'Jonny-Boys, where are you?'

On another occasion, Granny, anxious to cause me no further embarrassment, carried a chair with her during her search, and when she got to what she firmly believed was the right cubicle, put down the chair, and stood up on it, in order to look over the wall without strain. At the third unsuccessful attempt she arrived at the room of a very nervous young man who blinked a lot and suffered badly from 'incontinence'. Unable to sleep, he was looking up at the ceiling playing 'changing faces', when one of the most singular sights he had ever seen appeared over the top of him. It was Granny, wearing the latest creation from Madame Louise, her milliner of long standing – a large black felt with ostrich feathers, and a smidgeon of fruit and veg. This sudden apparition above him proved too much for the poor lad, whose loud screams caused Granny to take fright and fall backwards off her chair, mercifully without harm. I wish the same could be said for the startled youngster, but due to the severe shock he had received he promptly wet his bed. It is surprising, taking everything into consideration, that that's all the poor little chap did!

An interesting off-shoot of this is that during the war some years later, I was passed in Regent Street by an enormous black-moustachioed Officer-Cadet and was torn off the most terrific salute I'd ever received. A few paces on we both stopped and turned.

'I know you don't I?'

'Yes sir, we were both at the same prep school, I remember you were very kind to me.' I decided against mentioning the 'Granny reminiscence', not only out of deference to his finer feelings but also because he was about six foot four and could've killed me with one blow! As an officer he was much decorated for services to his country and is now a titled eccentric of enormous panache and charm.

Now to the staff. Mr Kendrick was a dear old buffer who should have retired years before, but he loved the boys and the boys loved him. He was with the school when it started and he intended to stay with it until it finished, or what was more likely, until *he* was. Mr Kendrick was our father, our mother, our confidant and what was more important, our 'shopper'. Every week he would make a list of the boys' requirements and hobble off to the shops to buy them. There were always 'crazes' at Wellington House – yo-yos, diabolo, paper gliders, rope-spinning, torches with red, green and white lights for signalling or reading under the sheets, crystal sets, even ants in glass cases. All these and more did Mr Kendrick buy for us and the New Hall would be alive with glider pilots for a week or two, then the cowboys with their lariats took over, followed by the circus perfor-mers, tossing their spinning and humming (6d extra) diabolo cones from one juggler to another. 'Oriental' yo-yoers took their yo-yos for 'walkies', they 'boomeranged' them, they 'looped-the-loop' and occasionally became so over-enthusiastic that they confused their string-hung yo-yos for conkers, resulting in broken bits of them flying dangerously around the room. I was a champion then, for I once owned a 'twelver' yo-yo. The ant lovers, however, were, after due consideration, summarily banished to the boot and shoe room.

Captain Thompson, MC, DSO was a tall, thin, ex-military gentleman of fine bearing, who was determined to take over as Headmaster when the 'Moon' retired. He regularly regaled us with lurid stories of the 14-18 war in Mesapotamia. 'Those damned Turks never took prisoners, you know. Before we could get to the battlefield and bring our wounded in, those diabolical Turkish women, looking for all the world like black widow spiders, would creep out with their long knives and hack the poor devils to bits.' It was Captain Thompson, and his heroic stories of soldiery that in 1939 made me join the Navy.

To be sitting at Captain Thompson's table was much envied. Every day you were obliged to move up one place to the right, bringing you, eventually, to a position next to the gallant Captain himself. What was so enviable about this position was that at breakfast, the Captain would take two 'soldiers' of toast from his own personal supply, spread them liberally with butter (no margarine for him), and then, under the excited gaze of twenty boys, carefully spoon a generous portion of Oxford 'Olde English' marmalade upon each slice. These he handed with great ceremony to the boys sitting on his right and left, who, knowing that it would be some considerable time before their turn came round again, took Mr Gladstone's admirable advice and chewed and savoured every delicious mouthful without haste.

Our French master was a Mr Hubert Riley CRO – what CRO meant was anybody's guess, and he considered any querying of its origin to be an impertinence. He was, he told us, half French, and stemmed from the Channel Islands, his father being a professor of some import and his brother the famous explorer and writer Quentin Riley. Quentin Riley visited the school regularly and gave us riveting lectures (with the additional showing of slides and props such as snow-shoes, sealskin coats and boots and blubber-lamps) on his adventures in the frozen North. Real Jack London stuff was this.

Hubert Riley was an out-and-out rebel. Small in height, he had the heart and moral courage of a cornered buffalo. In chapel, when the mighty Reverend Underhill rose to lead the choir in prayer, the congregation immediately rose with him. Not so Mr Riley. He stayed firmly seated, engrossed, so he would have you believe, in some fascinating, newly-discovered passages in his Bible. Or he would stare hypnotically at a line on his palm that had apparently appeared overnight. The tension was electric, the 'Moon' glaring at the 'Rebel', the 'Rebel' ignoring the 'Moon', until that split second, just prior to the bolt of lightning summoned by the Reverend to strike the impudent sinner down, when Mr Riley would slowly rise up, open his prayer book at the appropriate page, turn towards the by now apoplectic Headmaster and smile at him benignly as if nothing whatsoever had occurred. Result? Another game, set and match to the Rebel.

In class he was a terror, and with his close-cropped hair looked almost teutonic. He was an excellent teacher, however, despite his tart and bullying manner. 'Pertwee,' he commanded one day, 'stay behind. The rest of you, go.' The class made a hurried exit, leaving us alone.

'Yes, sir?' I said querulously.

'Why aren't you afraid of me?' he asked.

'Oh, but I am, sir.'

'No, you're not, you're just pretending to be. You're acting at being afraid, and you're not doing a bad job of it. You ought to take up the profession when you're older.' So spoke my first theatre critic, and for several years I continued to be amused by him. While others quaked, I shook, but with laughter. Not only was he witty, sharp-tongued and a mine of entertaining information, he was also a health nut, and when he, not Captain T., became Headmaster, all knickerbockers ('Don't allow a boy's sex organs to breathe'), Eton collars ('They garrotte the poor lads') and boots ('We're not living in ancient Peking') were immediately abandoned in favour of shorts, open-necked shirts, and soft sand-shoes.

H.R. taught me to be aware of, and take pleasure in, the many colours that were before me in flowers, trees and leaves, in the sky and the sea. He could hold you spellbound around a rock pool with his infinite knowledge of the minuscule life that lived there, and encouraged us to have aquariums in school and stock them with specimens that we had caught.

Wellington House had a large playing field and all around the perimeter under a low brick wall were the boys' gardens. Mr Riley was my 'old Adam' and under his careful guidance, I had the best garden in the school. I won prizes regularly, and cups, until by now a trifle blasé, I decided on a completely new approach. 'This year,' I mused, 'I will abandon flowers in favour of vegetables', and so it was done. A line of tall brussels sprouts at the back, clumps of thyme and rosemary, rows of elegant leeks, cheeky radishes and luscious lettuces, it was a sight any greengrocer would have been proud of. Not so the judges, however. They couldn't see the humour of the situation. The rebellious Mr Riley, sensing that in me he had found a kindred spirit, could, and gave me a star, 'for using my brain in an original manner'. He became a true friend and I regularly visited him and the school when later in life I was touring theatres in the vicinity.

W.H. holds some vivid memories for me, especially the Saturday afternoon boxing. There in the New Hall grudges were fought out under the strict supervision of a sports master. I remember one battle royal between two giant men, John Profumo, the ex-MP, and George Bowring of the shipping family. They fought it out over five two-minute rounds, and it is the most bloody battle in my memory. There just seemed no end to it. Eventually, the two evenly matched and exhausted gladiators were quite correctly given a draw. The two giants, I have just come to realise, were about ten years old and not much over five feet tall! But to a child's mind – like buildings, like people.

I thought I had a friend in Brother Backslider, John 'Freddie' Gibson, but I was mistaken. He was forever challenging me to Saturday jousts and, never taking 'no' for an answer, frequently bent and bloodied my already well-pronounced nose.

My forthright views on bullies and bullying, however, received a sudden kick in the teeth when my wife Ingeborg and I were entertaining two of my best school friends Nigel 'Podge' Neilson and Laurence 'Jolly' Jolivet and their wives to dinner last year. They, if you please, calmly informed the assembled company after some nostalgic reminiscence about bullying, that I, Jon Pertwee, was one of the school's prime offenders. Such perfidy! And to think that these were supposed to be very 'good' friends! I shall take solace in the belief that the whole thing was a pre-arranged jape, but between you and me, I'm not so sure!

★

There was also the most beautiful chapel at Wellington House, with very good examples of stained glass, oak pews, marbled floors, and a splendid piped organ, played upon with great relish and panache by a Mr Cameron. Up in the organ loft with him to do the pumping was a small shadow called Gaghan, who worshipped his own god, a 'graven image' in the form of Mr Cameron himself. He learned to play the organ like him, to walk like him, with his unseemly gait, bouncing up and down on the balls of his feet in great lolloping strides, to talk like him in a distinctive twittering ululation, to comb his black frizzy hair to sweep over his head in a frenzied bobbing arc. He even developed his master's unique style as a 'googly' bowler on the cricket field, that could best be described as the careening of a chronic sufferer from St Vitus's dance. A most excellent example of parrotry, but as Mr Cameron was never a particularly pretty sight, he was a strange choice for a young boy to emulate.

Into this ministrels'-gallery-cum-organ-loft came many visiting musicians and singers to enrapture the congregation with music and song of a higher standard than that we could provide for ourselves. Not that that should be denigrated, as our own standard was of the highest. The boys' choir was very good indeed and Mr Cameron a most able choirmaster. I myself had a fine treble voice and with the rest of the choir was recorded by Regal Zonophone on a 78 singing the inevitable double *Oh for the Wings of a Dove* and *Hear My Prayer*. I've got it hidden away somewhere to this day and am most anxious to find it so that I can prove to my children once and for all that I was not always a groaner.

But our star chorister was a young singer quite unsurpassed by even the world famous Ernest Lush. His name was Peter Pease, and when he sang the earth stopped spinning. The pure clarity and tone of those soaring notes entered my head and stayed there for life, and I was forever reminded of him when the young chorister sang the theme song for John le Carré's television series *Tinker Tailor Soldier Spy*. Peter Pease was sadly killed in the Battle of Britain and will be remembered by many from what was said about him in the classic book *The Last Enemy* written by Richard Hilary in 1941, but by me and all who heard him sing he will be remembered as a gift of God.

At least once a year the chapel gallery would be occupied by a certain 'Smelly' Satiswood, an exquisite violinist who introduced Bruch's Violin Concerto to me with memorable soul. The reason for Mr Satiswood's strange nomenclature was choice. The gentleman was a redhead and redheads as you know are a unique lot. Not only do they usually possess pale translucent skin, freckles and usually beautifully textured hair, but they also have a very distinctive odour. In most females it is the subtle musky smell of a perfume, but in some males this muskiness is potent to a degree. The chapel must have been 150 feet long with the gallery at least twenty feet up from the aisle, yet within seconds of Mr Satiswood coming to the edge of the gallery to play, the chapel would be permeated with the most extraordinarily pungent whiffy, niffy smell I have ever snuffed up.

Although we have been taught all about the speed of light, no-one to my knowledge has ever gone into the speed of smell, and to my mind this shows a gross lack of interest in a most fascinating phenomenon.

The boys' giggling reaction to the muscadine odour and the subsequent holding of noses and raising of handkerchiefs to nostrils, with accompanying *sotto voce* 'Poohs!' was unjust in the extreme, for the smell, as I have said, was by no means unpleasant and in any case was far outweighed by Mr Satiswood's exquisite playing.

Over the years I have frequently been jerked back in time to my place in the pew of that lovely chapel, where my nostrils were assailed by that peculiar and quite unique muskiness. I was attending an evening of boxing only recently at the Albert Hall, when right in the middle of a bout of considerable mayhem I cried out, 'Smelly Satiswood!!' My companions were not particularly bemused as followers of 'the fancy' are prone to shout out strange epithets and incomprehensible instructions to their favourite participants, and my cry might well have come under one or other of those categories. But the fact is, that involuntary cry had been wrung from me by that familiar pungent smell reaching my olfactory senses once again. Amidst all the reek of cigar and cigarette smoke, and the fetid odour of hot socks and armpits, the same distinctively redolent aromatic aroma of the red-headed Mr Satiswood came churning nostalgically through the noxious offensiveness to transport me back through time via nothing but my nostrils.

*

It is strange that Peter Dawson was my best friend at W.H., for he was 'academic and well behaved' according to his reports. Mine were by no means in the same category, as can be readily seen by the sample included among the photographs in this book. There was one thing you *could* say about my reports – that throughout my schooldays they were consistent – reading 'bad', or at best 'improving'. Peter used to take me out to tea at Kingscliffe, a smart hotel near Margate, whenever his parents or friends came down to visit him. Naturally when my parents or friends came down to visit me I was expected to do the same, and as we had so many visiting relatives between us, we were able to enjoy more outings than most. We became so close, that visits to each other's homes during the holidays became a regular part of our curriculum. Peter's family owned a beautiful Tudor house in Sussex. Here Peter's father, mother and sisters lived in considerable splendour with butlers, footmen, chauffeurs, and gardeners galore. It was a gloriously kept house, with Mrs Dawson, a gentle timid soul, keeping it ablaze with cut flowers and plants throughout the year. Her husband was a quiet introverted man who liked to be left alone. His command was my wish, for in truth I feared him, for all his introversion. He lived in the 'old way' and morning and night held prayers for family, friends and staff in the drawing room. A most solemn occasion, but one where all participation had to be at full voice, be it psalms, hymns or even prayers. These meetings were never long and in retrospect I rather enjoyed them. Sunday was different. On Sundays, Mr Dawson would demonstrate his prowess as a Hot Gospeller. For half an hour, as was expected of us, we stood in awe of him. Then suddenly an extraordinary change would come about. The entire family, except Mrs Dawson, would hurry to various corners of the room to collect their instruments, the girls their violins, violas and cellos, and Peter his clarinet. Gathering round their father, by now already seated at the Bechstein, they proceeded to play quite beautifully classical quartets in the 'Amadeus' mould.

I sat silently, both loving and at the same time hating their musicianship and expertise – the latter reaction being one of extreme jealousy at my inability to provide something of equal calibre.

The bedroom allocated for my first visit was situated by itself at the end of the west wing. This necessitated crossing the minstrels' gallery, overlooking the vast Elizabethan dining hall. There was at the end of this passage, a dark, oak-panelled room of perfect linen-fold, with a bathroom converted from an early priest's hole. A large antique bed faced this bathroom with the bedroom door on my right.

Sometime during that first night I awoke feeling desperately sick. So suddenly had this nausea attacked me that I had no time to find a receptacle and was promptly sick all over my bedcover. Mortified by what I had done I failed to notice the foul stench that permeated the room. Snapping on a bedside light I staggered into the bathroom heaving and retching. Eventually, feeling a little better, I proceeded to attempt a clean up. The bedcover had mercifully caught the brunt, and this I was able to wash out in the bath and dry, by wrapping it round the hot water tank in the cupboard. Putting the dreadful experience down to a 'bilious attack', I went back to bed and fell instantly into a deep sleep.

'Good morning, Jon, did you sleep well?' asked Mrs Dawson solicitously at breakfast.

'Yes, thank you, very well,' I lied bravely.

'Good, I'm so glad!'

I thought I detected a strange look pass between Mrs Dawson and her husband but decided it must've been my imagination. The next night at around the same time I awoke, attacked once more by the self-same nausea, only *this* time I smelt the reason for my retching, an odour so foul I am unable to describe it. Perhaps the smell of a long dead, fly-blown sheep would suffice. I sat up, my hand clapped over my mouth, when I saw the cause of all my vomiting. Between the end of my bed and the now open bathroom door, there was an undulating greenish shape in the form of a tree trunk. It was translucent and appeared to be bubbling like marsh gas. As the bubbles burst, so did the room fill further with the odour of noxious putrefaction. I was temporarily frozen in terror, but as soon as the 'presence' started to move towards me, I made the all-powerful effort that enabled me to get out of bed and fumble my way frantically out of the door. Hurtling up the corridor and screaming my lungs out, I ran smack into the arms of Mrs Dawson, who on hearing my screams had come out of her bedroom into the passage. Clasping me consolingly to her, she turned on her husband like a tigress. 'I told you to see that nobody was *ever* put into that room again. You just *won't* listen. From tomorrow that wing will be permanently locked and sealed.' No explanation was ever given and the matter was never discussed. Even Peter could not be drawn on the subject. Perhaps he was ignorant of the fact that his west wing was so well and truly haunted.

Since that time, I have had several strange encounters with the unknown, although I do not consider myself to be psychic in any way.

★

My all-consuming desire to be an actor took precedence over everything else at Wellington House. My studies were not so much 'shelved' as 'pushed temporarily to one side', to make way for the more important things in my life, such as writing plays and sketches, and trying to band my friends together to make up a company of players to act in them. The resultant side effects on my progress in scholastic matters were 'lowering' to say the least, but the Reverend Underhill did not seem particularly concerned at my lack of academic interest. By now, I think he realised that the theatre was all I thought and dreamed about, so the fives bat was 'retired' as far as *my* backside was concerned. From then on in he allowed me full rein, to 'brush up my Shakespeare', poetry, history, carpentry, and any like subjects that he felt would be of use to me in my chosen profession. He and Mrs Underhill encouraged and helped me to write, produce, direct, act in, apply the make-up and even provide the intermission music in many an evening of 'Pertwee's Delights'. The content of these entertainments I have completely forgotten, but Laurence Jolivet recently sent me the actual roneo'd programme sheet of the first show I ever put on. There is at the end a reference to 'Jack Sacosta's Saskatchewan Syncopators'. As, at that time, 'Jack Sacosta' (an alias of mine) was incapable of even blowing a raspberry on a bugle, I can only assume that the few popular tunes played by the 'Syncopators' were upon combs and lavatory paper, the 'Submarine Kazoo' having, to the best of my knowledge, not yet reached our shores.

An informative and entertaining few years, played out in a school with a great tradition and a perfectly splendid cast!

*

My penultimate chance of a reasonably academic education came when I left Wellington House at thirteen and a half and joined my two brothers at one of the world's oldest public schools, Sherborne, in Dorset.

I was in Abbeylands House, under the Housemastership of Mr 'Mauk' (why, I know not) Elderton, a completely ineffectual man, of little character but gentleness. He seemed frightened of his own shadow, let alone anyone else's.

I was informed that I must not chum up with boys of a previous term, as they were my seniors, and when new boys came the following term, I was not to chum up with them either as I was now theirs. 'Make friends with boys of your *own* term,' they said. This was difficult, in as much as there was only one other new boy in my term. He was a pimply Australian called Nooler, and I hated him on sight. So, what to do? I struck up a friendship with a kindred soul in the next house, one D. P. (Dippy) Walker. His Housemaster, Mr Parry Jones, very soon put a stop to that as 'Friendship between boys in different Houses is not to be tolerated!' Lonely now, I would visit Michael at School House near the main buildings. He was senior enough to have been allocated a 'study', a pokey little room furnished out of his personal pocket from a junk shop at an outlay of some four pounds. A poor place, but his own, and I envied him.

My 'place' was a bench-locker and a desk in the far corner of the Junior Day Room, where every few minutes, the cry of 'Fag!' echoed commandingly through its portals. It was always the last boy in the queue of fags formed outside the fagmaster's study that had to undertake the chore, and my desk being situated where it was made getting any place *other* than last in the queue a virtual impossibility! Therefore, in an endeavour to avoid this inevitable situation, I took to standing by the Junior Day Room door, reading a book, and ready the moment the fagmaster's study door opened, to anticipate his summons by hurtling up the passage to arrive *first*, instead of *last*!

The end result of this brilliant piece of logical thinking was to receive a vociferous complaint from the queueing fags that I had cheated.

Accepting their accusation as proved, the prefect switched procedures and said, 'Very well then, *first* fag!' . . . I was hoist with my own petard!

My visits to Michael were cold comfort as, 'It is not permitted to enter the study of another boy's house.' Standing outside the open window was all that was allowed.

'Not too long, I'm afraid,' said Michael's study-mate, 'it's cold enough in here as it is.'

I looked forward to these visits talking to Michael, and I distinctly remember laughing uproariously at a record of Sandy Powell singing his famous patter song *Can You Hear Me, Mother?* To think he went on making us laugh with that song until he died in 1982.

★

School routine was a rude awakening from the comforts of home. No extra half-hour in bed, and no relaxing in a leisurely hot bath. It was early rising and a cold bath.

First, a cacophonous hand bell was rung to facilitate wakefulness, followed by cries of 'To the bath, to the bath' from the supervising prefects. At once lines of completely naked boys with retracted penises formed shivering in the corridor outside the bathroom. Inside, there awaited three enormous baths filled to the brim with freezing water.

If the baths had been filled the previous night, it was not unusual for the 'preparing' fag to have to break the ice that had formed upon the surface.

The custom was to leap into the bath and, with nose held, immerse oneself entirely in the water, at the same time causing an icy wave to deluge the unfortunates standing behind. Any 'lagging' in the queue was promptly discouraged by the overseers' accurate flicking of the cheeks (buttock variety) with the corner of a wet towel. I have never been given a lucid reason for this pagan ceremony apart from 'It's good for you,' or 'Because it's been done since 1407,' and what can you say to logic like that, other than 'Oh, I *see*!'

It's always difficult when you really hate something, to understand that there can possibly be those who actually enjoy it. But lots of my contemporaries loved school, and partook with intense enthusiasm of those activities I so detested – early 'Long Runs', and 'Short Runs' and the downfall of the British Empire – 'Team Games!'

I never was very much good at rugby, soccer and cricket, although I had enjoyed fielding at long leg at Wellington House, because there, after each over, I was able to back slowly off the field, further and further into the tall grass, and at the precise moment when all attention was focused elsewhere, I would fall backwards into the weeds and wild flowers, and surprisingly remain there undiscovered staring up at the sun and the sky for the rest of the game. Only once was I caught *in flagrante* as it were, and that was by H. 'the Rebel' Riley, who just winked at me.

No, if you weren't into games at Sherborne, you had a pretty rough time of it. If you weren't a *scholar* that is. A scholar had carte blanche and that certainly *didn't* apply to me!

They say that the public school fagging system develops character, so let me give you a case in point and allow you to be the judge.

For some reason, perhaps the influence of the Dawson family's love of music, I decided to learn, of all things, the trumpet. Dad agreed and I started private lessons at a guinea an hour, with a professor of that chosen instrument. The lessons took place in the music-block some quarter of a mile's distance away from my house. In the middle of one such lesson, a fag came bursting into the music-room and with a quick apology for his intrusion, informed me that my presence was urgently required by my fagmaster, Carden.

'Why?' I asked.

'No idea, he just told me to get you, *quam celerrime*.' Fearing as always the worst, an accident to one of my brothers, or a death in the family, I excused myself and ran back to my house at full speed, arriving breathlessly before Carden's study door some moments before his courier. I knocked and entered.

'You wanted me, Carden?' I asked anxiously.

'Yes, I did, Pertwee, make me a piece of toast.'

I was temporarily speechless. 'A *what*?' I queried.

'A piece of toast – golden brown – and buttered, followed perhaps by another one.'

I couldn't believe it, here I was in the middle of an expensive music lesson, being called back to my house to make some lazy sod a piece of toast. My Gallic temperament burst into flame, and I let rip. 'Are you bloody mad? Are you crippled? Don't you know how to make toast? Well I'll tell you! You take a slice of bread, stick it on the end of your toasting fork, and hold it before your fire, allowing it to turn a nice golden brown. Try never to burn it, but if you do, *don't* be tempted to cover your misdemeanour by scraping it, otherwise some sadistic bastard like you, will beat your arse black and blue for anarchy.'

There is not much point in continuing this story, suffice to say that I was sent forthwith into the quad where I was given six of the best, in my gym shorts.

'Ladies and Gentlemen of the Jury, have you reached your verdict?' Of course you have!

This incident so rankled in my mind, that my career as a trumpet player never really took off, leaving Louis Armstrong to continue unchallenged as 'numero uno'.

The teachers at Sherborne were a bumpy lot. Amongst others there were 'Doughy' Randolph, 'Long-Bun' Thompson, 'Short-Bun' Thompson and 'Crippen' Hornsby-Wright. The latter in a class with a modicum of new boys, was wont to ask each such boy to stand up and give his name to the assembled class.

'Name?'

'Smith, sir'

'Name?'

'Tidmarsh Minimus, sir.'

'Name?'

'Pertwee Minor, sir.'

'Name?' (This to a small freckle-faced redhead in the front row.)

' – Er – Hornsby, sir!'

A suppressed titter ran through the class – Mr Hornsby-Wright peering over his glasses at the scarlet boy before him, switched his gaze to the boy next to him, 'And your name?' he queried.

'Er – Wright, sir!'

The class erupted with laughter.

'The cheek of those two, and on the first day of term, too, they'll catch it.' They most certainly did, and after a swift 'whacking', amid loud protestations and cries of 'But it's not fair, sir' – the two young 'comedians' were again requested to give their names.

'*Hornsby*, sir.'

'*Wright*, sir – *honestly*.'

The joke was – they were telling the truth!

The only time I ever heard a bigger laugh in a classroom, was when the normally careful 'Doughy' Randolph announced, 'I want to see Jon P. in my study immediately after lunch.'

Apart from numerous run-ins with the school's authoritarians, I also came in for a lot of bullying, that my Housemaster seemed unable, or unwilling, to control.

There were two boys senior to me called 'Smith' and 'Jones', for want of better names. These kindly lads took it upon themselves to become my personal inquisitors. On the night before the last day of term when rules mostly went by the board, S and J would swiftly get to work. Strapping me into my bed with luggage straps, and knowing full well how much time and trouble I had spent in the carpentry shops making gifts for my family, they took each individual piece and smashed it before my eyes. To make sure I was having a really good time they then rubbed a liberal amount of boot-black into my hair. 'That's nothing Peewee,' they said as they left, 'you just wait until tomorrow.' Bequeathing me a horrendous and intentionally sleepless night.

On another memorable occasion, I was placed kicking, biting and spitting into a large 'bumph' ('bum fodder' for those who didn't know) basket in the day room. The lid was closed and a pile of tuck-boxes placed on top to make escape impossible. I tried to hold out with courage but eventually I found the confined space and pitch-darkness overwhelming and all pretence of bravery left me. I cried and begged to be released, but this was food for the gods. Tears, cries, supplications, that's what bullying was all about. That's when you're *really* getting somewhere – you cry and you beg some more – 'Yeah, yeah, yeah, go man, go, now you're *really* turning us on.'

It seemed I had no friends or if I had they were not brave enough to risk tackling Smith and Jones, for fear of suffering the same fate and ending up in the basket themselves.

How long I was in that skip I shall never know, but it seemed like nine lifetimes. When I was eventually released I remember being unable to stand properly, as my confined position in the basket had given me cramp.

As soon as I was in control of myself, and ignoring S and J's threats of an awful fate if I 'sneaked', I hurried to the study of my Housemaster. I had been there once before, to receive a man-to-man talk on the dangers of masturbation, both mutual and personal, and a hint of the retribution (blindness perhaps?) that was likely to befall any perpetrator of this 'disgusting habit'. It seems that my being seen emerging from a copse with another boy already branded as an active homosexual, was enough to have me labelled as being 'tarred with the same brush'. The truth of this case of lack of moral turpitude, was that we had entered the copse for the sole purpose of:

1. Eating a tin of bully-beef;
2. Sharing a small bottle of beer; and
3. Smoking a 'Woodbine'.

'Ah, come in Pertwee, is there something I can do for you?' There certainly was! He could stop me from being hung, drawn and quartered for a start! It all came rushing out, a torrent of words and accusations listing every wretched moment of those last few hours, but whatever succour I had expected, I was bitterly disappointed.

'Yes, I see Pertwee, thank you!! Well, let me tell you that I know Smith and Jones' fathers personally. They are both Old Boys and certainly wouldn't tolerate their youngsters bullying. In my opinion you're taking all this *far* too seriously, I'm sure you'll find that it was all done in fun. Just normal high spirits at the end of term; eh? You really must develop a sense of humour in these matters. Try and see the funny side.'

I realised from his tone that I was not getting through, and could expect no help from him.

'Come,' he said, rising from behind his desk, 'we'll go and have a talk to them, I think you'll find both Smith and Jones will be perfectly reasonable.'

I was not prepared to risk their reasonability and excused myself from occupying his time any further. Somehow I managed to disappear sufficiently deep into the woodwork to avoid any further repetitions of Smith and Jones' 'fun' – for *that* term! But there was always the next, *and* the next.

★

'Boys *must* have labels on their bicycles,' said the Captain of House. 'You know the rules, Pertwee, and you know the penalty for breaking them. Get changed and into the quad for a "sixer".'

I had, only two days before, attached a brand new label to my bike, knowing full well that there was a blitz on. The fact that it was now gone, leaving only the string, could mean but one thing. It had been removed, and by whom it was not hard to guess. Smith and Jones were riding again. This I attempted to explain to my accuser but he quickly informed me that if I continued trying to place the blame elsewhere, I'd receive a double dose. The unjust punishment duly delivered, I went immediately to the bicycle shed to attach yet another label to my handlebars. The jesters S and J were there, lolling about, and watched me carefully as I tied the label on.

Several hours later I was stopped on my way to the lav by a bellow from the House Captain. 'Pertwee, you *still* haven't put a label on your bicycle! For defying me, I am going to give you *another* "sixer"!'

The complete injustice of it all was too much and I went berserk. I told my tormentor that if he came within an inch of me, I'd kill him and grabbed for a six-inch-long spiked pipe-cleaner, disguised as a fountain pen, that I had been carrying around as 'protection'. Whipping off the top, I looked down in dismay to find that the spike of my stiletto had been sawn completely through and all I was threatening the boy with was a pen-top. Smith and Jones were no fools and observant to boot. But there must've been a look in my eye that told the prefect this time he'd gone too far, and if he pushed me any further I was likely to go over the edge.

So he faded away, mumbling something about seeing the Housemaster. A lot of help he'd receive there. Although, if really lucky, he might have got a talk on the perils of venereal disease and how to avoid the contracting of same.

Shortly after this incident my father was called to the phone, told that I was 'impossible' and would he come and take me away. Rather than have the stigma of expulsion, I was to be 'superannuated', which means exactly the same thing.

*

And so, in this summary fashion my Sherborne education came to an end, and from my point of view not before time. But no reference to one's public school schooldays would be complete without referring to the 'School Song', those moving and martial compositions which have to do with playing the game, keeping a straight bat, being British, and breathing vengeance on the foreign foe. It's been said that to have a really good time at an Old Boys' reunion, you need to have had at least six 'floreat Salopias' before the dinner starts, so for those of you who have never had a School Song of your own, let me bequeath you *this* one. It's new so it can be used with impunity, without some 'beastly rotter' accusing you of pinching it from *his* school. The chorus is in Latin, naturally, but I won't insult you by translating it. It is to be sung to the tune of *Vivat Rex Edwardus Sextus* with straight face and no giggling.

Toe to toe with your comrade on the playing field of life.
With a hand to lend, to a fallen friend, when he's tackled in the strife.
Seize the ball of hope from the fly-half as it comes from the scrum of
   care,
Once it's in your clutch make a sprint for touch, let him hinder you
   who dares.
Then with your head held high,
Bravely sing, as you score life's try . . .
All together now. In omnia!!
Omne crede diem tibi diluxisse supremum,
Grata super veniet quae non superabitur hora.
Me pinguem et nitidum bene curata cute vises
Cum ridere voles epicure de grege porcum.

Just before I 'left' Sherborne for good, I walked and talked with my
father, trying to make him understand. His mood was one of sym-
pathy, but I don't think he or my brothers ever really believed in the
'Dotheboy's Hall'-Dickensian manner in which sections of one of
England's most illustrious schools were allowed to be run.

It was during this talk that I felt closer to my Dad than ever before.
For the first time we seemed to be communicating and listening to
each other, and I was certainly listening when he mentioned a 'co-
educational school' as a possible follow-up to Sherborne. The idea of
being educated with girls as well as boys made my heart sing. 'Now
that,' I thought, 'really *would* complete my education,' and so it did.
There and then, we plumped for Frensham Heights, near Farnham in
Surrey.

During the few ensuing weeks left to me at Sherborne, I managed to
stay out of trouble. Then followed a short holiday until I joined my
new school, where at last I discovered scholastic happiness.

It was one day as I was savouring the friendliness and companionship of Frensham Heights that I reflected on the misery I had
suffered at Sherborne at the hands of Smith and Jones, and decided to
send them a 'frightener' letter or two; letters such as 'Vengeance will
be mine, saith The Lord,' and signed 'The Black Hand'.

But the old saying 'out of sight, out of mind' seems, in my case, to
have applied, for the importance of the Black Hand's vengeance faded
remarkably quickly in competition with the close proximity of nubile
young ladies. I thought no more about S and J until years later in 1940
when, as a very fit Ordinary Seaman in His Majesty's Royal Navy, I
entered the bar of the Café Royal in Regent Street, in the company of

three other Jolly-Jacks. This was a favourite haunt of mine, for even as a humble Blue Jacket I was always made to feel welcome by Trevor the barman. Sitting at the bar and glancing to left and right to see if any of my old theatre friends were there, I noticed a sallow looking soldier sitting plumply and dejectedly in the corner. His face seemed vaguely familiar and I was fighting to put a name to it when it hit me like a thunderbolt. It was Smith, of Smith and Jones, and he'd walked right into the lions' den.

Putting down my drink, I walked slowly across to the man that I hated so much.

'Hello Smith,' I said jauntily, 'remember me?'

'No, I don't think so,' he replied, with evident disinterest. 'Should I?'

'You certainly should, but that's of no consequence. The important thing is, I've got something for you.'

'Oh, what?' he asked with more regard.

'This,' I answered and with that I hauled off and hit him such a beauty, that he left his bar stool at an angle of forty-five degrees and hardly touched the ground before hitting the opposite wall. My fury, bottled up inside me all those years, exploded, and if the combined forces of Trevor and my mates had not pulled me off him, I might still be in the nick for manslaughter.

Before sending the devastated Smith on his painful way, I gave him a message.

'If you see your friend Jones, tell him that if he ever comes into my line of vision, exactly the same thing will happen to him. Understand?'

He understood, all right. I had made sure of that.

Lightning, they say, never strikes in the same place twice: Well it did, for on my very next long-weekend leave in London, I was walking up Piccadilly on my way to Trevor's bar when I saw across the road, having his shoes cleaned by the Redcoat Shoeshine Man, an A/C plonk with a face of strangely knowable mien. Squinting to pull it better into focus, I stopped still – and paused for recollection. Then, with a bellow you could've heard in Harrow-on-the-Hill, I shouted, 'Jesus Christ, it's Jones!!' and with that I was off across the road after him, hotly pursued by my three self-same mates, crying 'Oh shit, not *again!*'

By this time the terrified Jones had got the message and was away down the alley, scattering all before him in an endeavour to get away from what seemed like four deadly assassins. Half-way down Lower

Regent Street, we could tell that here was a quarry in no physical condition even to run for a bus, so settling down to a nice steady jog I said, 'It's all right lads, relax, there'll be no fisticuffs this time, I promise you.'

'What're you going to do then?' they asked.

'Run the bastard down,' I answered.

And so we ran him across the Mall, and around St James Park calling out 'Remember, Jones, what happened to Smith, is going to happen to you.'

Just by Caxton Hall he collapsed on to the pavement, crying, 'Don't hurt me, *please* don't hurt me.'

'Come along, me old mate,' I said, any idea of further vengeance completely gone from my mind. 'You just sit here and have a nice rest. You've just had a bit too much to drink, that's all,' and sitting him on a nearby bench, normally occupied by winos, we went contentedly on our way.

'Did you see that, Nellie?' said an elderly passer-by to her companion. 'It's what I've always said, there's no-one as kind and thoughtful as "Jack" when he's ashore.'

★

It was in 1935, at the age of sixteen that I entered Frensham Heights which was under the Headmastership of one of the great educationalists of his time, Mr Paul Roberts. One of the originators of Bedales, he was a rotund, bald, genial man with a pronounced stutter and an abundance of charm. The school, a vast Victorian mansion, was an ancient pile of great importance, the previous owner having been an industrialist of note. Its main building, towering behind an imposing drive and a hundred acres of beautifully laid out parkland, housed, fed and slept us; its stables, with their half-opened doors, were our class-rooms. Above, in converted lofts, were the weaving looms, pottery wheels and kilns. There were also carpenters' shops, engineering workshops, green-houses, and a printing press. Thus we were not only taught in healthy, beautiful surroundings, but also to be very independent. The girls wove the material for curtains, cushions and bedcovers, and turned cups, plates, and mugs on the pottery wheels. The boys turned wooden plates on the lathes, and made the most original and comfortable armchairs out of four large pieces of wood and four small pegs.

We cultivated flowers and vegetables, learned how to repair and put back together our ancient tractor and Ford pick-up, and later on during my wonderfully happy sojourn there, I was helped and encouraged to dig out and build an open air theatre from the side of a hill, overlooking a small wood. It's still there, just – I saw it through the weeds only three years past.

In that same theatre, we put on amongst ourselves two stage productions of near professional standard. One was *Twelfth Night*, and the other – an extraordinary choice for a school play – *Lady Precious Stream*, the traditionally presented Chinese play that had had such enormous success in the West End of London.

They say asking an actor how he feels about critics is like asking a cow how she feels about flies! In my case, I have over the years been remarkably well-served by critics, and of such, this notice in the local paper was my first.

'The role of the "Wei", the Tiger General, knowing nothing and saying much, was filled by J. Pertwee in a very noteworthy fashion. His features were made to look, indeed, like "Nothing on Earth". He was a masterpiece of grotesqueness and his character was in keeping. The General had an impersonator here, who made the most of any situation and amused the audience immensely. J. Pertwee proved a "real live wire" throughout, and gave an outstanding performance.'

I was inordinately proud of that notice, and bought up the village shop's entire stock of the issue to impress my many friends and relations, although in truth I could have well done without the 'real live wire' acclamation!

For the first time in my life I really began to learn. Not because I had to, but because I wanted to. The teachers were interesting and knowledgeable of their subjects, and the curriculum was intelligent, allowing a student to work several one hour study periods consecutively, thus enabling him to complete the 'peak' set him by his tutor. In most other schools work periods of three quarters of an hour were the norm. A quarter of an hour to settle down, a quarter of an hour doing as little work as possible, and a quarter of an hour keeping one's eye firmly on the clock ready to pack up 'instanter' at the sound of its first 'ding'. In summer, we swam in a large open-air pool and there was nothing in the rule book about wearing costumes. Mr Roberts left that up to the discretion of the pupils. The junior school, of course, couldn't be bothered with such encumbrances, and leaped naked into the pool with freedom and joy, splashing and playing without embarrassment. Whereas in the main, the senior boys and girls chose their moments to swim naked with care and decorum. Naturally, as with all sex-conscious teenagers, a certain amount of surreptitious peeking went on from behind the laurel bushes, but once properly 'glimmed', the excitement of his or her nudity soon palled. 'Long live the bikini,' say I. But there was one young lady of eighteen, with a body you could only describe as bountiful. She was more aware of her body than any woman I've met before or since. She stood on the diving board in classic pose – one hand scooping her hair from the nape wildly on to the top of her head, the other hand flat on her golden hip, for she always displayed a perfect, even tan. Her head was back, her mouth half open, her back arched, her superb breasts held high. If she hadn't been so naturally beautiful, one would have had to laugh at her inimitable hokum. Paul Roberts approached her in mid-display one balmy evening and said, 'M-my dear B-B-B-ettina, don't th-th-th-ink f-f-for one mo-mo-moment that I am objecting to your s-s-s-plendid n-n-nudity or your irrrrrrevocable r-r-r-right to d-d-d-display it, but I d-d-d-on't want you to th-th-th-think you will quickly c-c-c-con-vert the w-w-world to n-n-n-akedness.' But it was thanks to Bettina's healthy attitude to sex that I became less inhibited over such matters. There was a Minstrels' Gallery over the ballroom and when the Saturday night dances were on below, I and a girlfriend would repair to the Gallery, lock ourselves in, and to the shouts of joy from below, add our own, vociferously. The element of proximity, discovery and danger added fuel to the flame.

School rules stated intelligently that pupils should only go out in threes, two girls and one boy, or two boys and one girl, so, whichever way you looked at it, you always finished up with a 'gooseberry'. Even your mate was loath to leave you alone with your girl. 'All very well for you,' he'd say. 'What about me? What am I going to do?' Exactly the same thing applied to a two-girl situation. Girls or boys, the old saying 'I don't think much of yours' couldn't have been more applicable.

It is often believed that in co-educational schools, sex is rife, and that the incumbents are permanently 'at it like knives'. I can assure you that in my day this was far from the case. The 'three' rule was closely observed and young love blossomed gradually, companionship and respect taking preference over fornication.

But there was one influence in the school that Paul Roberts could well have done without. His name was Peter Schamasch, a French boy well schooled in sexual matters, as his elder brother on his hols would, as a special treat, stand him the occasional short-time 'session' in one of

Paris's many brothels. Peter tried hard to bring the atmosphere of these seamy 'palaces of sin' back with him to Frensham Heights, and one night crept downstairs to the girls' landing, with three horny virgin boys he had recruited. Finding the room and its anxiously awaiting inhabitants, Peter and his cronies popped into the various beds of their chosen loved ones and proceeded to get down to some heavy petting, their bags of goodies and ciggies 'for after' placed neatly on the bedside tables. Before any actual insertions could be made, Paul Roberts and Mrs Roberts walked into the room. 'Well, h-h-hello! And w-w-w-hat have we here? A f-f-f-feast in the dorm? C-c-can w-w-we join in?' The sheepish eight shot bolt upright in their beds, the male participants' passions shrinking into insignificance.

'Y-y-y-yes of ccccourse, sir,' stammered Peter giving a commendable yet unintentional impersonation of the Head.

As I heard it, they then handed round the goodies, smoked the 'ciggies', and were bundled unceremoniously out of the room by the Roberts, with a 'Well, th-th-that w-w-was f-f-fun, we m-m-must do it again some day.'

The next morning during prayers, Paul announced a school holiday, to be spent at Frensham Ponds. There were to be races and games galore, and a good time to be had by all. By midday the 'Schamasch night-owls' were wilting somewhat, as they seemed to be the first picked for any of the more strenuous activities, be it athletics, games, running messages, climbing trees or chopping wood. By 6.30 we were back at school exhausted and happy, but the 'Schamasch gang' looked a little wan, to say the least. 'I've g-got a g-great idea,' said Mr Roberts after evening prayers, 'l-let's go on a na-na-nature ramble tonight, eh? W-w-what about it, P-P-Peter, you and your f-f-friends would appreciate that w-w-wouldn't you? You l-l-like staying up late at night.' At last the dawn! Suddenly we realised what the old fox was up to and that night, in the company of two other masters, he hiked that poor exhausted bunch of youngsters over half the county of Surrey. Around three o'clock in the morning they could take no more and collapsed in a damp heap on a log. 'What's th-this, g-g-giving up so s-s-soon?' he enquired with what seemed like sincere concern, but before Peter could reply, went on, 'You know P-P-Peter, the o-o-older I get the m-m-more I realise that ni-ni-ni-night-time is really b-b-best occupied by sleeping, d-d-don't you agree?' Last seen, he had hoisted the most junior member of the sex-club on to his back and headed back to the school, where as a man of middle years, his own bed was frantically beckoning.

There was a *real* teacher of men! Who could fail to respond to such simple, albeit wearisome, psychology?

★

From a very early age, I have always had a 'thing' about motorbikes. Michael owned a round-tanked 350cc Sidevalve BSA called 'The Green Bile', and I hankered after its like, desperately! So imagine my delight when I found that a mile or two from the school there was a large motorcycle garage run by three of the best grass-track riders in the country, Len, Sammy and Alan. At weekends whenever I could get away, I cycled over to the nearby race meetings to cheer on my heroes and inhale that wonderful smell of Castrol 'R', like a 'Bisto' kid.

On one of my visits to this garage, I spied a little black-tanked 250cc SOS trials bike. It was short and stubby with high handlebars and an almost straight-through exhaust. With its knobbly trials tyres it was a little beauty and I foolishly asked, 'How much?'

'To you, as a you're a friend, five pounds,' said Len. I should've known better, but I promptly bought it. Taxed and insured third party (whatever that meant), it came to seven pound ten shillings. Three shillings short, I was 'trusted' by friend Len and not feeling *too* guilty about 'whitish' lies concerning driving licences and previous riding experience, I wheeled the little monster out into the road to take her for a spin. She started on the thirteenth kick and bursting into a snarl, shot off in a perfect 'wheelie' nearly landing me flat on my back. Fighting to keep this mechanical version of Shadow under some sort of control I wove my way down the road towards Frensham Ponds, in spurts, jerks, and the crashing of gears. The expression on Len's face as I disappeared from sight was one of undisguised horror, for plainly this young idiot had never ridden a motorcycle before in his life. Roaring round a blind corner less than a quarter of a mile from the garage, I came to a T-junction. There was a low flint wall facing me belonging to the cottage behind it. Completely out of control I shot across the road, hit the wall, and knocked myself unconscious. Worst of all, I badly damaged the wheel and front forks of my precious machine. The occupants of the cottage were having tea in the garden when I joined them, from over the wall; and upon my regaining consciousness, sent for the doctor, who not only arranged for Len to collect what was left of my prophetically named SOS motorbike but also put my pushbike on his luggage rack, drove me back to school and promised to tell the Headmaster that I'd taken a toss over the handlebars of my (unfortunately for the veracity of the story) strangely undamaged bicycle.

Paul Roberts proved to be most solicitous and concerned at my 'cycling' accident and visited me in the san with many words of comfort.

At the end of that term, on my last day at Frensham Heights, we were queuing up to shake hands and say goodbye to Paul and his wife, when that funny twinkle came into his eye as he said, 'Well, go-go-go-goodbye, Jon, d-d-do take care of yourself on that bl-bl-bloody motorbike of yours, w-w-w-on't you.'

The old fox had outwitted the hounds once again. I loved him and wish there were more teachers of his calibre alive today.

There is a strange codicil to add to that story. Some fifty years later I was driving my son Sean down to his new school Pierrepont near Farnham, in Surrey, when, just as I was about to turn into the school drive, I vaguely became aware of a familiar cottage with a low flint wall and a small side road facing it. There was a sudden flash of remembrance of that heartbreaking day all those long years ago when I had rammed my newly bought motorbike headlong into such a wall. Could it be the self-same one? Stopping the car, I ran back to the T-junction and retraced the route I imagined my bike had taken before it struck. This manoeuvre brought me directly to the spot where the wheel and the front forks of my beloved machine had hit. There, for Sean and I to see plainly, was a badly chipped brick and a splintered flint as new and as fresh as if I had collided with it yesterday.

★

And so with a final burst of 'Dei Gratia sum quod sum', considerable relief and little education to speak of, I hang up my school cap forever and move briskly to the next age.

Chapter 4

I first donned my professional hat – number five in Shakespeare's list – before I became either a soldier or a 'serious' lover. The fifth hat should by rights, be that of 'The Justice, in fair round belly with good capon lined.' But what I actually put on, was I suppose, the cap and bells, becoming what I'd always wanted to be, an actor. Unfortunately acting as a calling is not exactly renowned for its justice, nor for possessors of fair round capon-lined bellies, for it is a fact that we strolling players frequently stroll more than we play – and you don't get paid for strolling!

However, completely undeterred by this, and a 'mature' seventeen, I announced to my father in 1936, 'Dad, I want to be an actor.' My father, having *been* an actor, at least didn't have those peculiar notions of the stage that some people still firmly believe in – that all actresses are grossly immoral, that all actors are effeminate, and that everyone connected with the theatre lies in bed stoned until noon, with two or more other people drinking champagne. He therefore received the news with commendable calm, reflecting no doubt that my academic prowess hardly fitted me for politics, science or the law, and contented himself by quoting George Moore who said, 'Acting is the lowest of the arts, *if* it is an art at all.' Dad was by then of course a Writer.

*

For my chosen and now parentally approved profession, help was offered by my Uncle Guy, a teacher at the Central School of Dramatic Art as well as the Guildhall School of Music and Drama, and as such, a friend and confidant of the principal of the former school, Elsie Fogarty. Small in build but a giant in personality, Miss Fogarty was a lady who struck terror into the hearts of all who came before her, but as a dramatic and voice teacher she was unsurpassed and had coached many of the 'greats', including Laurence Olivier. Uncle Guy was of the opinion that if I could only get past an interview with this she-demon, the audition and subsequent entry would be a doddle. So, employing all his wiles, he talked Miss Fogarty into seeing me.

I had prepared a piece taken from one of Uncle Guy's many works, *The Reciter's Treasury of Verse*, and presented myself clean and bushy-tailed to the great lady's office for inspection. She looked up at me towering above her for what seemed like an eternity, and then said, a trifle disparagingly, 'Humph!' My confidence began to ebb.

'Hand me that chair, if you would be so kind,' she said. I did so and, grabbing a newspaper from her desk, she rolled it up into what I could only assume to be a club with which to strike me, and stood up on the chair. Now eyeball to eyeball she commanded, 'Open your mouth.'

I did as I was bid, having no idea what was to follow. She then took the tightly rolled newspaper in her right hand, my chin in her left, and thrusting the paper into my mouth, said, 'Now bite hard.' Bewildered, I bit.

'All right, you can let go now,' she said tetchily, endeavouring to extricate the roll from my dental grip.

Getting down from the chair, she took the bitten newspaper over to the window to obtain a better look at it, and after studying the indentations from all angles, announced her findings.

'You've a malformation of the mouth, young man. Your teeth are set incorrectly in your jaw, causing your tongue, which is too big for your mouth, to stick through your teeth instead of resting *behind* them. The result of all this is a very sibilant 'S'. I'm sorry, I've no place for you here at my school, and I would strongly advise you to take up another profession.'

With this firm pronouncement, all my ambitions, my hopes and my dreams went sailing out of this hell hag's window. Then becoming firm of purpose I thought, 'I'll show her. Just you wait and see – I'll show her!'

As a consequence I auditioned for, and luckily (for there were numerous applicants) was accepted by the Royal Academy of Dramatic Art, to which, during my early days, I commuted daily by train from Caterham, where I was then living.

By this time I was the proud owner of a 150cc James 2 Stroke motorcycle, and one morning having ridden it down from the house, left it by the station padlocked to a lamp-post. You can imagine my chagrin, therefore, when I returned one evening to discover that not only had my motorcycle gone, but so had the lamp-post! If it wasn't the Council that had taken them away then it must have been a thief, and if that was the case what was the thief after? A new motorcycle or an old lamp-post? Luckily for me the motorcycle was found a few days

79

later lying in a bed of hollyhocks, but of the lamp-post there was never a sign.

One Sunday I found there was to be a 'Grand Talent Competition' at the local cinema, and I decided that the prize of one pound was a very sufficient incentive to enter. I had, a few weeks before, purchased an astonishing new invention from America called a 'UKA', a ukulele with a box of buttons attached on the neck to the frets. This enabled you, by depressing one of twelve buttons, to play a complete four string chord. The speed and accuracy of the chord changing was prodigious and your 'UKA' playing could, with practice, be made to sound as good and look as proficient and dextrous as 'Ukulele Ike' or George Formby. My entry for the contest was therefore effected, and singing *Leaning on a Lamp-post* and *The Window Cleaner* with great zest and élan, I was declared a popular winner – popular, that is, with all but the other competitors, who were unanimous in their condemnation of my employing a 'gimmick' to facilitate the chord playing.

Came the Grand Finale, where, as the winner, I was invited to step forward and once again entertain the audience with my humour, musicianship and song.

But the devil had been at work, and I was not half way through my hilarious rendering of *Window Cleaner* when the 'gimmick' suddenly became detached and fell slowly off the neck of the ukulele, to swing on one of its now broken strings, like Dick Turpin on a gibbet. As I was incapable of playing on four strings, let alone three, my performance came to a shuddering standstill, and to the accompanying jeers and cries of 'That'll show you, Faker!' from the delighted contestants, I gathered my broken junk together and hurriedly made for the exits.

★

I had always thought of Granny as being indestructible, so when that ample, bosomy lady began to fade away into nothingness I was completely shattered, even though I was a teenager at the time and old enough to understand and accept the fact that this beautiful creature I loved so much was being eaten away by cancer. Week by week, living as I was at Caterham, I watched her disappearing from my sight until she was so bodiless and fragile that I wished I could have taken her upon my lap for comfort and consolation. Being the valiant soul she was, she fought the demon, tooth and nail, but when she realised the battle was lost she accepted defeat with grace.

'I do not wish to die upstairs where I am alone and can see nothing.

Please put my bed in the sitting room where I can look out on the garden and talk with the boys.'

So it was done, and there she lay getting more and more skeletal, her dear face becoming transparent and bloodless as her life ebbed away. One morning with the garden door open to a beautiful day and the flowers ablaze with life she gave a deep sigh and gave up her own.

Uncle Guy and Michael went off to Caterham to see the undertaker and make arrangements for the funeral, leaving me alone in the house with Granny, for I wanted to stay with her. On tip toe, as if not to waken her, I went to the side of her bed and drew back the sheet that covered her wasted face. She looked quite serene and at peace, with the trace of a smile crinkling the corners of her mouth. For the first time in months she looked quite free from pain. 'So death can't be that bad,' I thought. Bending over I kissed for the last time the now cold lips of the one person in my life who had shown me nothing but unadulterated love. For me, the summer of 1936 was a dark one.

★

With Granny's death, I moved back to Dad's home and commuted to and from RADA from number 86.

In order to save the bus fare of a few pennies from Goodge Street tube station to South Kensington, I frequently walked the three miles plus home, often making a detour through the infamous 'Shepherd Market'. This beautiful corner of old London was, and still is, the workplace of 'ladies of the night', and as such was a great visual attraction for a virtually virgin boy such as myself. Just to be approached and spoken to by the beautiful 'young' ladies was a thrill in itself, albeit a vicarious one. They 'sashayed' their way up and down the streets, resplendent in shiny black very high-heeled shoes, form-fitting dresses and silver-fox capes, and seemed to me to be the epitome of glamour. Such was my naivety that for some time I genuinely believed that they were taking their dogs for a walk.

One day, I was stopped by a coloured girl of around twenty-five, the most exotic creature on whom I'd ever clapped an eye. She had long straight black hair that reached below her waist, and the full-fledged body of another Dorothy Lamour.

'Hello,' she said. 'Looking for a nice girl?'

'N-n-no thank you,' I stammered, 'I'm j-j-just on my way home.'

'What a pity,' she replied. 'Perhaps another time.'

'Y-y-yes of course, a-a-another time,' and with that interesting and witty rejoinder I sped away, scarlet in my confusion.

I thought about our encounter a lot that night, and decided that at our next meeting (for I was determined there should be one), I would talk to her properly. Ask her some pertinent and original questions such as 'What's a nice girl like you doing in a profession like this?' or 'What made you take up this kind of work?'

Unfortunately, in spite of all my careful preparation, at our next encounter the dialogue had not progressed very much.

'Hello again, what about coming back to my place for a little fun?'

'Er n-n-no thanks, I've g-g-got to g-get home.'

'What's your name?'

'Er, J-J-Jon Pertwee,' I answered, a touch formally.

'Mine's Touma, are you sure you don't want to come back home with me?'

'Q-q-quite sure,' I said, 'thank you just the same,' and once more I was off through the market like a dose of salts.

In the confines of my bedroom I thought the matter out and decided that the 'affair' had gone on long enough and that I would never speak to her again. After all, I reasoned, if I allowed it to progress any further I might finish up in bed with her and catch some dreadful social disease. Then there was the not unimportant question of money. If I was so skint as to find it necessary to walk home to save fourpence, I could hardly afford the undoubtedly exorbitant prices of Touma's loving favours.

So next day it was:–

'Hello Jon!'

'Hello Touma.'

'Coming?'

'I can't, I haven't any money.' So much for my *moral* intentions!

'Then how about a cup of tea?'

'Oh all right! T-t-thanks.'

My first get-together with a prostitute and I finished up having a cup of tea, not her!

She was a most companionable girl, of mixed Polynesian and Welsh birth and lived in a small flat in the market over a café, which was most convenient for sending things up. Two or three times a week, slipped in between her 'engagements', I would have tea with Touma in her tiny flat and be expected to admire all her touchingly 'kitsch' things. China figurines, colourfully embroidered pictures, satin cushions, Spanish dolls and shawls, and a vast collection of unsuitably named stuffed animals that covered her bed and presumably had to be removed to make room for each new client.

I should tell you here and now that my visits to Touma were social and not professional, although on quite a few occasions when business was slack, I was generously offered a 'freebie'. To my complete discredit I spurned this golden-skinned opportunity and tried to convince myself that I preferred to keep our relationship platonic.

I took a lot of convincing, that's for sure, but in truth, I think fear of the unknown had a lot to do with it. Oh! the agonies of adolescence when you're spotty, nervous and dying to be thirty.

*

Like most students, I defied convention in my mode of dress. But unlike today where it seems imperative to look as scruffy as possible, with torn jeans, ripped sleeves and Army boots, in the 30s the accent was on elegance. Hair was poetically long, corduroy trousers in bright hues were of the essence, and black elastic-sided boots from Anello and Davide, a must. I wore white shirts with Byronesque collars, my grandfather's Inverness cape with scarlet lining (later to be worn in *Doctor Who*), and to set the seal on my sartorial splendour, I carried an ivory-knobbed malacca cane, borrowed from my foppish father, who once said in my hearing to an insolent commissionaire, 'Steady, fellow, watch your tongue. I'd as lief lay my cane around your shoulders!'

No wonder I coveted that stick, after such a verbal association.

The girls mostly wore clothes of the flowing ethnic variety, in sinful black or virginal white; with hair hanging long and free, they looked utterly feminine and the complete opposite of today's slammerkin, with her spiky or shorn hair-style and accompanying draggle-tail look. What red-blooded male wants such a white-faced, unfeminine, boy-like girl for a bedfellow!

Unlike most students, however, I occasionally carried my mode of dress even further than the 'defying convention' stage, and lost no opportunity of playing character parts in 'real' life.

My brother Michael reports in *Name Dropping* that I was seen getting off a London tube train, on two crutches and wearing dark glasses, helped by an old lady. Moreover, he says that if I gave an explanation he cannot remember it. The explanation is simplicity itself. I was 'in character', and it would seem to have been a reasonably good performance, or the old lady wouldn't have been helping me.

I also remember donning, from time to time, full Highland dress, consisting of kilt, plaid, sporran and skean dhu, plus frilly shirt and jacket with ruffles at my cuffs.

I suspect Goldsmith would have said of me what he once said of the actor David Garrick: 'On stage, he was naturally simple, affecting. 'Twas only that when he was off he was acting.'

During my time at RADA my father was a Governor there, but let no-one ever accuse him of nepotism. That was something he was almost paranoid about. He would 'open doors' for me, but it was *I* who had to go in and get the job. For those of you inclined to disbelieve this, let me quickly inform you that my sojourn at RADA was predictably short. There were several reasons for this, not the least of which was that the Principal, Sir Kenneth Barnes, had given his considered opinion that I had no talent whatsoever.

The real trouble all stemmed from my refusing to be a wind. A Greek wind. The director, Mrs Wheeler, had cast me as a member of the chorus in Euripides' *Iphigenia*, and I can assure you there is nothing more unutterably boring than being a wind in a Greek play. Whilst everyone else is whooping it up and having a wonderful time, winds have to stay downstage left and go 'Woooooo!!' throughout the play with monotonous regularity.

I begged Mrs Wheeler to remove me from my duties as a zephyr and let me take a more active part in the piece, such as one of the soldiers who, in every Greek play, rushes on stage and informs the riveted audience that the most dreadful thing has happened 'right over there,' pointing (conveniently for the budget) just off-stage. But she would have none of it. It was a wind or nothing! I, anxious to become an actor, and not a flatulent noise-effects man, chose the latter. Sir Kenneth was not best pleased and sent for me to issue a severe reprimand. 'On top of all this,' he said, 'I understand that you have been writing rude things about myself and members of my staff on the lavatory walls.' Evidently it seemed that some light-weight author had written in red ink, in a handwriting remarkably similar to my own, 'Mrs Wheeler without Kenneth Barnes is like a fish without a bicycle,' an obscure observation, and mildly humorous, but nothing I would have thought to get one's knickers in a twist over. Sir Kenneth thought otherwise and decided he would pursue the matter further, so later that day I was summoned to his office again, to face my peers and let them decide my fate. On entering, I found the room to be filled with grave-faced students of both sexes sitting as if waiting for death. I certainly wasn't, and as I had no intention of doing so, I walked back out of the room and left them sitting there feeling frightfully silly. My father, having heard my side of the story and believing it, supported me to the hilt and informed Sir Kenneth via a letter delivered by my own hand (a nice touch that) that he intended suing for defamation of character and was engaging for my defence the services of one of the world's greatest barristers and KCs, Sir Patrick Hastings, and England's premier graphologist, Mr Charles Hoskins. As could be expected that was the end of it, and within a week the real lavatory chronicler had been caught red-handed.

But Sir Kenneth's opinion of my future as an actor remained unchanged, and I was expected to leave at the end of that term, although, as Sir Kenneth soon found to his chagrin, his opinion was not shared by one of the greatest talents this country has ever produced. We had been rehearsing a J. B. Priestley play and, as always due to the large number of students, each role was divided up into sections and played by as many as six different people. In my case however, I was to play two very small roles instead – a man who was murdered in the first act *and* the detective who found out who murdered him in the third. For the former part I sported a monocle, black moustache, hair parted in the middle, and an upper-class accent, and for the latter, a red wig, red moustache, raincoat, old trilby hat and a Cockney accent. The play was performed at the Academy's own theatre, the Vanbrugh, before a packed audience of students, friends and a celebrated adjudicator in the person of Mr Noel Coward. After the show Sir Kenneth brought Mr Coward backstage to talk to the cast, and while there, asked him if he had been entertained and if there were any students amongst us worthy of mention.

'Oh yes indeed there was a very good, very very young, young lady I thought to be absolutely excellent.' (If my memory serves me right this was Joan Greenwood.) 'The boy playing the man murdered in the first act shows definite promise – and the detective who found out who murdered him in the third is certainly not untalented. You have two actors with a future there, two young men definitely to be watched.'

I curled up with joy, not only at the great man's prognostication, but particularly at Sir Kenneth's discomfiture.

'What were their names?' asked Noel Coward.

'Er, Greenwood – Joan Greenwood,' replied Sir Kenneth.

'No, the two young actors' names?'

'Er, well it was the same actor actually,' mumbled Sir Kenneth, 'a Jon Pertwee.'

'Who?'

'Jon Pertwee.' This time louder.

'Any relation to Roland?'

'Yes. Son.'

'Ah, yes, I played in *Where the Rainbow Ends* with him when I first started. A talented man, with a talented son, certain to do well.'

I could have hugged him, because within hours I was to leave the Academy as a student who, according to the Principal, was incompetent, untalented, and with nothing to offer an honourable profession!

Some years later I had the pleasure of meeting the great character actor, Charles Laughton. 'I understand,' he said, lower lip curled almost to his chin, 'that you were thrown out of RADA?'

I flushed with embarrassment, for I was more than a little ashamed of that rebellious era and bitterly regretted the time that I had wasted.

'Yes, I'm afraid I was, Mr Laughton,' I replied.

'Good! Splendid fellow, then you're *bound* to do well! So was I! All the best people get chucked out of RADA,' he added as a codicil. Not strictly true, of course, but it certainly made me feel less guilty about a period in my life of which I was not particularly proud.

★

Due to my friendship with their two sons at Frensham Heights, on 'leaving' RADA, I was able to meet, audition for, and obtain a place in, Hugh McKay and Eleanor Elder's 'Arts League of Service Travelling Theatre'. This was a company of considerable prestige brought to it by the past presence in its ranks of so many well known actors – amongst them, Sara Algood, Sir Donald Wolfit, and both Baddeley sisters Hermione and Angela.

Its motto was to 'Bring the arts into everyday life' – something it did only *too* successfully! So many provincial Amateur Dramatic Societies copied the artistic principle and design of its portable stage, proscenium arch and lighting, and formed their own Companies, that, towards the end of the 30s, the ALS, as it was popularly known, was sadly forced out of business.

The ALS followed in the tracks of the old-time itinerant actors, known as barn-stormers, who barn-stormed their way across England. We travelled in a converted double-decker bus, the top half carrying the Company and the bottom half the stage, lighting, props and costume skips. The Company was small; a driver-cum-master-of-all-trades, a pianist, two character actresses, two character actors, a juvenile character actor (me), two young lady dancer-actresses, classical and folk, a mime (female), and from time to time, now an old man, Hugh McKay himself – dressed in a long black robe, he sang unaccompanied Hebridean folk songs quite hauntingly. There was a

86

standard printed programme of some 150 items, and each village or town could choose its own programme, as long as it contained at least two extracts from the classics, ancient or modern. The Bard of course being the foremost choice.

For the rest, there were song solos, dances (folk and ballet), sea-shanties, mime, monologues, marionettes and dramatic poems, ten of these latter items making up the remainder of the programme. A 'fit-up' Company, for that is what we were, played a different venue every night, hence the term 'a one night stand'. On arrival, the chosen programme would be carefully perused by the Touring Manager, the stage rigged by the men and the necessary costumes put out by the women. Sometimes, when there was no electricity available, our own carbide-gas lighting system had to be installed. The proscenium arch carrying the front tabs and wings was adjustable, and could be made to fit a large stage or a small platform. Scenery consisted of drapes or ingeniously designed cut-outs. Dimmers were the clay drainpipe and water variety. It was a fast, slick, well-produced show and quite deserving of its reputation.

For bed and board each member of the Company stayed the night with a different local family, something that was, in the main, enjoyed by both parties. It really was the rich man, poor man, beggarman, thief situation, for one never knew which it was going to be from one day to the next. If you wanted to know how the other half lived, this was the way to find out. On one occasion, I was staying in the house of a very rich mill owner who was also a collector of fine porcelain. Expressing an interest in his collection I was handed an egg-shell china plate to look at, and told that to appreciate its beauty to the full I should hold it up to the light between my palms. This I did, but due to the nerve-wracking quality of the situation, they were unusually moist, causing the priceless article to slip from my grasp and fall to the parquet flooring. Just prior to it shattering into a thousand pieces, I swung my foot forward as if in slow-motion and gently kicked it into the air under the horrified gaze of my host and hostess. It flew through the room in a parabolic arc to land quite undamaged thirty feet away on to a well-upholstered 'Chesterfield' settee. 'Hecky thump,' said my host, open-mouthed, 'do you often do things like that?'

'Every day' was the only reply that seemed appropriate at the time.

On the other side of the coin, I once stayed with a family in a tenement building. There were eight of them altogether and they lived in only two rooms, but that didn't stop them wanting to do their bit for the ALS, which they patronised annually. My host was impoverished, uneducated and illiterate, but managed in spite of all the cards stacked against him to be the most charming and generous of hosts. After the show his two small sons were sent out for supper – one to collect the fish and chips suitably vinegared, salted and wrapped in the *Daily Mirror* for 'starters', and the other to get pie, chips and green 'likker' sauce for the 'main'. I'd never tasted 'likker' before and found it to be delicious. There are only a few places left that serve it, but one in the East End of London is still patronised by the 'cognoscenti', Tommy Steele among others.

For 'finishers' my hostess had made a real bread and butter pudding, all crispy on the top with burned currants, just the way I liked it. Washed down with a half pint of old and mild and innumerable cups of hot sweet tea, it was a meal fit for a king.

The sleeping arrangements were not of the highest order however, but at least I was warm, for I had to share a bed with two of the small boys, who after a quick drag on a 'Players-weight' went speedily off to sleep. There's nothing better than two human hot water bottles.

Much art and entertainment had been brought into village and small town life by the ALS since they started in 1919 when facilities for village entertainment were practically nil, and although the need for travelling theatres does not exist to the same extent today, it would be a tremendous pity if they should be allowed to go out of existence altogether, for while they exist, they cater for all tastes, and give the grounding that every young actor and actress needs.

Certainly the time I spent on that final tour was invaluable, for not only did it give me practical experience as an actor, singer, dancer and mime but also a better understanding of the general workings of a stage, its lighting, scene building, set painting, and most important of all, how to start a cold internal combustion engine at six o'clock in the morning!

★

After the sad demise of the 'Arts League' I was determined to find employment in a good repertory company, a task even in the 30s far harder than one might imagine. But for the determined there was a procedure to be adhered to rigidly.

First, there were the compulsory morning visits to the offices of the principal Repertory Agents in England, Miriam Warner above 'Alkits', in Cambridge Circus and Nora Nelson-King (later to become Ralph Richardson's mother-in-law) in St Martins Lane. These were two of the scruffiest and most dilapidated places of business and singularly depressing to sit in for any length of time, so by the time it took the fifty or so out-of-work actors to get in and see either of these two self-important ladies, one's confidence was at a very low ebb. We sat on long wooden benches reading *The Stage*, *The Performer* and *Theatre World*, avidly scanning the ads and awaiting the imperious call of 'Next.' This command was followed by a quick splintering slide up the bench, until one was eventually positioned right before the appropriate Gorgon's door.

At the next 'Next', in one went. At your tentative 'Good morning Mrs Nelson-King' she would look up, wracking her brain for your name.

'Nothing today, dear, too tall.'

The following day the dialogue might vary, however.

'Good morning, Mrs Nelson-King.'

'Nothing today, dear, too short.'

The same reasoning was often applied when observing your age.

'Nothing today dear, too old,' or conversely, 'Too young!'

It was a soul-destroying experience, but at least we had the resilience of youth.

Inevitably, the day had to come when you were just right, but then there was always the grim question of your remuneration to go through.

'It's only a small part dear, you've played it before so you won't need much rehearsal.' (That meant, of course, that the Company wouldn't have to pay so much.) 'You'll get your return train fare of course.'

'Of course. How much does the engagement carry, Mrs Warner?' (Note the avoidance of ugly words like 'job' and 'pay'.)

'Ah! Well I've discussed the matter with Mr Hanson most carefully, and he is prepared to offer you two and a half.'

'Only two and a half, Mrs Warner?'

'Yes dear, two pounds ten shillings – none of your fancy threes and fours.'

Fancy threes and fours? You could hardly make ends meet on *four*, let alone two and a half. It was said of an old actor who when faced with the same situation, declared to a friend, 'Yes I know dear boy, it is not a large salary but I have it on very good authority that there is an excellent pork pie in Act Two!'

The next item on the out-of-work-actors' agenda was lunch at 'Ma' Phillips' 'Olde Lanterne Cafe' in Lower Wardour Street. Here you could obtain a first class home-cooked lunch of soup, meat-plus-two-veg, and a pudding, for one shilling and three pence (coffee extra). The 'Olde Lanterne' consisted of two rooms only, one in the back for the actors, and one in the front for the regular 'Nobs' who were obliged to pay two shillings and sixpence for the singular privilege of sitting at a private table and having two cups of coffee (inclusive). For the itinerant minstrels in the back room there was a very large pine table to sit around, the facing ends of which were permanently occupied by two ladies, one a large, busty, full-mouthed virago called Ione Kinkum and the other a slight, small-boned, introvert named Ella Starling. In all the years I patronised 'The Olde Lanterne' I never remember these ladies being anywhere or doing anything, other than sitting at that table.

In the opposite corner was a very small round table, for the very large round person of 'Ma' Phillips and her boss-eyed, greyhound-gambling husband Bill. 'Bill is going to the dogs,' said 'Ma', and on looking at him, even for a moment, one could see she spoke the truth. When 'Ma' could toil no longer at serving table, she would sink her splendid haunches on to a minuscule stool, and cry out 'Nellie, take over the front! I've got to rest me "plates".' In her hand she held a large wet dishcloth and God help the poor sinner who made the mistake of letting drop a single swear word other than 'damn', for before the epithet had properly left the lips she'd strike the offender across the mouth with the cloth with the speed and accuracy of a spitting cobra.

'We'll have no more of that filth, thank you, Mr Pertwee! Another one like that and I'll ban you for a week!'

That threat would've steadied Hitler, and all talk from then on was tempered with extreme moderation.

Above the table was a blackboard and on this 'Ma' would write in chalk any messages, or tips of jobs going. The film-extras casting office often rang 'Ma' and requested actors and actresses for 'special' work, where, because you provided your own clothes, the salary was more.

There was one 'regular' from the front room known only by the nickname of 'Prompt'. Twice a week 'Prompt' would invite an actor or actress to 'take luncheon' with him, and it says something for the mystery man that his invitation was never spurned. The invitee waited patiently in the back room until the host arrived, and then passed proudly into the front room to enjoy the rare privilege of sitting at a private table for two, and indulging in that extra cup of coffee. We were never able to suss out 'Prompt' (a military man, perhaps??), childless, unmarried, 'straight', not gay, and undoubtedly of means.

Otherwise how could he have possibly afforded paying out five shillings twice a week? At an outlay of ten shillings – 50p – he would've had to have been extremely well off.

Upstairs there was a little Jewish tailor called Mr Bloom, who, sitting cross-legged on the top of his work-table, kept his young actor friends' clothes in a reasonable state of repair. He wore thick pebble glasses to no apparent purpose, as they rested permanently on the top of his head and were never to be seen on the end of his nose. Mr Bloom and 'Prompt' became contender 'hosts', a situation we played on to the full as it afforded us a double chance of being 'entertained'. The only trouble was that Mr Bloom and 'Prompt', for reasons of rivalry, insisted on 'cutting' each other, something which the tailor performed with considerably better skill, naturally.

This feud placed the invited one in a most difficult position, for if he cut Mr Bloom when being entertained by 'Prompt' or vice versa, the chances of being invited again were remote in the extreme. It was best to let the 'cutters' have at each other alone and find something fascinating to observe on the ceiling until the 'joust' was over.

After an 'everybody out' from 'Ma' it was 'everybody in' to the accommodating Blue Posts pub next door, to prove one's heartiness and manhood by downing, with elbow well up, one pint of bitter. It was seldom more than one, due to the necessary financial outlay, but you had to kill time somehow until 'Ma' once more opened up her portals for tea.

For one shilling, you got a pot of tea, buttered toast or toasted tea-cake, jam and pastries, the favourites of which were 'Ma's' magnificent strawberry tarts. There, we sipped, nibbled and talked until closing time at six.

Sad to say, I don't think establishments like that exist any longer. And even if they do, the characters certainly do not!

For an occasional change of scenery, there was always the 'S and F' in Denman Street. This was a totally different ball game, for here, you had to have two requisites, a supply of pennies and an old play script.

Armed with these two essential items, you sauntered casually into the restaurant, purchased a cup of coffee (then considered outré), sat down at the counter bar, sipped the coffee and, turning the cover back so that no-one could see that the play was of an age, pretended to read it.

This afforded the reader a great opportunity for histrionics, loud laughter (to oneself), frowns, whispered exclamation of 'No, no, no' with accompanying clucks! and tuts! This performance was of course to convince *other* out-of-work-actors, that *you* were, as always, *in* work, and had just been given the script of a new West End play to read and consider.

Now came the *moment critique*. When all envious eyes were upon you, you advanced to the telephone booth (yes, that's what the pennies were for), and making sure you had left the door open, dialled, ostensibly, your producer or agent but in reality a friend or relation. Pressing button A you said, 'Larry? or Ralph? or Binkie? or Emile? or Prince? or Jack? This is Jon' or whoever. 'Yes I'm reading it now – what? Well, it's not *bad*, but I'm not sure it's really *me*. Let me sleep on it, I'll let you know in the morning. What? Oh all right I'll try and finish it tonight and I'll ring you at home with my decision.' (A nice touch that, hinting at an intimate knowledge of the recipient's ex-directory home telephone number.) 'Bye, give my love to Jean, or Barbara, or Rosalind or Jimmy!'

The phone would be replaced and the 'chicaner' would exit, smiling broadly at the envy he had successfully evoked in his green-eyed audience.

Strange to relate, I never met anyone who believed in the veracity of those performances for one single moment, yet they continued un-abated until the outbreak of war and then suddenly it was 'Tomkins here, sir. Speak German sir? Fluently, sir! In plain clothes as usual, sir?'

From then on, as far as the actors' daily agenda was concerned, you were on your own, though for preference you endeavoured to make sure it was otherwise.

I had come to accept my daily visits to the offices of repertory agents Miriam Warner and Nora Nelson-King as part of my life's rich pattern, and went through the ritual each morning as one in a trance.

This particular morning however, in answer to the call of 'Next', I went into the office, dutifully uttered my polite 'Good morning, Mrs Nelson-King,' and found to my astonishment that no longer was she wracking her brains for my name. Indeed, she knew it! And no longer was I 'too short' or 'too tall', 'too young' or 'too old'. In every respect I was perfect. Yes, Mrs Nelson-King was about to offer me my first engagement in Repertory – 'Repertory' meaning then a different play every week.

Chapter Five

The engagement was with J. Baxter-Somerville's Repertory Players at the Springfield Theatre, Jersey. With a salary of three pounds per week, and sharing digs in a dairy with Macdonald Hobley, or as he was then known Val Blanchard (his family name), I was a very happy young man. Our landlady, Mrs Le Mesurier (pronounced Ler Measurer) owned the dairy, and tipped the scales at some eighteen stone. One day in a fit of tactless exuberance, I asked her how she came to be so fat, and she replied, 'By laughing, my dear, just by laughing so much.' What a wondrous sight it was, to see all those 250 pounds of her shaking and quaking and shivering and quivering with uncontrollable mirth. Mrs Le Mesurier's theory of laughter causing fatness may well have been true in her case, but with me, it was a resounding failure. I laughed a lot but ended up looking like a beardless Don Quixote.

I'm afraid to say that I didn't last very long with Mr J. Baxter-Somerville's Company, due to a slight coolness that developed between me and the leading man Mr Peter Glenville, son of the famous principal boy Dorothy Ward, and now an eminent stage and film Director. We were performing a Dorothy Sayers 'Peter Wimsey' play, with Peter as Lord Peter and myself as the Vicar. In one scene I had to enter downstage left and warmly shake the hand of Mr Glenville. It occurred to me that it might be rather droll to have a raw egg in my hand on the first night. I, therefore, with a fresh brown one obtained from Mrs Le M's dairy secreted in my palm, shook Lord Peter's hand and chuckled merrily to myself when the yolk went up his sleeve and the white went down his trousers. The audience roared but Mr Glenville didn't, and thought it to be a very thin piece of fun. Trembling with anger, and without my knowledge, he at once phoned Mr J. Baxter-Somerville in England, and informed him that he would not remain any longer in a Company where he was expected to perform with buffoons.

'J. B.' taking his life into his hands straightway took a flight in a ten-seater twin-engined de Havilland from Croydon Airport, and landed perilously on the sands of St Helier. This was not an error of judgement on the pilot's part, but before the airport was built the beach was the only way of getting in.

That night, quite unbeknown to me, J. B. sat at the back of the Dress Circle to observe unobserved the threatened misbehaviour of this tiresome young man. He and Peter Glenville had been hugely unamused by the raw egg 'business', and were to be amused even less by what was to follow.

On summing up the case at the end of the last act, Lord Peter Glenville demonstrated that the murder had been committed in a most unusual manner. A hanging brass flower-pot containing an aspidistra, and suspended from the ceiling by a long chain, had been pulled back by the murderer and released at the precise moment his victim was passing the bottom of the stairs, the heavy pot swinging across and crushing the skull of the unsuspecting murderee. To prove his point, Lord Peter made a dummy of the victim by use of a large Victorian plant stand for a body and a cabbage for a head. Once released, he said, the brass flower pot would swing fast across the stage and to the horror of all assembled would strike the cabbage head such a blow that it would fly from its 'body'.

The achieve this splendid piece of Theatricalia, it was necessary for the long chain of the flower pot to be tied off in a perfect 'dead'. An inch out on either side and the pot would miss striking the dummy head entirely. That was precisely what I intended it to do. An hour before the show, when no-one was about, I shifted the 'dead'.

'And this, my friends, is how that swine killed poor Mr Arbuthnot,' explained Lord Peter with panache, and releasing the flower pot, was given the treat of watching it zoom down, missing the 'victim's' head completely and continue swinging backwards and forwards like the giant pendulum in Edgar Allen Poe's classic story. The laughter in the audience was tremendous.

But, as could have been expected, there was no laughter in the dressing room after, only censure and disapprobation. To no-one's surprise, including my own, I was once again summarily dismissed.

★

I had never expected to speak to J. B. Somerville again, nor he to me, but some years later, after the D–Day landings, I was sent by my then section of Naval Broadcasting to Jersey, to interview the locals on what their life had been like during the German occupation.

It was sad to see this normally sparkling isle so colourless, empty and depressed. The Jersey people were desperately hungry and short of everything. Having virtually no postage stamps, they cut two-penny ones in half and used them as pennies, and so on up. I bought a number of these stamps and later made quite a killing.

One evening I took a stroll up to the Springfield to have a look at the theatre where I had started my career. The park itself was jammed with German vehicles. Mercedes 540K open-tourers, superb Horchs and BMWs. Big BMW motorcycles with and without sidecars and a plethora of Volkswagens of every description, but there was one remarkable thing that all these vehicles had in common. There wasn't a car or motorbike with a full set of tyres on it. Unable to ship or fly any in during the last year of the war, the occupying German troops had resorted to binding strips of rubber cut from the walls of worn-out tyres around the rims, sometimes, in the case of the bikes and Volkswagens, even wiring on sacking. It was most undignifying for the Classic Royalty among them, to be so commonly shod. What a fortune lay there for a man of enterprise. Sad to say we will never see the like of such motor vehicles again.

Shedding a bitter tear, I walked into the large area under the auditorium of the theatre, to find that since the occupation, it had been used as a storage shed for the sacks of flour and grain employed in the making of bread for the occupying forces. No wonder the German troops looked hungry, for there was only one ten foot high wall of sacks left, and they'd obviously been eking them out. In a flash of memory I remembered that behind that wall was the scenery store, where all J. Baxter-Somerville's sets and props had been kept. So summoning an Army Sergeant I asked him to get some of the POWs to clear the wall of sacks from the door as I wanted to go in.

In twenty minutes the big scene door was clear and I entered the bay, the first man to do so in several years. It was Aladdin's cave. The store was exactly the same as when the company had left it in 1939, full to the brim with the 'old oak set' and all the other repertory theatre scenery clichés. There were skips filled with props and roll-cloths depicting hideously garish gardens and landscapes and many hundred-weight of timber for the construction of further horrors.

During the occupation, for want of fuel, the Germans had burned every sliver of wood that they could lay their hands on, including hundreds of beautiful mature trees. If they had known what was hidden away behind their grain sacks they would have burned the lot. So in order to protect my long-suffering old boss's property, I had the 'Soldaten' build up the grainsack wall again.

When I got back to England some three weeks later, I contacted J. B. Somerville and gave him the good news.

'Is that Mr Somerville?'

'It is.'

'This is your erstwhile *enfant terrible*, Jon Pertwee here.'

'Oh yes!' His voice took on a colder tone. 'And what can I do for you?'

'Its more a question of what *I* can do for *you*. Would you believe that I could metaphorically put hundreds of pounds back in your pocket, with just one simple sentence?'

'No, but tell me just the same.'

I told him and he was beside himself.

'What can I do to repay the bringer of such glad tidings?' he asked.

'Just give me another chance in one of your Rep Companies after the war, sir. I've grown up at last and wouldn't let you down again, I promise,' I replied.

'Then a position awaits you, Pertwee, you have my word on it,' said J.B. But the way things went for me professionally, after the war, I was unable to take him up on this offer, and sad to say, we never met again.

*

My dismissal from Jersey was followed by a somewhat thin period. Maybe my reputation as a jester had gone before me. I was obliged therefore to accept very small roles at Birmingham, York and Liverpool in the 'Tea is served, Madam' and 'The carriage awaits without, Milord' genre. I was also once given a script which read 'The curtain rises at Act One, in the library of the Duke and Duchess of Dillwater, where Elphinstone (me, of course) is discovered dead.'

*

As all good things come to an end, so do the bad things if you persevere, and my lean time finished in April 1938 when I was given the chance of joining the Rex Lesley-Smith Repertory Players, situated at the end of the West Pier in Brighton.

I was delighted to be living and working in this lovely Regency town, from which so many of my family had stemmed.

I was paid the splendid remuneration of three pounds, ten shillings a week and lived with a Madame Penison in the Victoria Road. I had a very comfortable room with crisp, clean French linen, and as this was the summer season, fresh flowers by the bed.

In the evenings if it was cold, there was always a crackling, coal fire to study by. Officially I had three meals a day, but in reality, far more, because the kitchen was always open if I felt like 'a little something'.

On Saturday nights, after the last show, two other lodgers from the company and I went down to the station, and at one o'clock in the morning collected Monsieur Leblanc, who was not only the chief chef at Frascati's Restaurant, Oxford Street, but also the lover of the voluminous Madame Penison. He would come with an enormous skip filled with all the 'goodies' he had purloined from Frascati's during the week, which were, he assured me, a chief chef's 'perks'. It contained half bottles of excellent claret and burgundy, spirits of every kind, and liqueurs. There were pieces of duck, pheasant, fish and salmon and sometimes the occasional dollop of caviar; profiteroles, tarte aux pommes and cheeses of every kind were in abundance. We lived like the proverbial lords. On Sundays, when my father asked why I didn't come home, I said with undisguised amazement, 'Come home? Come home and miss Ma Penison's family lunch? You must be mad!'

We were one family now, the family of Madame Penison and her lover. He would preside at the head of an enormous table, with all his 'children' around him. That room and board cost me the princely sum of thirty shillings a week(£1.50). From the residue of my three pounds ten shillings I ran a superb Ariel Square-Four motorcycle, paid for on HP at a few shillings a week, and worth a fortune now. I smoked a paper packet of five Woodbines a day, which cost me tuppence, and drank a quantity of rough cider at threepence a glass. As a healthy heterosexual I had many 'lady friends' and found that I still had enough left over to escort them out, buy them cups of tea and ice cream, take them dancing at Sherry's Dance Hall and generally lead the life of Riley.

We had an interesting routine at this theatre, a little policy called Twice Nightly, Twice Weekly, with matinees. You performed two plays a week. You rehearsed Monday morning and afternoon, and then in the evening you did a six o'clock show and an 8.30 show of the play you had rehearsed the latter half of the previous week. On Tuesday you rehearsed in the morning and afternoon and then in the evening performed the usual two shows. On Wednesday you rehearsed in the morning only, *not* in the afternoon, because in the afternoon you had a 2.30 matinee, and then of course the two evening shows as per, so you performed *three* shows on that day. On Thursday morning you started rehearsing the play for the following Monday, but in the afternoon did the dress rehearsal of the show you were putting on *twice* that night.

You can imagine the strain of doing that for a whole summer season, but somehow we managed it. I and some other members of the company used to learn lines by self-hypnotism. We used to take a sheet of cardboard, paint it black and put a pin hole through it. We would then prop it up with a lit candle behind it, put out the room lights and concentrate on the small dot of light, visualising a page of the play at the same time. As the dot got bigger, that would mean that your conscious mind was closing and your sub-conscious mind was opening. It was at that precise point that you could take a form of mental photograph of the page, which seemed on waking, to be imprinted upon the mind. This was fine, as long as somebody gave you the right cue, but if you got a 'duff' one, your brain would search in vain for the right picture. In this event there was, of course, bugger all you could do. There would be instant panic and confusion. The prompter et al would 'scream' – whisper – the lines at you, and everyone on stage would flap around like legless chickens until it was finally all rustled back together.

This at least was better than working from the infamous 'cue scripts' where you were presented with nothing but an inexplicable cue line on the small printed page and then your own line:

Sir John: '. . . my daughter.'
Gregory: 'That, Sir, is an unmitigated inexactitude.'
Sir John: '. . . fried on Thursday.'
Gregory: 'That is as maybe Sir John, but only once, I can assure you!'

And from *that* you had to understand what your part was all about. These cue scripts contained no description of the play, or your character, and it was only when you actually put it together in rehearsal that you discovered what the hell it was all about. We used cue scripts at Henley Rep, I remember. The only reason they kept that theatre going was that they had a bar-licence. The vulgar fellow that headed the Company made a lot of money from that bar. He didn't, as he so often told us, give a damn what was going on on the stage, as long as the bar and his customers were filled to saturation point.

I remember once at Brighton I had had a rather alcoholic luncheon with Michael. I said, 'I must get back, I've got two shows to do.' I was playing the gardener in *Love from a Stranger*, and, so typical of a young actor in Rep, was woefully overdressed in battered panama hat, striped wool shirt *minus* collar but *with* front stud, green-baize apron, cord trousers with string tied under the knees, muddy boots and of course the chin beard and deep lake lines of an 'Old Adam' the gardener make-up. As I was waiting to go on stage Rex Lesley-Smith approached me and said, 'Most interesting, but who exactly are you supposed to *be*?'

'"Old Willows", the gardener in *Love from a Stranger*,' I said, jokingly.

'Are you really?' he replied. 'Well, today we are playing *Candida*, you are playing Morell, and you're off!!' (meaning I had missed my entrance).

I instantly fell apart at the seams and croaked 'Oh my God, no!' From experience, we always had a young Assistant Stage Manager standing by, dressed as a maid, who, in a moment of crisis, could rush on to the stage with a tray and say, 'Good afternoon, mum. Would you like some tea? Take sugar, sir? Would you like a biscuit, madam?' and so she would 'prattle-and-pad-lib' on, while back-stage the panics and disasters of the occasion were being set to rights. Meanwhile in the wings, I hastily and painfully pulled the beard from my face, rubbed the gardener make-up into an unrecognisable blur, put my head round the door-jamb and, in my best clergyman's voice said, 'I really am most terribly sorry to have kept you waiting but I've been somewhat involved with a boll weevil in the antirrhinums. Have some tea, won't you? I won't keep you but a moment.'

With that I rushed off back to my dressing room, whipped on the clergyman's collar and the rest of his clerical outfit, re-applied my make-up and hastened back on stage before the exasperated Stage Manager had to make yet another pot of tea.

★

As the theatre was situated right at the end of the West Pier, in between rehearsals I would sit outside the stage door in the sun, relaxing and trying to get a tan. It was a quiet private little spot and few others found it. But one day, my favourite corner out of the wind was occupied by what my dear housekeeper Mrs Holman is wont to call 'a darkish person'. He was elderly, small, aquiline nosed, with a fine trimmed beard and a halo of frizzy black hair, and he was sitting in a deck chair staring dolefully out to sea with beautiful jet black eyes. Over his knees was tucked a travelling rug, and on his head a hard wide-brimmed hat, the like of which I had never seen before.

'Good morning, sir, lovely day,' I said, and then without thinking made one of those dreadful gaffes that we all make from time to time. 'Trying to build up a tan?'

He hardly reacted at all except to turn his head slowly in my direction and fix me with frightening black eyes. I was frozen by his gaze as a rabbit is by a stoat, and was quite incapable of movement or speech. He finally released me by saying softly, 'I think that would be like, as you say "carrying coals to Newcastle", don't you?'

'Yes, sir, I suppose it would,' I replied, and much relieved that he had not been too affronted I sat and talked to this strange little man for half an hour or so before excusing myself and going to work.

'Will I see you tomorrow?' I asked.

'Oh yes I expect I'll be here,' he said, adding wistfully, 'I've nowhere else to go.'

And so I struck up quite a friendship with this black man of mystery, for that is what he was, never talking about his past, future, friends or family. We talked trivialities only, whilst drinking endless cups of tea brought to us by someone I assumed to be his companion, a black gentleman who obviously came from the same country, and spoke to him in a strange tongue. This man was permanently at hand in a nearby shelter, reading books in an extraordinary print which I completely failed to recognise.

One day the old man failed to appear and after some weeks absence I could only conclude that he had either died or found somewhere else to sun himself. That is until, over my breakfast table months later, I opened my paper, and there staring up at me resplendent in a high ranking Army Officer's uniform, covered in orders and medals, was a picture of my old friend. The caption read 'HM The Emperor of Abyssinia, Haile Selassie, "The Lion of Judah", inspects the Brigade of Guards before lunching with his Majesty King George VI.'

What the Emperor had been doing on the end of Brighton Pier, unguarded except by the servant companion, I shall never understand. Perhaps after his tragic exile from Ethiopia no-one cared what happened to him and he just wanted to be left alone with his thoughts. It is hard to believe that in all the time I spent talking to him, he never dropped the slightest hint of who he was, or where he had come from – although bearing in mind that I talked the hind legs off an elephant, perhaps he couldn't get a word in edgeways. Plainly he was not old at all, nor in any way infirm, for he lived on, to return to his land once the Italians had been ejected and ruled his ancient Christian country for many years until the last revolution once more pushed him from his throne, leaving him to die in exile a lonely, broken-hearted man. To have lived in exile once is bad enough but to experience it twice must have been appalling.

★

One of my additional duties in Rex's Rep Company was prop-finding, and for a plug in the programme most local shopkeepers were more than willing to help. We badly needed a fur coat and I went to the only decent furrier in Brighton, 'A. Dudkin, Quality Furs', to see if he would lend us one. His reply was a succinct 'No'!

'But everybody else lends us things.'

'Then go to everybody else.'

'We'll put your name in the programme.'

'I don't want my name in your programme, I don't like your theatre, and I don't like you.'

'Mr Dudkin,' I said, 'don't beat about the bush . . .'

But he would have none of it, and Peggy Lesley-Smith was forced to settle for a woolly cardigan.

Revenge was sweet, however. In the early hours of the morning, armed with an extending ladder, we crept up to his shop and added a beautifully matching letter 'S' made by Rex's sister 'Frecks', to the furrier's shop sign, which, by the time we had left, read 'A. Dudskin, Quality Furs'.

★

One day I noticed an exciting advertisement in the *Evening Standard*. It read, 'For sale, fast hydroplane, airscrew propulsion, powered by 500cc twin Douglas motorcycle engine from a Bluey Wilkinson Speedway Machine. Snip at £5. Will deliver. Reply Johnson, 3 The Vale, Norwich.'

My five pound postal order was off by the next post and I anxiously awaited delivery. Within a week it was sitting on its trailer outside Ma Penison's, awaiting its first introduction to the sea. Mr Johnson had assured me that the little beauty was in excellent working order, handled like a dream and that although he had only driven it on the river, he was quite confident that it would be equally manoeuvrable at sea. The very next Sunday, aided by a friend, I trundled the trailer down to the water's edge, prior to launching. Here I filled its tank with petrol and gave it a thorough inspection. It was a small flat hull, built of half-inch marine ply, with a tiny cockpit, in which the driver would kneel over his steering wheel. This wheel controlled the five foot high canvas fin at the rear of the hydroplane, which in turn controlled the boat's direction. Just forward of this fin was a strong frame on which was mounted the Douglas twin with its two open exhausts, that drove the dangerously unguarded aeroplane propeller. The only controls, other than the steering wheel, were an exhaust lift, an accelerator and a mixture-control lever. The machine was started by a removable starting handle which engaged directly with the shiny flywheel, so distinctive of all Douglas engines. Duly inspected, the boat was launched through the surf and I jumped aboard. After a quick tickle of the carburettor and a touch of choke, I swung the starting handle. The compression was so great that when she momentarily fired, the starting handle kicked back and nearly took my thumb off. The strangled cries to the heavens that followed this momentary setback would not have been appreciated by the Bishop of Brighton. The second attempt, with the use of the exhaust lift, proved more successful, and the engine burst into life with a crackling roar. Throwing the handle into the well deck, I slid myself down behind the steering wheel and slowly eased the machine out to sea. After a few slow, testing turns I opened the throttle and with a prayer on my lips, felt the little boat rise up on its step and start on its bouncing, leaping way. At about 30mph I roared up the shore-line filled with elation. 'This is the life,' I thought. 'Who is this Sir Malcolm Campbell anyway?' After five minutes or so I began to get the feel of the thing and decided to thrill the holiday-makers crowding the West Pier with a demonstration of skill and daring, by shooting underneath them at speed without hitting the piles.

The first pass was a bit tentative, but on the second and third I shot through at full bore, doing at least 35mph, which on water seemed like ninety. At each pass, crowds would rush from one side of the pier to the other, shouting and waving as I whizzed beneath them. Amongst my many fans that day were 'Younkman' and his entire gypsy orchestra enthusiastically waving their violins. After some twenty minutes of beating up the West Pier, I bade farewell to my gesticulating audience and roared off to entertain everybody on the Palace Pier. Half an hour later, well pleased with my first sortie, I headed back to the ramp where I had left my trailer, to find two officers of the law patiently waiting for me. Lying off some twenty feet from the shore I courteously enquired if there was something I could do to help them. Yes, there was, they would be very grateful if I would kindly step ashore, where they could more easily arrest me, on (at a rough estimate) some ten charges. Amongst others, there was committing a public nuisance, disturbing the peace, and causing 'Younkman' and his orchestra to pack up and go home as no-one could hear a note they were playing. So 'Younkman' and his boys had *not* been cheering and waving at me after all! They and everyone else on the piers and promenades were being driven mad by the cacophonous racket of my open exhausts and had been frantically signalling that I should go away and leave them in peace. I was bitterly disappointed at this turn of events, and having no desire for a holiday in one of his Britannic Majesty's renowned establishments, I spurned the officers' kind invitation to step ashore and made for the nearby haven of Shoreham Harbour instead. There I tied the offending little beast to a friend's motor launch and made my way sheepishly back to my digs. 'Well hello!' said Alan Bromley, the Rep's leading man, 'Had a good day in your speed boat?'

'How did you know I've been in my boat?' I enquired.

'How did I know? Good God, everyone in Brighton knows, I was listening to the bloody thing for two hours!'

As Ma Penison's pension was well over a mile from the seashore, I dreaded to think what the inhabitants directly along the front must have suffered.

The next time out, I took more care and headed away from Brighton towards Worthing. The sea was rougher that day and I found that the craft was much less manoeuvrable. Unlike a boat with a propeller in the water, this craft had nothing but the rear fin to hold it on a straight course. Once at speed the undulation of the waves bounced the hydroplane about alarmingly and irrespective of its course and pitch the airscrew pushed it on unremittingly. It should've been obvious to anyone that disaster was about to strike, but I pig-headedly pressed on regardless, leaping, yawing, and pitching my frenetic way along the coastline. Suddenly, hitting a wave, the boat soared into the air, as if it was an aircraft taking off. The wind got under it, the airscrew kept pushing and I rose inexorably up and on until on reaching stalling speed the nose dipped and still going full chat, I headed down towards the surface of the sea at an angle of 45 degrees. Paralysed, I made no attempt to ease off the throttle, with the net result that the boat and I plunged into the sea at 30mph disappearing beneath the surface, like a cormorant after a kipper. A foot or so down the boat flattened out and my head rose above the surface to cleave through the water like the periscope of a submarine. From the shore it must've been a most laughable sight. It was not to last long, however, for after a few moments, to the undoubted relief of thousands, my ill-fated machine sank slowly to the bottom of the sea, never to be seen by human eyes again.

The long swim home gave me cause to think, and in retrospect it is my considered opinion that the watery death of the noisy little bugger was all that it deserved.

★

'Gentleman' Cliff Warner, my wrestling friend, came to visit me from time to time, and one night after the show we were involved in a unique situation. It was late as we left, for we had been sitting in my dressing room chatting, and making light work of some excellent claret that Cliff had brought down for our mutual consumption.

On walking the final stretch of the pier we heard from beneath our feet, faint cries of alarm and panic. Getting to our knees we peered through the slats to observe the shadowy figures of a young couple lying on the beach some thirty feet below.

'What's up, can we help you?' called Cliff.

'Yes, for Christ's sake help us! We're stuck!' came the agonised reply.

'Hang on,' I cried. 'We're coming.'

Bearing in mind the circumstances, I could've put it better.

Running at once to the spot we found the two lovers lying locked in the act of coitus in an agony of pain and embarrassment. As dogs when mating are inclined to lock together so did this unfortunate couple. The more he tried to withdraw, the more was the pain for his poor inamorata.

'What about a bucket of water?' I whispered to Cliff.

'Don't be bloody silly! That's only for dogs and that doesn't often work. We'll have to get them to the hospital,' he replied.

If you've never tried lifting two interlocked humans across a beach, and up a steep stone staircase, don't bother, because you haven't missed much. For apart from the immense physical effort required, there was the added irritation of a diatribe of unwanted advice from the coupled bundle of joy as to the manner and *modus operandi*, that should be employed to effect their speedy and pain-free transportation.

After what seemed like climbing Mount Everest without oxygen, Cliff and I eventually rolled the still groaning pair on to the curbside, Cliff covering their state of nature in true gentlemanly fashion by throwing his capacious Burberry raincoat over them. After several minutes, we managed to flag down a taxi. Opening the door, I turned to the raincoat-covered mound and whipping the Burberry off, Cliff and I commenced the well nigh impossible task of getting them into the back of the cab.

It was then that the cabby noticed for the first time the locked lovers.

'Ere wait a minute! What the fuck's goin' on?' he enquired.

'Well you see . . .'

'I fuckin' see all right, wot do yer take me for, Emperor fuckin' Nero?'

'Of course not. You see it's an accident.'

'Accident? It'll be a fuckin' accident if I lose my fuckin' cab licence won't it?'

'But they aren't . . .'

'Aren't? Wot d'ye mean aren't? They fuckin' *are*! Look at 'em. D'ye think I'm fuckin' blind or somethin'? Take 'em out of my fuckin' cab. I'm not 'avin them fu . . . er . . . you know er . . . er . . . here.' He foundered.

For having used the sought after word so unsparingly in his previous purple patch he found himself up the Oxford without a dictionary.

'Bleedin' perverts,' he muttered as he roared off into the night.

It took nearly an hour to find a cabby who was Samaritan enough to take the unfortunate couple to the hospital, but by the glazed look in his eyes, I'm convinced that he was sufficiently drunk not to have noticed even if a joyous twelve-up 'gang-bang' had been taking place in the back of his taxi.

★

After all that, what Cliff and I needed was a stiff drink, so we repaired to Sherry's, Brighton's infamous dance hall. There, in the long bar with a long whisky and soda in my hand, I came upon a pretty young lady and proceeded to chat her up. She seemed to be responding favourably, when Cliff, looking quickly over my shoulder, hauled off and hit me on the side of the head knocking me to the floor. As I fell backwards, furious at being assaulted by my own friend, a cloth cap sailed like a 'frisbee' over where my head had just been, and imbedded itself in the wooden panelling behind me. Cliff snatched it from the wall and showed me that the peak had had a dozen razor blades sewn into it.

'They can spin these things with great accuracy,' said Cliff, always a mine of information. 'If I hadn't knocked you over, it would've opened up your forehead like a zip-fastener.'

Just the thought of being 'trepanned' made me all but fall to the floor again. It seems that I had been flirting with the girl-friend of one of the 'Sabini Boys,' the vicious race-track gang later made famous by Richard Attenborough in the film *Brighton Rock*, and he, not being best pleased, had sent an armed flying saucer on its way to draw my attention to the fact.

★

One bright sunny day I was walking around the iron grating of the fishermen's part of the pier when I noticed a most beautiful young girl leaning over the railings and staring into the water. She was possessed of a remarkable stillness, for I watched her for quite some time and she moved not a muscle. She had long, straight black hair, large black eyes heavily browed, a full mouth and a perfectly proportioned body. I was immediately hopelessly in love, and advanced to plight my troth.

'Hello, a penny for them,' I said with startling originality.

'I was thinking what it would be like to drown,' she replied with devastating candour. I was stopped dead in my 'chatting-up' tracks. How do you follow a statement like that? Floundering, I still managed to pull something out of the bag.

'Nothing to it,' I said, 'I've done it dozens of times.'

She looked up and her beautiful eyes were moist with tears.

'Have you really,' she said. 'Did you suffer any pain?'

This was all together too much. The subject had to be dropped.

'What a morbid conversation for such a beautiful day. Why don't we share a cup of tea and a toasted tea cake in the Pavilion Cafe, and I can tell you what a wonderful actor I am,' I suggested, subtly informing her that I was in the profession.

'But I already know that, Mr Pertwee. I've seen nearly every show you've done this season,' she replied with the suspicion of a twinkle in her black eyes.

Over the tea and a chelsea bun, unrolled and fairly shared, I learned that her name was Louise Spitzel, that she was an eighteen-year-old Jewess, that her great-grandfather, once a Midshipman in the US Navy, had been present when the US fleet sailed into Japan, and was welcomed by a reception committee of Japanese Warlords on horseback and dressed in full armour. I learned also that her father was a successful businessman and that they lived in St John's Wood, London. (Hooray! Not too far from me!) I was not pleased though, to learn the reason for her presence in Brighton. She had evidently been ill and had come down with her mother to bracing Brighton to recuperate. She also had a sister, but I was not to bother about that as she was far too young for me, and would I like to meet her mother and her for tea the following day? I would, and hardly slept a second that night in anticipation of seeing again this quite beautiful creature.

Her half-American mother was a typical Jewish 'glass-a-tea', 'chicken soup', 'chopped liver and matzos' Mama, who plainly adored Louise and was unnecessarily over-attentive. She and I got along famously, and from then on she was in complete cahoots with me over my, and 'Kippy's', as I had now nick-named her, 'young romance'. Unfortunately due to her recent illness (as yet unspecified to me), Kippy had to be home and in bed by eleven o'clock. This gave us only an hour together after the show to ride up to the Downs above Rottingdean on my motorbike, and there to walk, talk, hold hands and kiss. During the day in between rehearsal times she would meet me on the pier and we would spend most of our precious time just staring at each other. Although I was pushing twenty, I had never been in love before and it hit me pretty hard. What with sleepless nights and not eating properly I started to look terrible, but certainly not as terrible as Kippy began to look.

'I'm taking Louise home at the end of the week to see her specialist,' said her mother. 'I hope we will see you in London. If so, whatever you do don't tell my husband that you're an actor. He hates actors and would immediately forbid Louise from ever seeing you again. Tell him you met her here while you were on holiday or something.'

That night after the show we rode up to the Downs and made a love pact which we signed, put into a tobacco tin and buried under a tree.

At the end of the season I couldn't wait to get back to London to see the girl I loved. She was pale, with a strange transparent look about her, and she still loved me, she said. Her father Cecil Spitzel and I took to each other at once, and after a few weeks of lies from me about what I did for a living, said, 'You know, Jon dear, you make me laugh so much you ought to be an actor!'

'Do you really think so?' I replied feigning surprise at his suggestion. 'Then would you have any objection if I tried?'

'Certainly not my dear,' he said, and to the complete amazement of his wife and daughters went on with his volte-face by saying, 'If there's anything I can do to help, let me know. I know a lot of the right people.'

Within a week I had obtained a job in my 'new found profession' and all the Spitzels came to see and 'enjoy'. To the delight of Kippy and her mother it seemed that I had got away with it. But our happiness was to be short lived, as indeed was Kippy. She had been feeling so ill again that her doctor had ordered her to stay in bed. I had just come out of her room after saying 'Goodbye' when I literally bumped into her father, who was standing ashen-faced in the corridor with a letter in his hand.

'My God, oh dear God, it can't be true! It can't, it can't,' he repeated silently over and over again. I led him into the sitting room where we sat alone, as his wife and younger daughter had gone out, and waited for him to tell me what was causing his terrible distress. It was not long coming, and when it did it was accompanied by a torrent of tears. The letter he held in his trembling hand was from a specialist, coldly informing him that the test had proved positive, and that his daughter Louise had contracted a virulent form of cancer. Her chances of surviving were slim, but he recommended surgery at once.

I couldn't take it in. I just couldn't believe that this beautiful girl could be suffering from anything so ugly!

Kippy was rushed to hospital where she was promptly operated on. The operation took little time, for as soon as the surgeon had opened up the abdomen, he found that his patient was so riddled with malignancy, that there was nothing he could do, but sew her up again.

The Spitzels just wouldn't accept his heart-breaking verdict, and started on a fruitless search for anyone or anything that could delay, however temporarily, their beloved daughter's inevitable death. They tried faith healers, homeopaths, acupuncture, even 'quack' doctors employing such obscure notions as the intake of sheep's liver to effect a cure. All this was to no avail and Kippy, like Granny, began to fade from our sight, but she never allowed me to see her unless she was looking of her best, with hair combed, lipstick applied and crisp white lace bed-jacket on. I would sit and read to her until she fell asleep, and then hold her hand while looking at her pallid, ashen face until I was gently led away into the sitting room by her mother. There we sat and inwardly prayed for the miracle that we knew in our hearts would not be forthcoming.

On an early spring morning, Kippy propped up on her pillows gently sighed her way out of my life. She looked, though colourless, just as beautiful as when I had first seen her looking into the water at the end of the pier. I remembered so clearly the eminently sad way she had turned to me and said, 'I was wondering what it would be like to drown,' and recalling the expression on her dear face, and the eyes filled with tears, I have often wondered whether she had had an early premonition of death.

drawing of my mother, Avice, by my father

My father, Roland (Photo by Angela Huth)

Granny with the hockey team she organised, 1919

An elegant portrait of my aunt
Decima, Lady Moore-Guggisberg

An early picture of Michael and me with Granny in the background

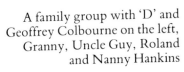

A family group with 'D' and Geoffrey Colbourne on the left, Granny, Uncle Guy, Roland and Nanny Hankins

With Michael and Granny at Caterham

Me, Coby and Michael

Uncle Keith Scholtz

My first infatuation, Peggy Burnell

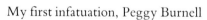

Louis de la Garde, my mother's second husban

Me with my father

Me at my most angelic at Wellington House

My first report from Wellington House — I was already an undistinguished pupil

With my school friend Laurence Jolivet in his father's aeroplane on a visit to Elstree Airfield

10, Downing Street,
Whitehall.

14th September 1931.

Dear Master John Pertwee,

The Prime Minister has asked me to tell you
that he has received your letter of the 10th
September, and to say how much he appreciates the
kind thought which prompted you to send 2/6d. as
a gift to the Exchequer.

Yours sincerely,

E. M. Watson

Master John Pertwee.

At the age of 12 I heard the Prime Minister talking about the country's unstable economy, and sent him half-a-crown. Downing Street responded graciously to this patriotic gesture

An early dramatic appearance in the open air theatre I started at Frensham Heights — I'm on the right, playing Sir Andrew Aguecheek

A lunch break at RADA, 1936, with William Dickinson and Ione 'Olde Lanterne' Kinkum. Dickie advertised himself as 'available for repertory' in *Spotlight* for years, but as far as I know never got a job

The Arts League of Service Travelling Theatre Company, 1937; me on the left

The ALS travelling theatre poster

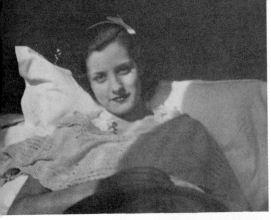

Louise Spitzel — 'Kippy' — in hospital

Cambridge Rep, in Shaw's *The Simpleton of the Unexpected Isles: l. to r.,* m Brandon Acton Bond, Sarah Church and Wileen Wilson. Sarah's fathe Winston, took us to tea aft performanc

Ordinary Seaman Pertwee J.D.R. P/JX178358

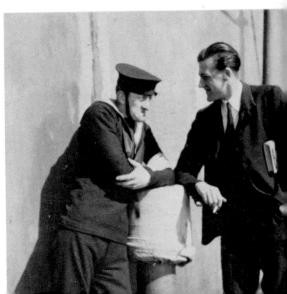

On the upper deck of *HMS Hood* with naval writer Geoffrey Clarke

HMS Hood at her best (Keystone Press)

WE, the undersigned, having made our acquaintance whilst
serving on board His Majesty's Ship HOOD during the year
of our Lord One thousand nine hundred and forty DO HEREBY
mutually and solemnly DECLARE that (Deo volente) at
precisely three o'clock in the afternoon of the first
Saturday of the ninth month immediately following the
month during which the present hostilities are officially
declared as having been terminated WE WILL MEET TOGETHER
at the statue of Eros in Piccadilly Circus London or at
the site thereof should the statue be demolished for the
purpose of renewing our acquaintance and celebrating the
occasion AND THAT such meeting shall take place on the
same day and at the same time from year to year for so
long as any two of us shall be still living NOTWITHSTANDING
that we may frequently meet in the meantime.

WE FURTHER DECLARE that in the event of any one
of us for any reason or reasons beyond our control being
unable to attend such meeting in person we will arrange for
a deputy to be present on our behalf AND that such
arrangement will not constitute a breach of this agreement.

DATED on board His Majesty's Ship HOOD this
Fourteenth day of April One thousand nine hundred and forty
one.

Jon Pertwee
Actor.

Geoffrey Clarke
Journalist.

Hanley. F. Johnson
Leading Writer R.N

R Russell
Property of Negotiator.

An 'Agreement for Post-War Reunion' made tragically only weeks
before the *Hood* went down

As a CW candidate in *HMS King Alfred,* Lancing: I'm second row third from the right, with Ray Roberts in the same row, second from left and Tommy Thomas fourth row third from left

I become an officer

The Isle of Man, 1941: Divisional Officer J. Pertwee of *HMS Valkyrie*

My beautiful 'Brescia' Bugatti

The 'Adolf Hitler' picture with which I
infiltrated *HMS Vernon* when I was a Security
Officer for Naval Intelligence

66 Chester Row, during the latter part of the war: I used to nip across the road to my friendly barber's for a shave, a cup of tea and the newspaper until the press caught up with me (*Daily Mail*)

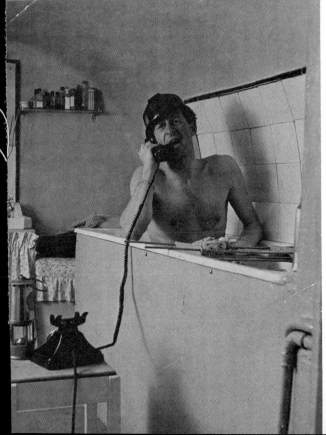

The bathroom at Chester Row — made from a coal hole, it was a perfect air-raid shelter

An early script conference with David Jacobs on left

BBC's *Mediterranean Merry-Go-Round: l. to r.,* Postman 'What does it matter what you do as long as you tear 'em up' Pertwee, Eric Barker, Margaret Lockwood, Humphrey 'Flying Officer Kyte' Lestocq, Pearl Hackney, Richard 'Lord Waterlogged' Gray, Barbara Summer and Horace Percival, conducted by 'Herr' George Crow

The Navy Lark 1961: *top,* Ronnie Barker, me, Michael Bates, Tenniel Evans; *centre,* Stephen Murray, Richard Caldicot, Leslie Phillips; *front,* Heather Chasen, Judy Cornwell (BBC Copyright Photograph)

With Ronnie Barker
in a relaxed moment
during *The Navy Lark*
(BBC Copyright
Photograph)

We did a special show aboard *HMS Belfast* to mark the breaking up of the real *HMS Troubridge* in 1975. With members of Her Majesty's Navy are: *back*, producer Alistair Scott-Johnston, Richard Caldicot, Stephen Murray, Tenniel Evans; *front*, Heather Chasen, April Walker, me, Leslie Phillips, Michael Bates

Her family tried in vain to get in touch with her through spiritualism, but I did not feel the need for such succour. My memory of the love she had had for me, and the love I still had for her, was sufficient.

Forty years later I was staying with D'Oyly John, an artist friend from the 'Olde Lanterne Cafe' days, in his cottage at Rottingdean. Excusing myself after dinner I walked up to the Downs where Kippy and I had gone together, and sitting under a tree in the gathering dusk, indulged myself in nostalgia. Suddenly I realised exactly where I was, and with a pen-knife started frantically to dig for the tobacco tin. Within minutes I had found it precisely where we had buried it all those many years ago. It was rusty and beginning to disintegrate, but not so much as to destroy the folded sheet inside, wrapped in silver paper taken from a packet of Players cigarettes. I held it up to the fast disappearing light and was just able to read in faded blue ink the details of Kippy's and my love pact. Moved near to tears, I sat silently for a few minutes before putting it back in its tin and re-burying it under the oak tree, where, to the best of my knowledge, it still remains.

★

For a short period after this, I was engaged by a Company at the Festival Theatre, Cambridge. Amongst others in the Company was a girl with the deep husky voice of a young Tallulah Bankhead. Judy Campbell was a tremendously talented actress and went on to become a very big star in the theatrical firmament. She had many fine attributes, and soon acquired a crowd of devoted admirers. Her dressing room was situated at the end of the passage facing the stage door, where, after the final curtain call had been taken, dozens of young blades from the University would gather in the fervent hope of catching a glimpse of this wonder woman. They were not to be disappointed, for Judy was very absent-minded and frequently neglected to close her door. Perfectly capable of taking off her blouse but forgetting to take off her hat, she would sit topless before her mirror while removing her make-up. The phalanx of waiting students could see everything, but Judy nothing. She was as blind as a bat, and it was only after removing her make-up and putting on her glasses that for the first time she could see in the reflection of her looking glass the goggling throng behind her.

Turning completely around to face her now silent admirers, she presented them with a full top frontal – the like of which few had ever seen before.

'Hello, darlings,' she cried. 'Did you want something?'

A highly unnecessary question as, from the looks on their faces alone, it was not hard to hazard a guess.

They were lucky to have had two bites of the cherry, however, for on appearing in Shaw's *The Simpleton of the Unexpected Isles* later in the season I had to play a scene with Judy as Prola in which I started off seated at her feet. The costume provided was so awful that Judy had made her own, and it consisted of little but a pair of briefs covered by a long, flowing dress of diaphanous white muslin, with a cross of wide red ribbon across the bust. At the beginning of the scene we were both seated, but at a given moment Judy was to rise up in anger and harangue me. Unfortunately for Judy, but fortunately for her acolytes, I was sitting on the hem of her dress, so that when she leaped up, the dress was pulled down. Without pause, the priestess Prola, now bared to the waist, went on ranting and raving until the end of the scene.

In the wings Judy, still unaware, said to me,

'My word, darling, weren't they a fabulous audience! You could've heard a pin drop during that last scene.' I was somewhat loath to point out the real reason for that hushed reaction, but plainly no-one else had any intention of doing so. It transpired later that the firm fit of the crossed ribbons had given Judy the impression that the top half of her robe was still very properly in place, and that nothing whatsoever was amiss. How wrong she was – *or* right, depending on your point of view!

Another girl in the Company was a very attractive, delicate looking redhead called Sarah Churchill, daughter of Winston, and a tremendous giggler. For one scene in *The Simpleton of the Unexpected Isles* we were directed to sit cross-legged for quite a considerable time on a line of wooden boxes, with Brandon Acton Bond on my left and Sarah on *his* left. Halfway through the scene, I whispered through clenched teeth, 'I've got to stand up, I've got cramp in my right leg.' So saying, I staggered haltingly to my foot. The leading actor, under the mistaken impression that I was going to say something said 'Yes?' and, on receiving no reply, dried up completely.

That was enough for Sarah, who went off into a paroxysm of near silent giggles. Within seconds we'd all caught it, and hardly a word was spoken as we snorted and gasped our way through what remained of the scene. Later, Peter Hoare, our Director gave serious consideration to the idea of my dismissal, but thank God, in Sarah I had not only a friend but a brilliant advocate, who pleaded so skilfully on my behalf that she was able to convince my complainants that I really *had* had a serious attack of the 'twingeing screws'.

Every now and then, Winston Churchill would drive over to take her and selected friends out to tea. I shall remember to my dying day that I was able to sit and talk, albeit nervously, to the greatest Englishman of my lifetime. He could talk to you about anything, and it was he who gave me this excellent advice – 'Never miss an opportunity to learn, my boy. If you find yourself next to a glass eye-ball maker at dinner, don't make him feel he's got to talk to you about something he knows damn all about. Get him to tell you how he makes eye-balls. You're sure to find it enthralling.'

If only I had taken written note of all the advice proffered by men and women of mark over the years, how much greater would be my comprehension!

The following one, however, *was* duly noted.

It was given during a party at the height of the evening when the drinks were flowing, the air was clouded with cigar and cigarette smoke, and a certain young actor was listening reverently to tales of theatrical bravura, recounted by that eminent actor Sir Seymour Hicks, who, irritated by the nervous tapping of his cigarette on the side of his cigarette case, observed, 'Don't tap your cigarette on your cigarette case, young man. It doesn't make an impression and only leaves a dent.'

Chapter Six

Putting Rep behind me, I returned to London late in 1938, determined to crack the West End wide open. To do so, I needed to be independent and fancy free, and therefore looked for a home of my own in the immediate environs of the West End theatres. I found just the place, a two-roomed furnished flat in a small house on the bottom corner of St Martins Street, below Leicester Square. On the first floor, it consisted of a bedroom-cum-sitting-room with an enormous divan bed, another small bedroom, and a bathroom. The decor was extraordinary: a mixture of bright emerald green paint and silver wallpaper. It was so 'kitsch' as to be almost attractive. What a find! Convenient to my Agent, Maurice Lambert of Film Rights, whose office was literally round the corner in Whitcomb Street, it had a garage for my motor-bike, a wonderful pub opposite owned and run by an old Frensham Heights friend, 'The Olde Lanterne Cafe' just up the road, a telephone box in Leicester Square (where if you knew the system you could phone the world for free!); and best of all it was only a few yards from stage door of the Prince of Wales Theatre, from which came an unending stream of beautiful girls. My personal inamorata, Bunty Darling, one of the principal show girls, had a key to the flat, and whether I was there or not would use it as a refuge from her cacophonous dressing room.

'Bring any of your friends,' I said, 'they're always welcome.' They were certainly made to feel so by *my* friends, who just couldn't believe their luck. My popularity became legion.

'Let's go up and see old Jon,' they said, 'he's a first class chap, and so amusing.' I didn't suffer any delusions however, and knew exactly where the real attraction lay.

Beneath my bedroom window was an area of the pavement most popular at night with 'Ladies and Gentlemen of the road'. There would come 'Old Molly', 'Tiger Tim' and 'Brown Paper Jack' to lay themselves down and sleep.

'Old Molly' was an infamous alcoholic known to every Magistrate in London. Her tipple was a mixture of 'Big Tree' Burgundy and methylated spirits, which did her absolutely no good at all. Settling down for the night she opened her sack, and laid out neatly before her all the important things she would need during the next few hours. Two sardine tins, four odd pieces of string, some apple cores, several empty boxes of matches, a mummified orange and a Kia-ora bottle of her special concoction, known in the trade as 'Red Biddy'. After consuming but half of this nectar, 'Old Molly' was roaring and having to get up at 5.30 in the morning to go to the film studios, I opened the window and shouted, 'Put a sock in it, Moll, there's a love. I'm *trying* to get some sleep.'

'Fuck off,' came the ladylike reply, and unable to top that, there was nothing else for me to do, but obey.

Tiger Tim was so named because he communicated not with words but by roars.

'Good morning Tim, lovely day,' I'd say.

'Roooaaagh,' he'd reply.

'Did you sleep well?'

'Roooaaagh,' he answered. If one was lonely and felt in need of verbal intercourse, then the toing and froing of conversation with Tiger Tim inclined towards the monotonous.

One was far better served by talking to Brown Paper Jack. He came by his name for the obvious reason that he preferred to dress in brown paper and string, than in ordinary layman's clothes. Swathing himself in brown paper had many advantages, in that:-

1) It was adaptable to all weather conditions – in winter six more layers could be tied on, and in summer three or more layers taken off;

2) Wrapped up nicely, dirt couldn't get in, making the washing of his person unnecessary; and

3) If it rained and the paper began to disintegrate, a few fresh layers would quickly put the matter right.

The only real disadvantage was that Jack was a fire hazard. Nightly, against avuncular advice from passing members of the Constabulary, Jack would build a fire for the combined purposes of warmth and cuisine. He could produce a 'fry-up' on the lid of a biscuit tin that was, so I have been informed by previous honoured guests, unsurpassable.

The only trouble was that if 'Old Molly' had been amongst the invited she would treat Jack to a few slugs of the Biddy by way of gratitude for the excellent repast. This was inclined to have disastrous results, as Jack, after a few snorts, would fall forward into his fire and instantly turn himself into a human torch, only to be extinguished by liberal cups of tea thrown over him by the other guests.

Shortly after the war, the Director of a picture I was working on needed a tramp.

'I know the very man,' I said, describing Jack. 'Bung us a few quid to give him and I'll make sure he turns up on the right day.'

Jack had moved to his country residence under the bridge at Chislehurst, and it was here I found him, crouched over his fire, in a crisp new brown paper suit.

'How would you like to be in a film, Jack?' I asked.

'Does it pay?' said Jack suspiciously.

'Four pounds,' I replied, 'plus your meals and rail fare.'

'That's all right, Mr Jon, my sister's got a jam-jar. She'll bring me down, and I'll save a oner.'

'6.30 then, Jack, and don't be late.'

'Don't you worry none, Mr Jon, I won't let you down.'

By 7.30, the Director was worried. By 8.30, frantic!

'The whole day's shooting hinges on the tramp,' he screamed. 'Where the hell is he?' Once again I searched the 'extras' dressing room. There was no sign of Jack, only a little man in an ill-fitting blue serge suit, with a short back and sides, sitting in the corner.

As I made to leave the room, he got up and said, 'Are you ready for me yet, Mr Jon?' It was Jack. Jack, as few had ever seen him. It transpired that as I had completely neglected to tell him that he was wanted as a tramp, he assumed that he was wanted for his looks and his talent. In order not to let me down, he had had a shave, a haircut and borrowed a fifty-shilling suit from his brother-in-law.

I never saw Jack again and was saddened by his disappointment at not becoming a 'film-star for a day.' Perhaps I was responsible for his retirement from the road and his adoption of standard dress in preference to brown paper and string.

★

In his bachelor days, the splendid character actor Sydney Tafler frequently borrowed my flat for Trysts and Assignations and his astonishing virility could be readily ascertained by counting on the bedroom floor the number of circular pieces of pink paper that separated the pessaries in his tubes of prophylactic 'Gynomin'. Sydney pretended to be a bit put out when joshed about this, but in actual fact he was preening!

★

The years of 1938 and '39 were a busy time for me. I obtained a small part in *Judgement Day*, a heavy drama concerning the trial of Van Der Lubbe, the wretched pawn in the Berlin Reichstag fire trial. It starred young Glynis Johns in one of her first leading roles in the West End, my cousin Jill Esmond, Leon Quartermaine, W. E. Holloway, Andrew Osborne, the late Peter Bull and a mort of others whose names escape me. But the uneventful run was made memorable by the highly original wit of Peter Bull who played the mentally retarded Van Der Lubbe. Peter always made me laugh inordinately and I was forever saying so to my wife Ingeborg. One day years later whilst we were parked in the Kings Road, Chelsea, Peter, whom I had not seen for many years, came breasting down the street towards us. Peter being made of considerable stuff did not walk, he breasted.

'Look,' I cried to Ingeborg in delight, 'here comes Peter Bull, *you* know, the man I'm always telling you makes me laugh so much.' Ingeborg looked dubious as the alleged humorist breasted abreast of my car.

'Peter, Peter, how are you?' I cried in pleasurable anticipation of some witty repartee. Stopping and bending his not inconsiderable bulk to bring his face down level with the windows to see who it was that had so enquired after his health, he said, and remember I had not seen him in four or five years, 'Ah, there you are!'

I at once collapsed into quite helpless laughter, almost sinking under the steering wheel. By the time I had sufficiently pulled myself together to talk with him, he had typically gone, making me go off into yet another bout of hysterics. Ingeborg, whose colloquial English was not very good at the time, never cracked a smile, and to this day fails to find Peter's statement to be as truly humorous as I have always found it.

★

The other memorable part of the *Judgement Day* run happened in the last act, when one of the judges, despairing at the travesty of justice unfolding before him, turns a pistol on himself and blows out his brains, rather than be a party to any further legal impropriety.

On this unforgettable occasion, the veteran actor W. E. Holloway made his impassioned speech in defence of true justice, said, 'Farewell', turned the gun to his head and fired. There was nothing to be heard but a metallic click of the trigger – a misfire. He re-cocked the gun, and again said, 'Farewell' – louder this time. 'Click', another misfire! Nothing daunted, the many years of experience took over, and taking the gun by the barrel the old gentleman proceeded to set about himself with the butt, intent on beating his brains out. Unfortunately, as the final killing blow struck home, so did the panic-struck Stage Manager pull the trigger of the spare pistol kept in the wings for such an emergency. The result of that loud report going off, at the precise moment that Mr Holloway made the 'killing' contact on his cranium, was one of shameful hysteria which would have been quite correctly reported in the media as 'There was laughter in court.'

★

In the same year, my father's new play *To Kill a Cat* was being cast, and I begged to be allowed to audition for it. Luckily I didn't have much competition and landed the juvenile lead. The stars were Clifford Mollison in one of his first non-dancing roles and the sexy Enid Stamp-Taylor. The Director was the comedy star Henry (Harry) Kendall, who, when given the opportunity, preferred to approach young gentlemen from the rear, as opposed to another lady in the cast who preferred to approach young ladies from the front.

During a love scene where I was supposed to take this lady's face in my hands and kiss her, she turned to Mr Kendall and said, 'Harry, don't you think it would be more in keeping if I took Jon's face in my hands and kissed *him*?'

'Wonderful, darling, an excellent suggestion, do it!'

It might well have been 'more in keeping' with her way of life, but it certainly wasn't 'macho' in mine.

I was just about to protest, therefore, when she grabbed my face, pressed her full mouth to mine with unladylike fervour, and hurled herself on top of me, flattening me into the sofa. My muffled cries of protest went unheeded, until, with a sharp arching of the back, I was able to dislodge this aggressive limpet and send her flying to the floor.

'Heavens to Betsy!' cried Harry Kendall. 'What on earth's the matter with you? You're behaving like a Vestal virgin!'

There was little point in trying to explain the heterosexual's point of view. The actress was furious at being baulked and Harry was later equally displeased by my humourless and hostile reaction to his frequent administration of the top dead centre 'goose'.

So what with this and that and my immature and bellicose response to being 'fancied' by a member of my own sex, I was downgraded, when the play opened at the Aldwych Theatre, to understudying the more pliable Mr Grey Blake. For some reason that I've never understood, the lady I had this disagreement with was also given the order of

Valkyrie starts P.173.

Found this in our cut-price bookshop here & could not resist it after reading a few pages itno!

the boot, and her part was taken over by a clever young actress called Elizabeth Gilbert. She also happened to be married to my brother Michael, so perhaps I was wrong when I said earlier that my father would never tolerate nepotism.

Another member of the cast was the tall, dark haired, dark eyed and statuesque beauty, Margaretta Scott. Her personal attitude to dress was highly original and she was often to be seen wearing a large wide-brimmed black felt hat with feather, and a voluminous black cloak. One day on entering the famous 'Ivy' Restaurant, she was spied by the most regular and famous of their customers, the wickedly witty Dame Lillian Braithwaite. 'Ah look,' she whispered, sufficiently loud for all the neighbouring sycophants to hear, 'there goes the lovely Margaretta Scott, on her way to York, I see!'

If it hadn't been for my friendship with London's youngest Stage Manager, eighteen-year-old Shaun Sutton, later to become my overall boss in *Doctor Who*, it would've been a very galling and theatrically frustrating engagement.

In this same year, aged nineteen, I appeared in *Goodbye Mr Chips* at the 'Q' Theatre. On recently studying the programme, I found that in a very large cast, there was not a single name apart from the star, the late Raymond Lovell, that I recognised. I concluded that they were either dead or had retired from the profession – a somewhat alarming indictment of a life in the theatre.

I also did my first broadcast that year, narrating *Lillibulero* with Leo Genn and Ralph Truman. This interesting piece, directed by Michael Barry, was produced in Northern Ireland and walking through the streets one evening, I was almost knocked off my feet by a tremendous explosion from a nearby basement. On enquiring what on earth it could be, I was calmly informed ''Twill be the lads blowin' up de masonic temple again, oi'll be thinkin',' the reasoning for such dislike of 'masonry' being beyond my comprehension. As, equally, was the explanation given by a landlady in Dublin, at the discovery of a dozen or so holes through a wall in the bedroom. 'Ah yes; well yer not to worry yerself about dem, Mr Pertwee, they're just dere to remind us of the troubles.'

During that stay in Belfast, presumably because of the import attached to the subject matter of the broadcast, we were invited to have lunch with the Prime Minister of Northern Ireland at Government House.

For some reason, best put down to insecurity, I was completely unnerved at being seated to the Prime Minister's left, and while he talked to the guest on his right, I sat silently rolling up bread pellets. Eventually, he turned to me and in an endeavour to put me more at ease, asked politely what I would like to drink.

'Er j-j-just some w-w-w-ater, thank you, sir!'

'Mary, pour Mr Pertwee some water will you,' he said, utterly bewildered at such an unusual request. After all, he must have thought, I'm not exactly unknown for the quality of my cellar.

The young maid, who was plainly as nervous as I was, went to the mahogany sideboard, picked up a beautiful Waterford decanter and poured me out a large goblet full. The inside of my mouth felt like a compressed beer mat, so I downed most of the glass in one draught. The effect of this action was immediate and awesome; my breathing stopped; I quickly changed colour from surprise pink to scarlet through to blue; my eyes stood out like a terrified Pekinese with Bright's disease; and as I threw the glass over my right shoulder, my feet came up smartly under the table with such force that a large proportion of the silver, crystal and china left the surface by about six inches with quite disastrous results.

After the panic resulting from this embarrassing exhibition had died down, and some semblance of order had been restored, the PM conducted an immediate inquest.

It transpired that Mary, the young maid, was new to the job, and instead of pouring me fresh water from the jug, had poured me neat Kummel from a decanter, and I, in my nervousness, had gulped it down in one.

'It's sorry I am, sorr,' she said, 'but they both looked the same to me.'

She was right of course, poor soul, but by heaven they didn't *taste* the same, *nor* were they the same proof.

★

In the cast of *To Kill A Cat* was a character actor by the name of John Salew. He was doing very well at the time, working in films, theatre, and on the radio. This was a medium that I very much wanted to crack, and in meeting John Salew in Whitcomb Street early one morning, fate must've taken a hand.

'Ah Pertwee, just the man I wanted to see,' he cried. 'Can you do a West Country accent?'

Could I? Dammit, I'd lived half my life down there. If I couldn't do *that* dialect, I couldn't do any!

'Yes, Mr Salew, I think so.'

'Then get yourself to this studio in Bond Street at once,' he said, handing me the address. 'Tell them I can't get in today, I'm filming at Denham.'

Now at the time Mr Salew was playing various parts in famous soap operas such as *Marmaduke Brown* (the *Waggoners Walk* of its day), *Backstage Wife*, *Young Widow Jones*, *Mr Reeder* and *Stella Dallas*. These fifteen-minute programmes were broadcast five days a week from Radio Luxembourg and Fécamp.

Needing no further bidding, I tugged my forelock for Mr Salew and, thanking him profusely, shot off to the Bond Street Studio, and told them why I was there.

The Producer was Jack Hayes-Hunter, a very live-wire American, who to put it mildly was not best pleased.

'That bastard's too clever by three quarters,' he yelled. 'What in Christ's good name am I going to do now?'

'Well you could try letting me have a shot at it, Mr Hunter,' I suggested. 'I'm here and you've nothing to lose.'

'True,' said Jack, and took me at once into the recording booth. The star, Ernest Clark, and the rest of the cast quickly put me at my ease, resulting in what I hoped was a reasonable performance.

The next morning I received a phone call from my Agent, Maurice Lambert (by coincidence, also John Salew's Agent), to inform me that Jack Hunter had been sufficiently impressed to offer me the part permanently at two pounds two shillings a programme – and, because he was so angry at Mr Salew's 'unreliability' and 'lack of professionalism', all the rest of his parts as well.

'You clever schmock,' said Maurice, only employing such endearments to good friends, 'I represent John Salew, as well as you, so how in Moses' name am I going to explain *this* to him?'

'That's your problem,' I replied, 'you're the flesh peddler, not I,' and although Mr Salew never spoke to me again, at least I had cracked the world of commercial radio. For the next two years, I did around twenty to twenty-five fifteen-minute shows a week and at two pounds two shillings a programme, I was pulling in between forty and fifty pounds. A fortune for a young actor in those days. This added increment enabled me to pay the price down on another motorbike, a V-Twin 1000cc Brough-Superior, refurbish the flat, buy two new suits from Hector Powe at three pounds ten shillings a go, and to afford the luxury of Miss Carlotta Joachim Sid'Kithan, a beautiful live-in lover. She was from Ceylon, half Dutch, half Singalese, and was by far the most exotic creature I had ever met. Usually gentle and soft of voice, she was at times as fiery as a Tasmanian Devil. She wore sarongs of silks and cottons and taught me the many ways to tie them. I've worn sarongs on the beach, on my boat and in bed ever since, and have collected lava-lavas, pareu clothes, lunghis, and kikois from all over the world – most useful and colourful garments. The Tahitians, who are very sexually orientated, say, 'They are quick to put on, but even quicker to take off!'

Carlotta was a great cook and taught me to appreciate the pleasures of good eastern food. The delicious smell of succulent curries wafted down St Martins Street to delight my home-coming, but probably vexed Mr Harold Macmillan, whose publishing house was right next door. Old Molly, Brown Paper Jack and Tiger Tim had no complaints, however, as they frequently came in for the left-overs and rice, which Jack would mix up with a threepenny tin of Heinz baked beans or a tin of pilchards.

Carlotta's languid sexuality, outward calm and aura of restfulness, made me, for the first time in my life, want to stay at home. She made the kitsch flat look almost beautiful with vases of flowers everywhere and single blooms in her hair. Carlotta sat mostly on the floor, sewing and making things, with her long black hair swinging in a single plait over her shoulder. Friends continued to drop in, but they were now of a somewhat different genre, no longer the frantic ones forever on the prowl, but those who liked to sit, eat and talk. It was my first introduction to peaceful domesticity, with the added advantage of tender instruction into the art of love.

The British film business was at its peak around 1938–39 and there was then no stigma attached to an actor for being employed as an 'extra' or 'crowd artist'. Stewart Granger, Michael Wilding, Richard Attenborough, Laurence Harvey had all been extras in their time. To work in the crowd meant a very early rise to enable one to catch the train down to Denham, or any one of the numerous studios in London's environs, for a 7.30 call. I soon got used to the routine, however, and learned that 5.30 in the morning is often by far the best part of the day.

After checking-in to the studio with the third assistant, it was off to the canteen for breakfast. It was there that I met John Churchill for the first time, and over the weeks learned from him all the tricks of the 'extra' trade. After his breakfast, John would check-in for the film for which he was sent down, then in the lavatory surreptitiously change into some other clothes that he had brought with him. Cloth-cap, raincoat, that sort of thing. Then putting on some spectacles he would check in with the third assistant of a completely different film as Harry Farnsbarns. Denham was so big, that it was possible to have several films on the floor at the same time. This done, he would escape from the lot through a hole he had previously made in the fence, jump on his hidden motorbike, and roar off to other studios in the area where he reported for duty with a different name and in a different guise in each.

Armed now with several chitties, he returned to the Denham studio from where he had originally started, excusing his tardiness with the most inventive collection of excuses I have ever heard. Recurring attacks of dysentery, beriberi, and malaria were amongst his favourites. He could never have topped my favourite 'sorry I'm late' excuse from the late great Max Adrian, however. Max was always late and the Producer was getting very icy about it, saying that if it happened once more, he would reprimand him before the entire Company or even replace him. The next day Max was later than ever and everyone waited with bated breath for the inevitable excuse.

'My dears, I'm terribly sorry I'm late,' said Max, 'but I just *couldn't* stop crying!' Everyone, the Producer included, was naturally far too embarrassed to ask anything further.

But to return to Denham. Throughout the day John, having found some quiet place to hide, would read the papers and sleep, rising only for the natural functions, lunch and tea. 'You see, old boy, to do well in this racket, your face must *never* become familiar. Once it does, once it becomes recognisable to the Assistant Directors, you'll cease to get work. If you *must* appear in a scene, stay well back. You don't want the Director saying, "What's *he* doing there, we saw *him* yesterday," do you? So keep out of sight and be seen as little as possible. Just remember a "nonentity" *always* gets plenty of work!' And to think that I, determined to be noticed by the Director and his assistants alike, had been pushing myself to the front, in the expectation of being picked out for instant stardom.

Once the day's filming was through, the extras went to the third assistant, had their chitties signed, collected their money and went home. The salary was one pound, one shilling a day plus any overtime – more if you wore costume or dress clothes and still more if you wore your *own* dress clothes. I'll always remember those pathetic advertisements placed in *The Stage* by out of work actors and actresses. Heavily abbreviated to save cost they ran: 'Exp chtr Actrs own wrdrb sks mplmnt sprir rep coy rmnratn opn to ofr rply rgntly bx 1072', viz – 'Experienced character Actress, own wardrobe, seeks employment in superior Repertory Company, renumeration open to offer, reply urgently Box 1072.'

But John Churchill *couldn't* go home – not yet! He had the rounds of all the other studios to make, getting all his chits signed and collecting all the ensuing cash.

How he got away with it I'll never know, but he did, and made a great deal of money out of it into the bargain.

We were both in *A Yank At Oxford* with Robert Taylor and Vivien Leigh, playing undergraduates, and as we were permanently on location, John, finding it virtually impossible to hide himself successfully did a complete volte-face and taught himself to play the bagpipes. And there's no way of staying well back with *them*! In between each shot, the skirl o' the pipes could be heard over the generator's hum, and for those who liked it, a good time was had by all – all but the sound–man that is! No-one believed that he could have reached such proficiency in such a short space of time, but he did, and to the infuriation of all other competitors, went on to win the Pipe majors' world bagpipe championship. The haunting sound of John Churchill's laments were with us until he went off the join the Army in 1939.

It was not until he joined the Commandos, however, that John became a real star, for amongst his other accomplishments, he was a champion toxophilite and taught his men the ancient art of bowmanship. His was the only Commando unit that went into action with sten guns *and* bows and arrows, which they later used to tremendous effect in raids on the French coast.

It was in the famous raid on Vaagso in the Lofoten Islands off the coast of Norway that John had his finest hour. Commanding this epic raid he marched up and down the quay playing *The Cock o' the North* on his pipes, under a hail of German bullets. Utterly undaunted and badly wounded he spurred his men on to achieve one of the most successful raids of the war. For this act of sheer bravado he was very highly decorated (the VC if I remember correctly) and was properly dubbed by the press and the PR department at the War Office 'The Mad Major of Vaagso'.

I've just remembered another example of his original thinking.

'I'm only doing this sort of work, and leading this kind of life so that I don't have to use my brain,' he said. 'That way, when the day comes that I really want to use it, it will be virgin fresh, and quite uncluttered by unnecessary flotsam and jetsam.'

If there is any reader who can tell me what happened to John

Churchill and his present whereabouts, if he has any, I would be very grateful.

★

In 1939 I worked in three other films, of whose content I remember little. There was *Dinner At The Ritz*, *A Young Man's Fancy* (an unfortunate title) and *The Four Just Men*. It was in this film, playing the part of a young politician, that I spoke my first lines. My father, Roland, apart from writing the scenario, also played a tiny part. But when watching it on television earlier this year, I found to my dismay that I, with much the larger role, was not mentioned on the credits. Roland was consistently awful in the little he had to do, but looked distinguished. I, conversely, looked undistinguished and wasn't at all bad. In fact I would've been much better if I had had the cutters on my side. But I must have pleased the Producer, Michael Balcon, for on watching me go through the scene he asked my father standing nearby who I was.

'That is my son!' replied Roland.

I think that was the first time he had ever cheerfully acknowledged parenthood.

The scene involved my haranguing a large crowd of worker 'extras' outside some factory gates. We had started on the scene fairly late in the afternoon and the Director was most anxious to get the shot in the can, and not have the expense of recalling the crowd for a further day. This was quite opposed to the wishes of my many friends among the 'extras', who were equally anxious that I should muff my lines and screw everything up to ensure that they *were* called for the following day. I was in a cleft stick! What to choose – popularity, or the chance of setting my foot on the ladder-of-stardom's bottom rung? I chose the latter, which later cost me every penny I had just earned on placatory pints of ale for my many aggrieved associates.

★

Theatre-going in those days often provided work for artists *outside* the theatres as well as in.

To obtain a cheap ticket in the Pit or the Gallery before the war necessitated a long wait in a queue. This is where the many buskers came into their own. There were the Bowler Hatted Sand-Dancers (à la Wilson, Kepple and Betty); a jazz band called the Happy Wanderers, consisting of a heterogeneous collection of veteran musicians, dressed quite differently, but always wearing what appeared to be prison-

123

officers' caps; a black gentleman who recited nothing but *Othello*; a red-bearded gentleman, who by previous arrangement with the black gentleman, recited everything *but Othello*, and a lady with a club-foot who had a voice of such devastating power that later, when the air raids had started, she could, when requested by the Wardens, summon stragglers to the shelters by impersonating an air raid siren more penetrating than the original. There was also an elderly violin-player in funereal black with the long white hair of a Paderewski; and an assortment of bouncy entertainers in the 'Cheeky Chappie' mould. Each would arrive at a queue, wait patiently for his or her predecessor to do his or her 'bit', and go round with the hat for donations, leaving the pitch for the next diseuse, monologuist, minstrel, jongleur or contortionist.

During these various and varied entertainments, a familiar West End figure was frequently to be seen strutting purposefully past the waiting queues. In appearance, he resembled nothing so much as 'Struwwel-Peter', with his unkempt shoulder length hair flowing behind him as he walked, his furled umbrella's ferrule rapping a regular tattoo on the pavement.

What the purpose of this routine promenade was remained a mystery for many years, until one day a jealous street-artiste of little worth let the cat out of the bag. All London's buskers, it seemed, were under the control of a 'union', and this union was administrated by one man, 'Struwwel-Peter'. Every pitch was allocated by him, with the buskers working in whatever order and duration he designated. To make sure that his members were adhering strictly to union rules, and would not forget to pay their weekly 'dues', he strode the pavements several times a day, to let them know that 'Big Brother' was watching, and that they had better toe the party line or else.

I was queuing at the 'New' for the great Olivier–Gielgud season, when the little old white-haired violinist arrived at the curbside.

'My Lords, Ladies and Gentlemen,' he said with quavering voice, and judging the quality of the audience well. 'Today I should like to play for you, the Bruch Violin Concerto, thank you!' and with that, the sweet old man proceeded to play the great work with surprising style and soul. Half-way through, there suddenly appeared at the curb one of the 'Cheeky' ones who, against all 'union rules', and only a few feet away from the old violinist, took from his pocket a piccolo and started to play very piercingly *The Sailors' Hornpipe*. So the old violinist upped his volume a touch. With the piccoloist promptly following suit, the battle of wills and notes was on, the contest continuing unabated until the saintly looking old violinist could stand no more. Removing the violin slowly from under his chin, he turned to the offending flautist and said with remarkable clarity, for all the 'Lords, Ladies and Gentlemen' to hear, 'Fuck off, you piss-hole!'

The piccolo player was so taken aback that he pocketed his piccolo and scarpered. To shouts of approbation and a shower of coins, the old gentleman was prevailed upon to continue his piece without fear of further interruption. Though I do not doubt that at the next buskers' union meeting, the General Secretary Mr S. Peter issued the piccolo player with a temporary suspension for not abiding rigidly by union rules.

★

Let us pause here for a brief résumé of my life's successes to date. 'Superannuated' from Aldro and Sherborne; 'asked to leave' RADA; fired from Jersey Rep; nearly ditto at Cambridge and downgraded in *To Kill a Cat*. Not bad for starters was it? But success in commercial radio had just about tipped the scales back in my favour and no longer was poor Maurice Lambert getting the same reaction when putting me up for a job. 'Him? You must be joking.'

War clouds had been gathering, and it looked as if, having just turned the corner, I was likely to be pushed back round it again.

It was bad luck for Michael too; he had just had an enormous critical hit with his first West End play *Death On The Table* in which he collaborated with Dr Guy Beauchamp, the renowned osteopath. Michael, the youngest playwright ever to have a play presented in the West End, had also recently signed a very good film-writing contract with Michael Balcon at Ealing and having just recently married was badly hit when war inevitably broke out.

Chapter Seven

'Then the soldier
Full of strange oaths, and bearded like the pard,
Jealous in honour sudden and quick in quarrel,
Seeking the bubble reputation.'

I was paying a rare visit to my mother's cottage, Blewbury Mill in Oxfordshire, when she called me to the radio to hear Mr Neville Chamberlain's chilling declaration of war. I had had nightmares over the years, involving the trenches, the hand to hand fighting, the bayonets and the rats. Joining the Army therefore, was definitely out, and even though Michael had pre-empted the declaration by joining the Territorials with his brother-in-law, I would not be moved in my resolve. The Air Force? No, that must also be a non-starter; the thought of being trapped in a burning aircraft terrified me. How anybody found the courage to do what the last war fliers did is beyond my comprehension. Especially the bomber pilots, who, night after night, hour after hour, allowed themselves to be shot at from above and below, awaiting philosophically, by the law of averages alone, a fearful end.

So, apart from being a conscientious objector (which needed the greatest courage of all), what was there left but the Navy? Nothing! The trouble here was the question of my seasickness. Over the last few years, on our way to France, I had regularly joined the Dover-to-Calais passengers as they tossed, heaved and retched their way across that violent channel. The groans, moans and smell of those Tourist Class lounges will remain in my memory forever.

But, and it is a *big* but, ships were clean, food was regular, action when it took place, was at a distance, and therefore death, either dealt or received, was impersonal, not forgetting the *best* reason that 'all the nice girls love a sailor'. I took a little longer to join up than Uncle Guy would've wished, but the threat of receiving a 'white feather' disappeared as soon as he saw me in my full seaman's rig.

Of course, before the Navy would have me, I, like everyone else, had to undergo a strict and very thorough medical examination. It is when one has a service medical that one realises that there is no medical practitioner in whatever field you care to choose, that can compare in skill and knowledge with serving Medical Officers. Go to any civilian doctor, or even specialist, for a check-up and what happens? You are given blood tests, eye tests, electro-cardiograms, X-rays and God knows what! The serving Medical Officer scorns such devices. He can tell everything there is to know about your medical history, physical condition and mental ability by two very simple tests. These are known in medical circles as 'The Cough' and 'The Sample'.

They're both embarrassing, as those of you who have undergone them will know. In case anyone hasn't, let me describe them briefly. First the Sample. Here, you are given a small test tube – one and a half fluid ounces capacity approx – told to retire behind a curtain and return with your sample in the tube. It is at this point that people are divided into two distinct categories. Category A, those who cannot produce a sample at all and Category B, those who can start, but, having started, cannot stop. I began as a member of Category A, and was getting rather worried when suddenly, and entirely without warning, I transferred sharply into Category B. However, I duly produced my test tube – plus a few spares – and was given my second test. The Cough. For this you are attired in nothing whatsoever, except a slight blush, and stand facing the MO, who then places a couple of icy fingers on a very intimate part of your person and says 'Cough!' A rather unnecessary request because in that position, there isn't much else you can do *but* cough. And that one small cough tells the keen mind of the MO if you've got flat feet, hardened arteries, galloping consumption or dandruff and if you haven't – bang! You're in the Navy, me old shipmate.

For my part, I was not 'bearded', but a clean shaven sailor, and soon full to the brim with strange oaths. At least they were strange to me then. Now you can hear them almost daily on children's television. Sailors are a rum lot. In general conversation their language is not by any means out of the top drawer, and the use of the number one four-letter-word is a must. In fact, it is almost mandatory to insert it between every word of more than one syllable, e.g. – 'Yer, abso-fuckin-lutely.'

By the same token, the epithet should also be liberally dispersed *between* words, such as 'Hey Peewee! Oo's this George fuckin' Bernard fuckin' Shaw then?'

But in mixed company, or within hearing of the female sex, I seldom heard a sailor use a naughty word. They had the remarkable ability of switching from a conversation festooned in 'fucks' to language more in keeping with a cleric's tea-party.

So, had you been passing Portsmouth Barracks in late 1939 you would have seen the transformation of a raglan tweed-overcoated, flat-capped civilian Pertwee being turned into Very Ordinary Seaman Pertwee PJX178358, a tough, ruthless, cold-blooded war machine.

Having changed from the raglan tweed into the sailor's serge, I was paraded on the barrack square, with the rest of our rag, tag and bobtail lot, for inspection by our CO, Commodore 'Hooky' Walker, so named for the piratical brass hook he had in place of his right hand.

A three-badge Able Seaman (always referred to as a 'Stripey', his stripes being a sign of long service) had advised me during the previous evening's meal:–

'When joining the Andrew [Navy] mate, you must make up your mind what you are going to be. A bastard or a cunt.'

On reflection I chose to be the latter, and just for a lark, to set the seal on my decision, turned up for that inspection sporting a rimless monocle à la Erich Von Stroheim, as opposed to one of the Bertie Wooster gold-framed-on-a-string variety. The effect the appurtenance had on 'Hooky' Walker was startling, and for a moment no words issued from his mouth, only steam. Thrusting his quivering hook into my face he demanded, 'What is that?'

'A monocle, sir.'

'Sailors don't wear monocles. Take it out.'

'But I need it, sir.' I pleaded, 'Without it I might fall down.'

'You'll fall down all right by the time I've finished with you,' he said, and turning to my Divisional Officer, barked, 'Put this man in my report.'

The report was somewhat muffled as far as the Commodore was concerned, for nothing could be found in the King's Rules and Regulations that forbade sailors on the lower deck from wearing monocles. Before I was dismissed, with no stain upon my character, 'Hooky' Walker called me over to his table and whispered, 'Pertwee, will you do me a personal favour?'

'Of course, sir,' I said. After all, I could afford to be magnanimous.

'In future, when I am personally taking inspection, would you make a point of leaving your monocle in your ditty-box, and thereby save me the indignity of dying publicly from apoplexy?'

The whole of this confrontation had gone down a storm with the other matelots in my division, especially with a bunch of villainous

Scots from Glasgow who promptly dubbed me 'Marmaduke'. My connection with radio's *Marmaduke Brown*, I suppose, adding grist to the mill.

So as 'Old Marmy' I became probably the first lower deck sailor in His Majesty's Royal Navy ever to wear a monocle. The only trouble was that contrary to the reason of threatened instability offered up to the Commodore, due to the quite incorrect prescription of the eye-glass, I was more in peril of falling down from keeping it in, than taking it out.

So there I was in Portsmouth Naval Barracks, waiting for a draught and marching almost incessantly. Just how one learns to fight battles by marching round parade grounds I've never understood, but whatever service you're in, you march. We used to have to take it in turns to give the commands and, when my turn came, the CPO in charge, one Chief Petty Officer Branch said, 'Rightho, Pestwee! March that column of men to the end of the parade ground, turn 'em about, and bring 'em back 'ere in front of me.'

'Aye aye, Chief,' I replied confidently and gave the order, 'By the left, quick march!' I waited until they'd gone some fifty yards and then shouted, 'Squad, habout . . .'

'Not yet, Pestwee,' said CPO Branch, 'I'll tell you when.' By this time they were getting out of earshot, so I shouted, with all my might, 'Squad habout . . .'

'*Not yet*, Pestwee,' said CPO Branch. I was just recovering from my last effort which had turned my face purple and caused my eyeballs to protrude, when CPO Branch said, 'Right lad, now!' Rallying what little vocal resource I had left, I screamed, 'Habout turn!' A scream that was heard by all at the back, some in the middle, but none in the front, so that they all started to go in different directions.

'Dearie me!' said CPO Branch. 'Oh dearie, dearie me. What a *very* nasty mess! Get 'em back together, lad.' Fighting to clear the mists that had formed before my eyes I breathed in deeply, clenched my teeth and my gluteals, braced my feet and gave the piercing screech, 'Haboouuuttt teherrrn!!!'

This time they *all* heard it and dutifully turned about. As you can imagine the result was chaotic. They all banged into each other, and several fell over . . . it was ghastly. There was a long pause then, in a voice broken with emotion, CPO Branch said, '*Now* I know what they mean when they say "Marines will advance in columns of fours and matelots in fuckin' great heaps."'

When watch ashore, to get away from the noise of the mess deck and the considerable chore of lashing and unlashing my hammock, I used to stay in the Sailors' Rest, or Aggie Weston's, the establishment of a long dead philanthropist whose generosity allowed a sailor to have a clean bed and a hearty breakfast for ninepence. It was in such hostelries that I was later to spend many nights of terror during the air-raids. It seemed 'a better 'ole' (as Bruce Bairnsfather would've called it) to die in. But for all the warmth and succour that these excellent hospices afforded us, I couldn't have been happier to make the acquaintance of my cousin Guy and to enjoy all his subsequent hospitality.

I had been walking through the barracks, when I saw bouncing towards me a man of unseemly gait, a battered old felt hat on his head, a blue navy raincoat, shining resplendently with age, a cardboard dog collar and the most ill-assorted collection of teeth I've ever seen. It transpired he was the ex-Chaplain to the Royal Family and the present Senior Chaplain to the Royal Navy, and rejoiced under the strange nickname of 'Reckless-Reggie' Churchill, referred to by all as 'Reckless'.

He was never without his gas-mask, which he would wield as a Biblical sling, and as we came abreast, true to form, he dealt me a stunning blow with it between the shoulder blades.

'Ah-ha! and what have we here? A new boy methinks!'

Not particularly perspicacious of him as my uniform was so new, it could have stood up by itself.

'Yes, sir,' I replied, unsure if a salute was in order.

'Name?'

'Pertwee, sir.'

'Pertwee, eh? Follow me at once, Pertwee,' and he was off, lolloping and bouncing his way across the parade ground his gas-mask swinging in great concentric circles.

Arriving at his office, he thumped me into a chair, picked up his telephone and asked the operator to connect him with 'Paymaster Captain Guy Pertwee, the Admiral's Secretary'. I froze.

'He can't . . . I mean, I can't – a Captain? Oh God no!'

'Hello Guy? Reggie here. I've got another Pertwee in my office. What? I'll ask. Who's your father?'

'Roland, sir.'

'Roland? The writer?'

'Yes, sir.'

'He's Roland Pertwee's boy. He's a cousin is he? Send him round for tea? Right, he's on his way.'

Filled with fear and trepidation, I duly reported for tea at Cousin Guy's beautiful Georgian house in the Dockyard. The door was opened by a three-badge Able Seaman called Dogges, who, eyeing me with considerable suspicion and distaste, ushered me into the presence.

Guy and his family looked upon me with much more approbation however, and I was very quickly put at my ease.

The Captain was a short, grey-haired, handsome man, with a chestful of decorations and a great capacity for kindness. He was a cousin of my father's and he knew of every Pertwee living or dead: it was he who had assisted the Abbé Jean de Perthuis de Laillavault to compile the extremely complex Pertwee family tree. His wife Carmen was an Officer in the WRNS, as was their very pretty daughter Jill. But there was going to be no 'hanky-panky' here. I knew which side my bread was best buttered on.

Guy immediately offered me a permanent room in his house, saying that I could come and go as I pleased, and just to let them know when I wanted to dine with them at night, for I was always welcome.

So I bade a fond farewell to the Sailors' Rest and Aggie Weston's and stayed with my cousins at every possible opportunity.

Unfortunately, my bed was so comfortable that on quite a few occasions I ignored the ringing of my small alarm clock and was 'adrift'. These misdemeanours resulted in my receiving several days' 'jankers' and confinement to barracks. The jealous Dogges was certainly not going to be of any help to me here, so I bought myself a large alarm clock that would've wakened Rip Van Winkle. The only trouble here was that Guy and his wife didn't have to be up at five o'clock in the morning as well. So, the offending article went under my pillow, where its Big Ben tick-tocking, kept me awake *until* five o'clock in the morning, thus making the alarm section of the clock quite unnecessary.

Seated one night at dinner with Guy, his family and several married service friends, I was addressed by my cousin from his position at the head of the table.

'Jon, dear boy, have you prepared your prick?'

I was more than a little startled by the directness of the question, and duly hedged, 'In what way, sir?' He must be drunk to bring up such a subject before ladies.

'Good God, boy, don't you know how to prepare a prick?'

Dreading his answer, I nonetheless admitted my ignorance of this unknown aberration, and replied with clever ambiguity, 'Not exactly, sir, no.'

'Very well then, I'll tell you.'

A pregnant hush had fallen on the room.

'First of all, you must soak it in rum for several days.'

Obviously a most difficult procedure to follow if you have other duties to perform at the same time.

'Then you wrap it in a bit of canvas, and whip it with tarred twine.'

This was dreadful. In front of the fair sex he was actually encouraging masochism. The extraordinary thing about this mortifying dissertation was that I seemed to be the only one present to be in any way shocked by the frankness of his discourse. The rest of the guests were either eating like the good trenchermen they were or nodding sagely at each new instruction.

'Then you leave it like that, soaked, wrapped and bound for several weeks.'

This was getting worse. Now he was advocating bondage! Still no-one challenged the good taste of his subject, and continued to partake of the excellent fare before them without pause.

'Finally,' said Guy, the bit now well between his teeth, 'your prick is ready for use. All you have to do is undo the twine, roll back the protective canvas an inch, and holding your prick firmly on the table or a block of wood, cut thin slices off the end of it.'

At this final outrageous suggestion, goggle-eyed and scarlet, I almost slid under the table from the embarrassment of it all. Guy, seeming somewhat surprised at my startled reaction, said, 'Of course, all that information is of no earthly use to you if you are not a pipe-smoker.'

Oh my God! To have gone through all that, only to find out that all he was doing was explaining how one should prepare a Naval issue of tobacco leaves for use in a pipe. Incidently, the correct word and spelling of this prepared length of tobacco is p-r-i-q-u-e. Bearing in mind its idiomatic use, I wonder which came first, the chicken or the egg.

The dreaded Dogges always served at table, and when he got to me surreptitiously played little games, like taking the dish away before I had time to put the serving spoon back safely, hoping that it would fall to the floor, and, by splattering the carpet, so embarrass me that I wouldn't come again and no longer put him, a 'stripey' of twenty years' service, to the indignity of waiting on a three month, hostilities-only, Ordinary Seaman. The situation had to be rectified, for if

Dogges' dilemma continued, my life in the barracks, where he was a king, would become untenable.

One night some weeks later, while taking coffee in the lounge after dinner, Guy said to his wife, 'Where the Hell is Jon? Everytime he gets up from the table he disappears, he can't be in the loo all this time.' A search was instituted and to my chagrin, I was soon discovered. Jacket off, I was at the sink washing up, with a beaming Dogges sitting on the kitchen table, finishing off a bottle of excellent claret while spurring me on to further effort. To the great credit of Guy and Carmen, they retired unseen, and it was only later that Guy opined that by virtue of my volunteering for such onerous duties, my life in the barracks was likely to become *much* more tenable.

★

For some reason, I decided that I should better benefit the 'Andrew' by becoming a Wireless Operator, and was duly transferred from Pompey Barracks to *HMS St Vincent* in Gosport, just across the harbour. Life was just as intolerable as in my previous barracks, but it had one great saving grace, its Chaplain, the Reverend Charles de Candole, who quickly became a close friend and has remained one ever since. Charles, with great perception, noted those men who found the transition from home life to barrack life to be beyond the limits of tolerance, piled us into an old 'Swift' open tourer, his dog-collar relegated to a dresser drawer, and took us on regular country pub-crawls. His friendship, remarkable outspokenness and permanent good nature almost turned me to religion – not quite, but almost – and when, years later, I was about to marry for the first time, there could be no other choice but him to perform the ceremony. I even went so far as to suggest that he performed the ceremony the second time I got married, but Ingeborg, quite rightly, objected on the grounds that it would not be in the best of taste.

There was a hundred-foot high masthead in the square of *HMS St Vincent* with all the ropes and rigging of an early sailing vessel. Up this mast and out on to the cross spars, all new recruits were sent, both for exercise and for development of the character-building quality required to perform such feats of derring-do.

Unfortunately, as previously mentioned, I suffer from acute vertigo, and when my turn came to scale the masthead's dizzy heights, I baulked.

'Come along lad,' said my Divisional Officer with uncontrolled glee, 'it's only a little way up – off you go, or it's ten days Number eleven for you!' ('Number eleven' was a most arduous punishment.)

So up it I went, but coming down it was quite a different matter. On the way up, you look up (no trouble there), but to come down, one's inclination is to look down (aye and there's the rub). Where to put the feet was the question.

I had arrived at the top spar with little trouble, and was starting on my way down when I broke out into a cold sweat and froze to the mainmast. No amount of wheedling, cajoling, threats or intimidation from Officer, Petty Officer or friend could prise loose my iron grip on the mast. In the end a 'Killick' (leading seaman) had perforce to rig a bosun's chair, and strapped in, I was ignominiously lowered to the ground, to accompanying jeers and cat-calls from the rest of the ship's company. 'Marmy', it seemed, was not only a cunt but a coward. (The first appellation was wholly acceptable, but in the 'Andrew' the second would never do.)

On my twenty-first birthday, 7th July 1940, feeling more than a little jaded that I would not be getting a traditional twenty-first party at home, I decided to invite Carlotta down from London, take a large hotel room for the weekend and invite all my friends to join us for a bit of a shindig. Carlotta agreed wholeheartedly, and arrived laden with dishes she had previously cooked in the flat. Filling the dingy room with flowers she soon had the whole place looking festive, and I was just beginning to cheer up and look forward to the occasion, when I was stricken with the most agonising tooth-ache. It was so bad, there was nothing else for it but an immediate visit to our infamous 'Toothy', Lieutenant Clarence Allworthy, RNVR, who by reputation was trained by Spanish Inquisitors. With me stretched out rigidly on his converted barber's chair, the Lieutenant looked into my mouth and said, 'Ah, yes, just as I thought, it's the jolly old impacted wisdom, chaps. Not to worry, we'll have the lot out quicker than a Stoker sups his rum. Nurse, gas please.'

With that, she clapped the claustrophobic mask over my nose and mouth and let me have several deep whiffs. 'There, that should do it lad! So away we go!'

It *didn't* do it though, and although I felt like a giggling schoolgirl (the natural effect of laughing gas), there was absolutely nothing to laugh at at all. I had not inhaled anything approaching sufficient gas to deaden the pain of the extractions and was at last able to comprehend the agony my Granny must have suffered, when as a young girl she had had her tonsils hooked out by the roots, without the benefit of any anaesthetic. In all, my nautical torturer extracted four wisdom teeth, two of which felt as if they had the roots of a 300-year-old oak tree. They were so long, that when the 'Toothy' started pulling, with his knee against my chest for better leverage, I imagined my toes were slowly curling upwards, and to set the seal on a good job badly done, he was unable to stop the bleeding. After studying an ancient tome, probably passed down to him by Merlin, he decided on a solution. Two large cotton wool and gauze wads were soaked in turpentine, and placed between the two bleeding sockets on both sides of my jaw. A tight bandage was then tied over my head and under my chin, making the opening of the mouth for either speech or the intake of food and drink an impossibility. Thus throughout my entire twenty-first birthday celebration I sat in a hospital bed with nothing to remember it by, except a mouthful of turpentine wads as a gift from His Majesty.

The Senior Nursing Sister, no doubt swayed by that 'very present help in trouble', the Reverend Charles de Candole, took compassion on me and allowed Carlotta and my friends to hold a party at my bedside. It was for me the most cheerless celebration of my life! I just sat there glowering and tasting turpentine, while they made merry by drinking my drink, eating my specially prepared food, and falling in love with Carlotta, who was looking at her most infuriatingly desirable.

★

Around this time *HMS St Vincent* was in the process of being turned over from wireless operator training to something else, so all 'Sparkers' were shifted to *HMS Collingwood*, a recently completed stone-frigate nearby. Living conditions were better, and there was even a car park, where, for a week or two, ratings' cars, including a brace of Bentleys and a Rolls, were allowed to park. It wasn't long, however, before the Staff Officers' eyes began to turn green and the practice was told to cease forthwith. It was here in *HMS Collingwood* that war became for me a grim reality, no longer the cold war, so far removed as to seem almost non-existent, but a howling, screaming, death-dealing war that shattered the nerves and the ear-drums. It started with the first air-raid siren to be heard in our vicinity, and was quickly followed by the arrival of a swarm of Stuka dive-bombers, bent on destroying the Fleet Air Arm base at Lee-on-Solent, not two miles distant. They came in out of the sunlight and proceeded systematically to bring down every barrage balloon that surrounded the aerodrome, making nonsense of the claim that their presence would hinder all bombing attacks.

At the first sound of the siren, we were ordered to take refuge in our ground-level air-raid shelters, but as soon as I heard the distinctive scream of a diving Stuka, I was up through the escape-hatch like a rabbit out of his bolt hole, to sit on the top of the shelter with a few other ingenuous idiots to watch, for the first time in my life, death being delivered in reality and not on the silver screen. As each balloon exploded and flopped to the ground like a wet rag on a string, we cheered like excited schoolboys at a football match, and it was only when the Stukas started to strafe and bomb the airfield that the reality of the situation began to strike home, and the cold sweat of fear began slowly to ooze from my pores.

After the first wave, a bunch of us were hurriedly trucked over to Lee to assist in extricating the dead and wounded from the bomb-damaged buildings and generally making ourselves available for whatever task was most urgent at the time.

It was while we were helping to push a damaged aircraft off the landing field that the Stukas attacked again, but this time it was me they were after, or so it seemed, for one plane, flattening out after his perpendicular bombing dive, saw us and started to fire his twin wing-mounted machine guns – I was by this time running for my life, in an impossible endeavour to reach the safety of a ditch before he could get me. But for some reason, maybe that he was too near for the line of his fire to centralise, as I fell over exhausted and run out, the bullets kicked up the ground to the right and left of me like mice scuttling through dust.

From that moment on, war was a serious business, never to be taken lightly again. I was determined to do what was expected of me, but never in such a foolhardy fashion that my chances of living were likely to be diminished, a decision that stood me in good stead throughout the rest of the war.

One night in 1940, the sirens wailed and to my horror the church bells rang. That meant only one thing – invasion. Hurriedly lined up outside our Nissen-huts we nervously awaited instructions. Then started a rumble of coastal gunfire which continued unabated throughout the night, and was of no help at all in my efforts to control my inner fears.

At last a Chief Petty Officer arrived before us with a lorry, and proceeded to issue every alternate man with an ancient Ross training rifle. These were rifles with a difference, in that they were innocent of either bullet or firing-pin, and possessed a splendidly solid barrel. When I politely drew the Chief's attention to this deficiency, he said,

'Not to worry lad, they're all like that!'

'But what am I supposed to do with it?' I asked.

'Well, son, you could wait until the parachutists get within reach, then nip out of yer hidey-hole and break the buggers' legs with the butt before they can hit the deck.'

To every other man, he gave a pick-axe handle with an iron tip, saying, when asked the same question as I had previously asked, 'Well now lad, in case the leg-breaking caper don't work, you could try shoving the handle up to the bastard's armpits when he isn't looking!'

So the tough, ruthless, cold-blooded war machine of the King's Navy sat round the perimeter of a field throughout the night, filled with foreboding at the inevitable outcome. There was a road running up from the coast due north, and across this had been constructed a considerable deterrent to the impending invasion. From two perpendicular gate-posts, a telegraph pole wrapped in a single strand of barbed wire was swung across the road by the use of a cart-wheel attached to its end. Normally, the pole could be moved freely back and forth, but out of regard to imminent attack from the German hordes it had been chained and padlocked to the post. The fact that there were several acres of flat, unbroken fields to the right and left of it, seemed not to have deterred its brilliant innovators one iota. Happily for us all, word of this barbed barrier must've reached Hitler, who was evidently so frightened by the combination of this unsurmountable deterrent and the prospect of having countless armies of men with bruised ankles and sore behinds, that he called the invasion off.

I have read anything I could lay my hands on and avidly questioned every war historian I have ever met about what really happened that night. What was all that gunfire, and was there really any truth in the rumours that were rife at the time of hundreds of German dead being found washed up and hideously burned, all along the south coast? Rumour had it that this was the result of our releasing oil fuel from secret storage tanks hidden under the sea, and igniting it as the invasion barges passed overhead? I have never been given a satisfactory explanation and presumably it will remain one of the Second World War's great mysteries.

What we got away with at that time is now legend, but I still shudder at the thought of what would really have happened if we had attempted to repel the invader with solid-barrelled rifles, pick-axe handles, and the Home Guard's infamous pike.

*

In the company of several friends and shipmates, I went up to London on a week-end leave and walked right into the worst air-raid of the war. Arriving at Victoria Station, we found the city ablaze. Flames and showering sparks soared skywards, as the exploding bombs burst in the heart of the holocaust. The sky was criss-cross alight with the beams of searching searchlights and the continuous cacophonous banging of the ack-ack batteries assaulted the ear-drums. Air-raid Wardens exhorted us to take shelter in the underground station below, which turned out to be packed with people, who looked as if they had moved in for the duration.

All along the platform were hundreds of triple-tiered bunk-beds, with whole families encamped around them. They sat on rugs, air-mattresses and folding beds, on boxes and stools, reading, talking, singing, eating, drinking and sleeping. Nightly they came, and by mutual agreement occupied the same territory. They brewed-up continuous pots of tea and shared what food they had with such casual safety-seekers as ourselves. Never in our history have people been so compassionate to each other. It was as if the whole heterogeneous population of Britain had suddenly become one big family.

After an hour or so of refuge, my companions decided that they would risk going out in the continuing raid, as they were anxious to get home to the welcoming arms of their loved ones. I demurred, as I had a strange premonition of disaster and after saying goodbye, went back down the underground to sing the night and the cataclysmic air-raid away. Denis Breeze, the writer brother of Alan Breeze, Billy Cotton's vocalist for many years, wrote in an article published just after the war that his first sight of me on that awful night was 'A tall lanky sailor sitting on top of a bunk-bed with a borrowed guitar in his hands singing songs to an admiring throng, as if he had been wound up.' The next morning, bleary-eyed and voiceless, I walked into the chaos of that devastating attack, and on seeing the smoking ruins thought how lucky I was to be alive, a feeling made all the more poignant when I found on returning to barracks that two of my companions that night had been killed. Not by the enemies bombs, but by the falling shrapnel of our own ack-ack guns. My premonition had served me in good stead!

Some weeks later, returning from another few days leave, I was crossing the 'Hog's-Back' near Guildford in a coach, when a German Bomber returning from a raid on London found that he still had a 'gash' bomb on board, so opening his bomb-bay doors he dropped it on the nearest moving object he could see in the moonlight, our coach.

Luckily he missed, but he punched a nice big hole in the road ahead of us that we promptly ran into. At the time, I was sleeping, with my head up against the window and when the coach lurched on to its side in the ditch, my head pierced a neat hole through the glass. The extraordinary thing was that although my head went *through* without any trouble, willing helpers found it next to impossible to get it *back*. At the same time they implored me to keep still, as sharp slivers of glass were surrounding my neck, and any unnecessary movement might sever my jugular, or my throat at best. My eventual extraction was carried out with great good humour and jocularity, those inside gently knocking the glass away with a jack handle, and those outside stuffing handkerchiefs over the slivers to minimise my chances of being decapitated. Throughout all this, pretty ladies gave me deep puffs of their Woodbines, a three-badge AB gave me innumerable 'gulpers' from a medicine bottle of illicit rum, and a good time was had by all.

But it was when I was lying in a hospital bed in Guildford, recuperating from mild concussion and a stitched head, that for the first time I gave serious thought as to what war really meant. This was not surprising, for I was completely surrounded by examples of its futility. Alongside me there was a young seaman who had been burned so badly when his ship was torpedoed and set on fire, that practically every inch of skin had been flayed from his body. He was hairless and black from head to foot from the burns and the purple 'gentian violet' that had been painted all over him, with what was left of his skin turning up in dry flakes everywhere. Mercifully his face had avoided the brunt of the flames, but the rest of his body was horribly scarred. Quite unable to wear clothes (the weight of them would've increased his agony) he lay naked and silent, on a mattress filled with water. Every hour on the hour throughout the day and night, four nurses would come to his bedside and gently turn him round, to make sure that he didn't stick to the mattress. First on to his back, then on his right side, then his left and finally face down with his head twisted round to enable him to breathe. Throughout this agonising routine, he never uttered a word of complaint or any cry of pain. He was the most stoic man I had ever met, and my affection and admiration for him grew day by day. He talked only of the future, never of the past; of what he was going to do with his life after the war; of his wife and two sons and where he was going to take them on holiday, to do what, because of the war, they had never been able to do. To take them to the seaside to swim and play cricket on the sand, to fish, to play football and climb every mountain. All those magic things that have been dreamed of by fathers since the beginning of procreation.

But in spite of his desperate will to live, he died, lying on his side with his eyes staring into an unknown destination. He looked so dreadfully sad that his fight for survival had failed and all his best laid plans for the future had come to naught.

Had I not been so young and blessed with that particular combination of idealism and recklessness that only youth seems to possess, I doubt that I would have emerged from the war as a relatively well-adjusted young man. But at the time I felt that fighting for my country was not only my duty but also a very personal challenge. I saw the cruel realities of war as bold adventures; the destructions, the sufferings and the unnecessary deaths as heroic examples of patriotism.

Only towards the end of the war did I develop a determined sense of survival. Dying for one's country may be the ultimate sacrifice but it also is a waste of a life, and I didn't want to be just another casualty in a war that was nearly over.

And now, when I reflect upon the years I spent in the service, I feel that the war was an essential component of my existence. It taught me many things, but above all, it gave me a deep respect for human life.

*

My stay at *HMS Collingwood* as a trainee telegraphist came to an end for much the same reason as my many short stays at school, i.e. an inability to keep up with the rest. I had a good ear for morse but found the involved 'procedure' very difficult indeed. I could read and send with great rapidity, and could talk to other 'Sparkers' when travelling on public transport by blowing and tonguing the morse on two fingers held over the lips, the passengers being much impressed by our skill. But as for the rest, it was all utterly beyond me, so with kit-bag packed and hammock lashed, I returned to Portsmouth Barracks where I was promptly relegated to Very Ordinary Seaman Pertwee once again.

That same night Pompey greeted me with one of its worst raids ever, and for the first time since the advent of war, I was able to fire at the enemy. Detailed off as a Lewis-gun drum-loader I squatted on an ammunition box on the roof of the barracks, and loaded bullets into the drums for the Leading Seaman gunner. After an hour or so's lull, the 'Killick' excused himself and went off in search of tea, or relief, or somesuch, and left me alone with the gun. Within minutes the bombers were overhead, with searchlights sweeping back and forth over the cloud banks in an endeavour to catch an enemy plane in their glare.

'Where in God's name is that bloody Killick?' I thought, and then, 'What the hell! I'll take over and personally save the barracks from destruction.' So I got behind that ancient Lewis-gun on its equally ancient tripod and sprayed the unseen enemy with a hail of perpendicular fire that must've been, at a minimum, 8000 feet short of its target. But I was really into the John Wayne role now, and would've fired off every drum, if it hadn't been for a shout from an irate Chief Petty Officer below, 'You up there! Stop firing that fuckin' gun, before you kill somebody.'

It seems that the spent bullets from my Lewis had been falling in a hail on the heads of other gunners and fire-watchers on the parade ground below. So being the loyal Englishman I was, I ceased fire, preferring to let the enemy fly on unscathed than risk helping them by wiping out members of my own side.

★

The nightly bombing was so bad around this time, that Guy and his family went off to the country for a long leave and shut up the house. In order to get a modicum of sleep when off duty, rather than being ignominiously blown out of bed in Aggie Weston's or any other Sailors' Rest, I decided, with a bunch of the lads, to clamber up Portslade Hill overlooking the city, there, under the lee of the old forts, to camp down for the night with ground sheets, blankets, some scran, a box of ticklers (Naval issue cigarettes) and my trusty old 'uka', which, when accompanied by song was a splendid adjunct to keeping 'Old Marmy's' popularity to the fore.

It was a horrible yet breathtaking sight to see the city below us being systematically destroyed. From the flames of the burning buildings, we could see quite clearly the changing silhouettes of the poor city's death throes. But not without a tremendous fight did Pompey go down. The ack-ack fire put up was staggering in its intensity and the searchlight crews were no slouch at their job either. From our high, safe, vantage point, sipping beer and munching wads, we watched with fascination as the enemy bombers appeared over the city and nightly set it afire, accurately dropping their bombs smack in the centre of the maelstrom. Many was the plane we saw, caught in those unremitting beams of light, shot from the sky, one German pilot landing, unfortunately for him, right in the middle of a bunch of rather boozed-up matelots below us.

But somehow the old girl hauled up her skirts, dusted herself off, tied up her wounds and got ready for the next assault upon her ancient and esteemed person.

When the final bell rang to mark the end of the contest 'Old Pompey' came out battered but unbowed, and a clear winner on points.

★

Robert Newton, the celebrated actor (my association with whom almost made my life *un*tenable again) appeared shortly afterwards. He was outrageous, impossible, disrespectful, aweless, mocking, derisive, contumelious, usually plastered and I loved him.

The first thing he did was to obtain by fair means or foul, four watch cards which enabled him to go ashore at night whenever he wanted. Next he found an 'oppo' (friend) who would bury him during the day in the middle of the hammock nettings (the area where all the lashed hammocks were kept). The 'oppo' would construct a tomb of hammocks and Bobby would crawl in through an igloo-like entrance with two torches (for the reading of several paperbacks), some cold sausages, of which he was particularly fond and a goodly supply of booze. He would go in sober, come out drunk, and seemed to have the bladder control of a camel. The object of this secret hiding operation was, of course, the avoidance of anything resembling work or duty. If he was rumbled, he talked his way out, with offers of orgiastic nights in his suite at the Queen's Hotel Southsea, and promises of endless supplies of succulent starlets for the discoverer's delight. All balls of course, and although he did have a permanent suite at the Queen's it was never used for anything other than straight-forward piss-ups.

With the blitz now reaching intensity, Portsmouth was strafed almost nightly. Bombed house clearance parties were formed, with a dozen or so sailors taking a Naval truck to the scene of a bombed building to assist the shocked occupants in rescuing their few pitiful belongings. Bobby excelled in this operation and the expression on the faces of the assisted, once they saw who their principal assister was, was a sight never to be forgotten. Bobby would promptly strike out the booze and have the wretchedly unhappy people laughing and rolling about in less time than it takes a cat to catch a mouse.

Once our mission was completed we were under orders to return to the barracks immediately. Our team worked with far greater zest, speed and humour than the others, for two very good reasons. One, we were all well under the influence of the demon, and two, that as soon as we had finished our assignment, Bobby would imperiously demand that the driver should take us to his 'personal' barracks with all speed, which meant that within minutes we were all happily ensconced in Bobby's suite, enjoying the fruits of his unending hospitality.

There was one night in barracks, however, that Bobby and I were determined not to miss. A celebrated Shakespearean actor was coming to Portsmouth and would give one performance of the Bard for the edification of the incumbent bomb-happy sailors.

The actor was not long into the piece when a very inebriated Glaswegian, seated directly behind us, called out, 'Hey John, sing us a song!' During the ensuing laughter, Bobby and I shrank into our seats hoping that if we were seen by any of the cast, there would be no assumed association with the drunken Scottish toss-pot.

It came again, 'Hey John, sing us a song!'

By this time we were almost *under* the seats with embarrassment for the courageous but foolhardy star, who, nothing daunted, pressed on with his soliloquy. Suddenly with frightening clarity for one at least five sheets to the wind, the barracker conceded his request for a song, with yet another entreaty: 'Okaaay John! Show us your prick instead.'

The hall erupted.

'Oh Christ,' said Bobby, 'I can't take any more of this, let's go and have a drink', and with the use of one of his many watch cards that's exactly what we did.

Any chance of Bobby being put up for a commission went to the wall when, at a party he was giving in his suite for Officers and friends, he told a teetotal Paymaster-Captain drinking orange juice, that if he didn't like the drink that Bobby had provided, he had better 'piss-off' to some other party where 'old poofters' would be better catered for. The 'old poofter' did just that, and returned a few minutes later with the Naval Patrol, who before us all, promptly arrested Bobby on a charge of gross insolence to a Senior Officer.

As Bobby was being marched ignominiously out of his own party, he turned to the assembled Officers and guests, and said, 'If I can't stay at my own bleeding party, I don't see why you should, so you can all piss-off.'

To save the embarrassment of a court martial and the subsequent explanations that would've been asked as to the reason for so many Senior Officers being present at a lower deck sailor's shindig, Bobby was sent to sea in a trawler. 'That'll show him,' some thought, 'that'll teach him to respect a Naval Officer.'

They could've saved their breath, for within minutes of meeting the tough ex-fishing-boat skipper from Hull, Bobby was away at full mouth.

'Righto me old mate, I'll go and get us some decent booze, a hamper of choice foods, and we'll be off into limbo on a great old cruise.'

The bemused skipper, like so many before him, was unable to say him nay, and (as Navy chroniclers have it) was last seen standing on the bridge with Bobby, holding a bottle of VAT 69 in one hand and a smoked salmon sandwich (purchased from God knows where!) in the other, heading out over the horizon with the sound of a fine song echoing melodiously down the wind.

Chapter Eight

And so to sea. There was no point in cramming a six foot two and a half inch Ordinary Seaman into a small C Craft submarine with low-beamed Tudor cottage headroom. Looking at the plaster and lint dressing stuck on my forehead, the Captain said, 'That wound's taking a long time to heal up, lad.'

'I haven't got a wound, sir.'

'Then why are you wearing that dressing?'

'So I won't get one, sir.'

So on 29th November 1940, the Navy, with perfect logic, put me into one of the biggest battle cruisers in the world, *HMS Hood*. Laid down in 1918 at the end of the First World War, with a normal complement of 1,341 men, rising to 1,768, she weighed some 42,100 tons and could cruise at speeds of up to thirty-two knots. So fast could she go, that when running the North Sea on Russian convoys, if the weather was too heavy for the accompanying destroyers, they would lie in line astern of us so that we could break a passage through the towering waves for them. But even then they had a considerable job keeping up with us.

The *Hood* was stationed at Scapa Flow in the Orkney Islands of Scotland. This necessitated a miserable two-day, two-night train journey to get there. It was on this mortifying trip that I discovered for the first time the possibility of sleeping stretched out sideways on the net luggage-rack overhead. With two of us similarly perched 'up top', there was that much more room for the lads below, who, placing all their kit-bags and hammocks between the seats, were able to lie full length, head to toe, like a pile of snoozing puppies.

We eventually de-trained at Thurso, a small port some fifteen miles from John O'Groats where the climate was colder than a witch's besom. There we were given our first hot meal for 48 hours, served by some kind Scottish ladies of the WVS who chatted continuously to us without the courtesy of any reply, for, so strong was the dialect, there was hardly a soul amongst us that could understand a single word they said. Refreshed, we boarded a horrid little inter-island steamer and set off for Lyness passing Flotta and the protective waters of Scapa Flow where the *Hood* lay moored. What a magnificent looking ship she was, lying there so low in the water. Her lines were nothing else but beautiful; a strange simile to apply to a weapon of war, but nonetheless true.

I was to be a Foretopman in the fo'c'sle, port-side. Meaning I was up the front on the left. I was allotted an area to hang my hammock right over the mess-deck table, and a lock-up steel locker for my cap and 'ditty' boxes, the latter being a 'must' for every sailor to put all his personal 'goodies' in. Traditionally the lid held photographs of progeny, wives, mums and dads, and in the case of bachelors, snaps of their 'parties'. A strange word – meaning, in lower-deck lingo, a girl-friend. As: 'Would you like to see a snap of my party?' or 'Bet you've never seen a party like that?'

It was a 'general-messing' ship, in that you had to take your turn drawing the stores and doing the cooking. And let me assure you, the standard of cooking was expected to be of a high level. The fare chosen daily by members of the Mess was simple, yet had to be cooked just right – or else. After two weeks of this I had found an amenable 'Stripey' who for 'sippers' would relieve me of all future mess duties.

The word 'sippers' has found itself a favoured place in the Royal Navy, and I had better explain just how and why.

In 1655, a British Admiral by the name of Vernon ingratiated himself to such a degree in the eyes of the West Indian Government that they vowed out of immense gratitude for their country being saved from invasion, that from that moment on every lower deck sailor in the British Navy above the age of eighteen would receive a daily tot of Jamaican rum, free, gratis and for nothing.

Admiral Vernon, who always wore breeches made of a coarse silk and mohair material called grogram, was known affectionately by his men as 'Old Grog'. Therefore, after his rum deal had been put into operation, a grateful Navy always referred to rum as grog. If you were at sea and you were in a hard-lying ship such as a submarine, destroyer, frigate, MTB etc., you got your tot neat, but if you were in any other kind of ship, you got your grog two and one, that is, two parts water and one of rum. The main purpose of this desecration was to prevent seasoned sailors from saving their daily tot for a few days, decanting it into a bottle and then going on a blinding piss-up with one or more oppos similarly stocked up for the occasion. If you were a teetotaller, however, you could waive your tot and earn yourself an extra threepence a day, but anyone who did so was a fool, for rum was

146

a remarkably valuable bargaining agent. Before I expand on this, let me explain some Royal Navy rum terminology.

grog: As previously explained, was traditionally two parts water, one part pusser's (Paymaster's) rum – 95.5 proof 54.5% alcohol.

tot: 1/8 pint rum, the standard daily ration.

neat: Rum without water.

sippers: A small gentlemanly sip from a friend's rum issue.

gulpers: One, but only one, big swallow from another's tot.

sandy bottoms: To finish off whatever's in a mug when offered by a friend.

splice the main brace: A double tot for a job well done, a decision made only by the Captain.

the framework of hospitality: Where three sippers equal one gulp and three gulps equal one tot.

Now to its value:– during my time on the lower deck, for two sippers daily, my hammock was unlashed, hung in a prime position, lashed up the next morning and put away in the hammock nettings by a kindly three-badge disciple of Bacchus. For a further daily gulp, another old rumpot would do all my dhobi-ing (washing). He was a real mother to me, and as I was reliably informed by my hammock lasher, would've been a lot more, if I'd given him half a chance. There was nothing really homosexual about him, said my informant. It was just that when at sea, having a young 'oppo' to 'care for' was an old Navy tradition. It was further said that the expression 'chuff' [carryings-on] for 'duff' [pudding] was not without a certain element of truth. Perhaps food was the only article of barter left to those young men unlucky enough not to have a tot to bargain with, but to me bartering with pudding seemed a bit beyond the pale.

Two more sippers relieved me of many mess-deck chores, like washing-up, drawing stores, and food preparing. So you can see why I called anyone a fool who took threepence a day in lieu. If you were popular with the lads, on your birthday you were asked to visit the various mess-decks and partake of a little rum, the quantity depending on your popularity.

In my case, on one birthday I was in luck, or in retrospect, perhaps out of luck, for 'Old Marmy' was sufficiently liked to be invited to 'sippers, all round' by two or more mess-decks of a dozen or so ratings. My rum intake therefore was around 36 sippers, which plus my own tot, nine sippers, equalled 45 sippers in all. Within ten minutes I was falling down drunk, and remained so for two days and two nights. Endearingly, I was joshed, picked up, picked up again and finally hidden away to sleep it off, my mates performing my duties and keeping my watch for me. Everything would've been just fine, if, on waking several hours later with a mouth like a shark's overcoat, I had not asked a passing Samaritan for a gallon of water to slake my raging thirst. This proved to be a fatal request, as unbeknown to me, a quantity of water thrown on top of a quantity of alcohol starts the whole process off again, and within minutes of drinking it, you are once more a roaring screaming drunk. Then and there I decided that what I needed most was to go for a nice run in the recreation area, and to shouts of encouragement from the assembled, tried to impersonate a wall of death rider. The only trouble was that some inconsiderate bastard had left a bench lying across the track, causing me, on every lap, to strike it halfway up my shin, and pitch me forward on to my face. Once or twice was good for a laugh, but after witnessing six of these classic 'arsers', some well-meaning spectators took compassion on this bloody, battered and bruised rubber-ball of a pissed sailor and put him gently back to bed.

'Happy Birthday, Marmaduke,' they cried.

'Cheers,' I replied, hiccupping through two split and bloody lips.

When I finally came out of my stupor and with a blinding hangover, I became aware of a very sore forearm. Squinting, I observed, wrapped neatly around it, a sheet of Izal-impregnated lavatory paper held in place by two elastic bands. I tried to think what purpose this flimsy cover was achieving and lay back to give the enigma my fullest consideration. It was a useless exercise and quickly abandoned. There was only one thing left to do, remove it and look. The bands were off in a jiffy but the toilet paper was more tenacious, and took a few painful moments before revealing all.

'Oh God, no! I can't be!'

But I was, I'd been tattooed. A green and scarlet cobra was squirming itself into a question mark on my forearm. In the middle was a small letter C, which I could only assume stood for Carlotta. On the other hand perhaps the choice of subject had been taken from a child's spelling-book and the C stood for cobra. God knows where or by whom this work of art was done, but whoever it was had executed quite a fair job and it doesn't seem to have upset too many people over the years, except maybe a few young female ophidiaphobiacs, and that was a pity.

★

We had gone to sea within hours of arriving on board and from that moment on, we were hardly ever at anchor. Our flagship *HMS Rodney* (a battleship with its stern cut off to conform with the Geneva Convention) lay, on the other hand, almost permanently at anchor. It was said by nautical wags that she couldn't move, due to being hard aground on the millions of her own milk tins that she had ditched over the side.

My battle station was down in the bowels of the ship winding a small wheel. Somehow with the aid of other wheel-winders our mutual endeavour enabled *Hood*'s gunnery to reach a greater state of accuracy.

Normal watch duties ranged from looking after ropes, cleaning the heads [lavatories], scrubbing and stoning decks and generally looking out for enemy ships or planes.

The deck-scrubbing I could tolerate, by allowing my mind to wander to more pleasurable things, like Carlotta in her sarong with a flower behind her ear. At other times I behaved much as earlier seamen before the mast had done, by singing sea-shanties while scrubbing. The rousing rhythmic songs were soon taken up by my fellow scrubbers and although looked upon with suspicion by the Petty Officer in charge, were allowed to continue, as the work seemed to be getting done with greater speed and efficiency.

To go to the 'heads' for duty or relief when at sea in rough weather was the cause, on one's first few visits, of not a little laughter. The pitch of the ship was remarkable. Doing twenty-five knots in mountainous seas, she would slowly rise some thirty feet into the air, shaking, vibrating and shuddering at the effort of forcing her bows through the middle of the gigantic greenbacks before her. Once through, she would shoot forward like a greyhound off its leash, to a point where there was no sea immediately beneath her bottom. This caused the 42,000 ton man-o'-war to drop like an elevator out of control and land smack on the surface of the sea far, far below. The amount of water thrown up by the massive ship's impact was past belief and indelibly imprinted on the minds of all those from other ships who had ever witnessed it.

But to return to the matter and manner of going to the 'heads'. Leaving the mess it was necessary to make one's way right forward to the bows, for that is where the lavatories were situated. If the ship was on its shuddering and shaking way upwards, this journey was well nigh impossible, the force of gravity being so strong as to make any forward progress practically non-existent. Feet seemed to be encased in divers' leaden boots and refused to move more than two inches up and three inches forward. Once the apex of the rise had been reached, however, the whole situation was reversed and as the ship dropped into her coalminer's lift routine, the caught-short sailors would metaphorically swop their divers' boots for ballet pumps and tippy-toe downhill with tiny steps at tremendous speed, under absolutely no control whatsoever. This combination of mountain climbing and on-points ballet dancing, finally brought the now bursting sailors to their ultimate goal, the 'heads'.

In these lavatories, to prevent the sea flowing back up the soil pipes when she dipped her bow down deep, non-return flaps were fitted under the water-line. Unfortunately, in North Sea waters, we dipped so deep, and so rapidly, that the flaps were lifted instead of closed, allowing the water to surge back up the pipes. So if you were one of the uninitiated, the following would happen. You entered the doorless loo, sat upon the seat, and with trousers around the ankles, did your business. The ship would then commence its downward plunge, causing the sea to by-pass the retaining flap and surge up into the bowl. The water level would then rise, until before you knew it, your offering had been deposited into the unsuspecting trouser below. This calamity caused riotous laughter from the cognoscenti, who would then instruct you in the ancient art of 'dodging'. For this method, you advanced trouserless and under-pantless to the bowl, hovered over its port or starboard side, until the water level had begun to subside, swung your buttocks quickly over the porcelain to make your deposit, then whipped the bottom back again out of immediate danger. This procedure could be continued as required and when all was done, the defecator would dart for safety.

Strange to relate, there were always volunteers to be 'Captain of the heads'. I suppose the Captains valued the independence of the position; at least they were in charge of something, unsalubrious as it was.

My one regret on joining the Navy was the curse of seasickness. To give you an idea of how afflicted I was, a messmate, Leading Seaman Bob Tilburn, one of only three survivors of the later disastrous explosion, has told the following story when being interviewed on radio or TV. On one occasion when we were lying at anchor in Scapa Flow, one of his mates came up and said in jest that a force ten gale was coming up and that we were really in for a blow. Evidently the more he fabricated, the greener I became, and within a very short space of time I was up on deck heaving my guts out – the only seaman on record to have been sick in harbour, except, as history would have us believe, for Lord Nelson.

On the bulkhead where my hammock was slung, there was a mess cupboard for the crockery, and to make the endless journeys to the 'heads' and 'A' Deck less frequent, I obtained a medium-sized jam tin to be sick in. This I partly filled with water and disinfectant and left on the top of the cupboard where it would be handy during the night. A creature of habit, I removed, emptied and recharged it with disinfectant daily, but the best laid plans sometimes go awry. For one stormy night after using the tin to good effect I was called out on an emergency watch and inadvertently left the offending article on the top of the cupboard. An ill-tempered leading-hand of the mess, looking for the jam, found my tin, and on seeing its contents was not very well disposed towards me for sometime. My hammock position was promptly given to another more deserving sailor, and I was relegated for the rest of my time in *Hood* to sleeping on a hard wooden bench in the mess-deck. Arms folded across my chest, and with my head resting on my cap for a pillow, I slept like a baby and after a few nights' practice nothing short of a hurricane would have pitched me off.

The most heartfelt want of any sailor at sea was privacy and a man would go to any lengths to find it. Behind a cupboard, on top of a cupboard, or in a cupboard, he would lay out his hammock mattress and make himself a little home-from-home. I was luckier than most on three counts. First, I was in charge of a rope-locker on deck. This was about seven foot long, four feet high and with the ropes coiled and piled up at one end, left sufficient room for my mattress, ditty box and 'things'. With a pusser's torch suspended from the deckhead I spent many a happy hour reading, writing letters and generally revelling in the privacy this minuscule iron cell afforded me. With the locker catches down, I was unassailable. Photos of my dear ones were stuck on the bulkhead allowing me to dream undisturbed of peace and tender loving arms enfolding me. These 'cabouches', as such havens were traditionally known, were quite accepted by the Officers and Petty Officers and could be occupied during daylight hours without fear or hindrance, although two men in a 'cabouche' with the door closed and locked off, was likely to be frowned upon. You wouldn't believe how many of my mates were able to get themselves into that ridiculously confined space for a smoke and a crack (chat).

Years later, a portrait painter friend actually painted my portrait in there. His name was Philip Steegman and he had many years before served as an Officer in the Royal Navy. He was laconic in the extreme, and with his affected manner made me laugh a lot. Philip possessed a cigarette case given to him by the National Broadcasting Company of America, which was inscribed 'To Philip Steegman, the only man to have said "the" word over the National Hook-up.'

It seems he had spent a lot of time in India painting Maharajahs and Maharanis and was quite an authority on the country. 'Tell me, Mr Steegman,' said an NBC interviewer as Philip was passing through America, 'what do you know about these magic men of India? You know, these – what do you call them? Ah yes – these fakers!'

Philip bridled.

'You have said the word quite incorrectly, sir,' he said. 'The correct pronunciation is . . .' and here he paused to give his pedantic instruction its full effect – 'Fuck – here.'

Which when spoken together, at normal speed, Philip assured me, was the only way the word 'fakir' should be pronounced.

On another occasion he showed remarkable bravery in the face of the enemy, or stupidity, depending on the way you look at it. We were on a Russian convoy off the north coast of Norway manning an after 'pom-pom' gun. Freezing cold with a temperature well below zero, we had been on duty without food or anything to drink for hours. This was the position that brought us within range of the German Focke-Wolf reconnaissance planes, who, on sighting us, would immediately call up their submarine 'Wolf Packs' and give them our exact position. The U-Boats would then come in and wreak havoc with our convoys. On one, the disastrous PQ17, we lost a total of twenty-four ships, Merchant and Naval, twenty-three belonging to the United States and UK, and one Dutch. 166 men were killed.

We had been watching one such Focke-Wolf go round and round as always just out of range, for an hour or more, and our nerves were beginning to fray a little around the edges. On a previous occasion our Gunnery Officer, feeling as frustrated as we now felt, had sent up an RT message to the German pilot. Speaking in English he had said, 'You up there, can't you go round the other way, you're making us dizzy.'

Back came the reply, also in English. 'Certainly, anything to oblige the British,' and he did. Just to make sure that the German pilot didn't take any liberties, the Gunnery Officer ordered the high-angle guns to loose off a few rounds. Small black puffs of smoke appeared well beneath the circling plane.

'How's that?' said 'Guns' on the RT.

'Not out,' answered the obviously anglophile German pilot.

As we sat, becoming more and more dejected, a young Midshipman, wrapped in two duffel coats and looking for all the world like a babe in swaddling clothes, came up to the gun and proceeded to give us a right tongue-lashing. The gun was dirty, we were dirty, the ammo was improperly stacked and altogether we were a disgrace to the Navy. Philip stood it for a moment and then fixing the wretched 'Snotty' with ice-cold eyes he said,

'Piss off, you bum of impudency! You booby, germinated outside lawful procreation! I was a Naval Officer before your birth, and have no intention of listening further to your infantile burblings. So away with you, before I kick you in your under-developed testicles.'

The Midshipman's jaw fell lower and lower and then with an expression of such abjectness that I was inclined to feel sorry for him, he turned and slowly walked away. We never saw or heard from him again. I think his ego must have been pricked to such a degree, that he decided he would imitate the 'ooslem bird' and disappear up his own orifice.

My second lucky count was in having as a friend the 'Jack Dusty' of the ship, CPO Geoff Pope. Geoff had an office to himself with a big desk and a home-made bunk for his much needed afternoon siestas. Being in charge of stores, he had easy access to the rum barrels, in consequence of which his office reeked of it, as did CPO Pope. Delivering a message one forenoon, the Chief asked me my name.

'Pertwee?' he said. 'Any relation of Roland?'

'My father,' I replied. It transpired that Geoff was an avid fan of my Dad's and had read everything he had ever written.

'Would you like a signed copy of his latest novel?' I asked artfully.

'Sit down, lad, and have a tot,' said Geoff, and from that moment on we became the best of friends. When work was slack and the sea was flat, I would call in for a grog and a chat, but if it was rough, Geoff let me crawl in under his desk with my jam tin, and seemed quite impervious to my noisy discomfiture.

Geoff would often pump me for stories of my father and never seemed to tire of them, so I regret all the more that I never got him that promised signed copy before he, too, went down in *Hood*'s action with the Bismarck, on May 24th 1941.

Lucky count three, was my friendship with the Second in Command of the Royal Marines on board, Lieutenant Davies. This was a somewhat dangerous situation for him, as having a lower deck rating as a friend was unheard of, and could've been suspect. But this delightful man found ways of getting me into his cabin that defied any criticism. Running errands, discussing ship's concerts, tuning his guitar, and translating (very roughly) passages of French poetry. Once in, I was made very much at home and over endless cups of tea, laced with some of Geoff's 'neaters', we talked and talked. He was quite besotted by the theatre and the arts, and despairing of finding a kindred spirit among the Officers on board turned to me. Thank God he did!

One of his more unenviable duties was to censor part of the crew's letters home. This censorship was unfortunately essential as letter writers often included, quite unintentionally, vital information, that would prove disastrous should it fall into the wrong hands. Lieutenant Davies also had the well nigh impossible task of running to earth those lusty lads who had given *nom de plumes* and aliases to various female conquests in port. Among the favourite names to be assumed was Able Seaman Derek Topping. When the arm of a derrick or crane is about to reach the perpendicular, the operator would shout 'Derrick Topping' meaning the crane arm had almost reached its limit. This pseudonym was frequently given after a night of love and passion, to minimise chances of identification should the sound of tiny mistakes be heard pattering up the companionway. Another much-used name was Able Seaman B. M. Lever. The initials B. M. standing for breech-mechanism, and lever referring to the lever on a gun that opens and closes the breech. So pathetic letters of remarkable similarity would arrive with envelopes marked SWALK (sealed with a loving kiss), possibly reading:

Dear Derek,
You said you was going to rite but you never. I am now three months gone. I am disperate has I am begining to show – wot are you going to do about it? Rite soon.
I.T.A.L.Y.   Doris.   – P.S. H.O.L.L.A.N.D.

These impassioned pleas were posted on the ship's notice board and brought forth little response other than cruel laughter. Derek Topping and Basil M. Lever should've felt very ashamed of themselves. (I.T.A.L.Y., I should explain, stood for 'I trust and love you' and H.O.L.L.A.N.D. for 'Hope our love lives and never dies'.)

It was my friendship with Lieutenant Davies and Geoff Pope that kept me going through some of the most wretched and despairing periods of my young life. Time spent with my mates on the mess-deck was fine, but in small doses only; for any long period, the noise and the subject matter of general conversation was one of boring and monotonous repetition, 'parties', poking and booze, booze, poking and 'parties'. For finding me even temporary relief from it, I gave them both much thanks.

Sad to relate, Lieutenant Davies also went down in *Hood*, just after I had attended his very jolly wedding in Edinburgh.

When at anchor in Scapa Flow, off duty liberty men used to go ashore to taste the pleasures of Lyness night-life. This, for the majority of the men, meant going to one of the enormous NAAFI canteens and, armed with Naval issue coupons, imbibing their allotted two or three pints of beer. Clever barterers, however, always managed to collect a pocket full of additional coupons, which allowed them the long-looked-forward-to opportunity of going on a monumental 'piss-up'. After several such outings I sold my beer coupons and opted for other joys of the flesh. With two or three friends I would take an early liberty boat to Kirkwall, go ashore and walk the starkly beautiful island of Mainland for hours. The strange quality of light up there at dawn and dusk is unique, and to all young painters I advocate a visit. The furthest I ever went on one of these excursions was when we hitched a tractor ride to the opportunistically-named village of Twatt.

During one leisurely walk we came across a little croft in a hollow where, after passing the time of day with the crofter's wife, we were invited in for tea. This tea came under the Naval-slang heading of 'Big-eats' and consisted of tea (pots of it), lashings of bread and real butter, scones, oat and fruit cakes and simply oodles of home made jam, the precursor to all this being a tremendous plate of sizzling eggs and bacon. How, and from where, all this magnificent rationed fare came, we certainly didn't ask. Suffice to say, we accepted their gracious hospitality the first time, but mutually agreed that on all future visits, the high tea should be properly paid for. If my memory serves me right, the sum in question was one shilling and sixpence per head. About seven and a half new pence.

These visits to the McKenzies continued over a period of quite a few months and it was on one of our last sojourns there that old Mac said, 'Well, laddies, yer a guid, well-behaved lot of young gentlemen, and because of that Mrs McKenzie and I have a mind to let you meet our daughters.'

A hush settled on the room. What daughters? We'd been to the house half a dozen times and never had sight nor sound of any young women.

'Have they been away then, Mac?' I asked, puzzled.

'Nooo, they've no been awa'.'

'Then where *have* they been?' I enquired, perplexed.

'Locked in the cupboard, where else?' said Mac, seeming surprised at the naivety of my question.

At that, he bade Mrs McKenzie to go to the bedroom at the end of the house and release the poor incarcerated girls. Within minutes, chattering like cheeky budgies, Mrs Mac and her three daughters entered the room. They were not of startling beauty but their well-scrubbed, white-toothed, rosy-cheeked look made up for any such deficiency. From the chuck-up they made it seemed impossible to believe that throughout all our previous visits they had sat so silently and for so long in a locked-up clothes closet.

Judging by the lusty light in their eyes, I was never quite certain whether the incarceration protected them from us, or us from them. All I do know is, that as the weather got colder and the evenings drew in, the word 'bundling' kept cropping up in Mac and Mrs Mac's conversation. This was accompanied by the downcasting of eyes and a pretty flushing of the cheeks from the daughters.

The ancient custom of 'bundling' was native only to the wilder parts of Scotland and the Islands and had been practised by young girls and their menfolk, affianced, or 'just good friends', for centuries. The idea was this. In winter, when temperatures fell to zero and below, in order to allow the old folk closer access to the fire, the daughter or daughters were allowed to take their men to their beds fully clothed, for warmth and verbal, not sexual, intercourse. The latter possibility being made impossible anyway by the simple expedient of tying the young ladies' legs together with rope. The same procedure was then carried out on the young man. The calvinistic and God-fearing father, having checked the prospective lovers' knots, would take leave of the young couple and return to the warmth of his wife and the fire.

This ancient Scottish rigmarole was probably more than sufficient to guarantee the intactness of the crofter's daughters' hymen with a local lad, but in retrospect I think it was just as well that this turned out to be our last visit, for there was not one of us that would've been averse to a bit of 'bundling' with a Miss Mac and seamen, as you know, are fair devils when it comes to the untying of knots.

★

As I mentioned previously, the matelots not interested in the nature surrounding them amused themselves in the NAAFI bars and games rooms that had been built for that specific purpose. There was not a single habitable dwelling within sight, other than a small cottage that rested alongside the footpath leading from the wooden jetty to the canteen. This little cottage was completely surrounded by barbed wire, making access by any unlawful intruder impossible. If you looked carefully you could see the eyes of the occupier peering expectantly through the lace curtains of her front room as the sailors made their way to and fro.

Some months before, this widow-lady of advancing years had been roisterously taken by an inebriated sailor, and was evidently so enthused by the almost forgotten experience of intercourse that she became something of a man-eater. Like a black Tarantula she silently lay in wait for her prey, and, as they rolled drunkenly by, would nip smartly out and drag the poor unsuspecting victims into the net of her boudoir. The barbed wire entanglement was, therefore, erected not so much to keep the befuddled sailors out as to keep the voracious widow in.

One night a drunken Stoker from the *Rodney* was arrested by the Naval patrol for committing bestiality with a sheep. At the hearing held on board the flagship, the prisoner's defence was unique in Naval annals. Here it is:– not verbatim, of course, as sadly I was not present . . .

'Stoker second class Robinson,' said the Prosecuting Officer, 'what have you got to say, in defence of the charge laid before this enquiry, that you did, on 21st March 1941 at 2230 hours, commit an act of bestiality with a sheep, the property of one Angus McTavish, farmer of this parish?'

The Stoker thought for a moment, clearing the clouds from his mind and replied with what must be one of the classic rejoinders of all time.

'Sorry, sir. I thought it was a Wren in a lamby-coat!!'

There was a temporary silence in court followed quickly by the rumblings of barely controlled mirth.

'You don't usually find a female member of His Majesty's Women's Royal Naval Service running around a field on all fours, wearing a sheepskin-lined overcoat turned inside-out, do you?'

'Well, sir,' said the undaunted Stoker, 'up here in Scapa, you never know.'

The previously controlled laughter now broke through the retaining walls of the twenty attending Officers' stomachs, the resulting reverberations of that explosion of unseemly mirth being heard in mess-decks throughout the fleet. We never heard what actually happened to that drunken, depraved, but none-the-less delightfully droll sailor, but the general consensus of opinion was, that in view of the great laugh he had given us, he should've got off with a caution.

But the unusual nature of the charge started something of a feud between the lower deck crews of *Rodney* and *Hood*. It began when several hundred *Hood* seamen lined up on the fo'c'sle to give three rousing cheers to the flag ship, 'offed-caps', and instead of replying 'Hooray' to the Captain's 'Hip-Hip-Hip', bleated 'Ba aaa!!!'

As we were all facing the same way, with Officers and non-commissioned Officers at the front, it was hard to pin down the perpetrators.

There was only one recourse left to the CO and that was to stop all shore leave for several days. That really put the cat amongst the pigeons, and by the time our leave had been restored, we were champing at the bit to take on our rivals in *Rodney*.

That night in the company of a phalanx of boozed-up *Hood* shipmates, I was weaving down the jetty prior to boarding our liberty boats, when we spied fifty or sixty liberty men off the *Rodney*, waiting to be picked up by their boats.

'Let's see if the sheep-loving bastards can swim,' cried a primed torpedo-man. With unanimous agreement we linked arms and, advancing slowly, systematically swept the poor unfortunate men straight off the end of the jetty into the sea. Inevitably a few of us up front went in the 'oggin' with them, as the pushers at the back couldn't differentiate in the dark between *Rodney*'s crew and ours and didn't know when to stop. The drop from the end of the jetty was some fifteen feet and the resulting shouting and general hubbub from the tumbling men was tremendous. Apart from that the water was freezing and we realised that if we didn't get out quick, someone was going to drown. Suddenly the feud was forgotten, albeit temporarily, and everybody started helping everybody else to safety. Strange how immersion in cold water will kill off passion, in *all* its forms. The serio-comic end to the foray was that quite a few of the more drunken participants, being capless and therefore unidentifiable, ended up in the 'Lions' Den' by finding themselves aboard the wrong ships.

From that night on the crews of the *Rodney* and the *Hood* were understandably never again allowed ashore at the same time.

★

From what I have written in the last few pages it would seem as if wartime at sea was one endless sky-lark, but this was far from the truth. The combination of lack of privacy, living conditions and the weather with its freezing cold were enough to break the spirit of far stronger men than me. When high-up in the main-mast on 'look-out' duty, wrapped in two duffel coats, two pairs of trousers, two sweaters, two balaclavas, two pairs of socks, winky-warmer and one pair of seaboots, I was still frozen to the marrow. As the bow dropped, the resulting spray would fly up and instantly freeze, the ice particles hurtling over the ship and endangering any unprotected men on deck. Where I was, up in the spotting-top, I have seen icicles whip past my head that I swear could have impaled me and brought about my instant demise. What a way to die in wartime, to be stabbed to death by an icicle. They were lonely, lonely times up there, and terribly sad ones too, when one saw so many ships and men go down on those vitally important convoys to Russia. The submarine and air attacks were inevitable and punctual, for one knew almost to the hour when they would come. As soon as we reached a certain latitude off the northern tip of Norway we could expect attack, and got it. From stygian darkness the bright flashes of torpedoed and burning merchantmen would light up the night skies, and to the crash of gun-fire and the muffled thud of exploding torpedoes and depth charges I came to realise the true horror of war at sea. The *Hood*, weaving and dodging an evasive course to make her own destruction a more difficult task for the U-boat Commanders, was never a very happy ship, and no-one had much confidence that she would come out best in any action with a German boat of equivalent size. We were an old ship in comparison to the *Bismarck* and we carried nothing approaching the same amoung of armour. I think we had only one armoured deck and once the heavy anti-magnetic mine gear had been installed, Mr Churchill ordered that in order to ensure her speed was restored to that of the fastest enemy battleship, all our unnecessary weight should be removed. This it seemed included the thick armour-plated hatch covers over the fifteen-inch gun magazine-hoists – hence the feeling amongst the ship's company that if she ever came to grips with a German battleship, she wouldn't remain long on the surface.

Our Master-at-Arms, Jimmy Green, was of the 'old demon' school. An immense man with a huge stomach, he could move, when he wanted to, at the speed of light. When we were closed-up for action with the main hatches shut, it was necessary to climb through a small circular one situated in the middle of the main hatch. This presented no problem at all to CPO Green – he would ram his body up the hole as far as it would go, then placing both hands over his gargantuan gut, press sharply and firmly inwards. Like a child squeezing a balloon, his stomach would suddenly overflow over the top of the hatch-cover and he was up and away. To go down below, all he had to do was reverse the procedure. It was a wonderful sight if you were ever standing beneath, to see that massive mound of flesh appear like magic 'Before Your Very Eyes!' Jimmy was involved in a running battle with a bunch of seamen called Macdonald from the Island of Stornaway. They all had the same name, were all closely related, all talked at once in an incomprehensible dialect and only found rapport with some Scottish seamen from the Gorbals in Glasgow, who were equally incomprehensible.

One forenoon, this heterogeneous collection were working up in the bow on a damaged 'blake stopper' (an enormous clip that held the anchor chair from running free). The seas were gigantic and it was necessary for all hands of the working party to wear safety lines, to prevent their being washed overboard. Not so Jimmy. In oilskins and seaboots he was up there with them, moving about free of any incumbrance and shouting out salty, unwelcome instructions over the howling wind. Suddenly as the bow dipped, a huge wave caught him and swept him straight overboard. In seconds the frantically waving man was gone from sight.

'Thank Christ fer that,' said one Macdonald.

'Serves the loud mouthed bastard right,' said another.

'I hope to Christ nothin's happened to him,' chimed in a Glaswegian, his eyes twinkling with glee at the fat Master-at-Arms' demise. It was unanimously decided that out of respect for the dear departed, all work on the 'stopper' should cease forthwith and they would repair to the mess-deck for a cup of hot 'kai' (chocolate). Unbeknown to them, Jimmy had been swept along the port side of the ship and as he drew level with the quarterdeck, the deck had dipped low, miraculously allowing him to be swept back on board. Grabbing a rail to prevent his onward rush, he was quickly assisted to safety. Without pausing for even momentary ministration, he swept through the ship dripping water from every cranny, and burst out on to the bow just as the mourners were on their way to the wake.

'All right you bastards, get back to work, or I'll spifflicate the lot of you,' he bellowed. It was a good thing that most of the lads were still on safety lines, otherwise the shock and subsequent paralysis they received, would've been party to their own disappearance over the side.

Jimmy cheated death twice in a very short space of time, as due to a sudden transfer, he narrowly missed going down in *Hood* with all the others.

When I was appearing in a Sunday concert for Billy Butlin in the late 50s Jimmy made it known that he would like to see me. Expecting his massive frame to appear around my dressing room door, you could imagine my surprise when a gaunt, thin figure with haunted eyes, weighing no more than ten stone, appeared there instead. His old Scottish adversaries had finally got their wish. Something had indeed happened to him. Perhaps the shock of that terrible experience and the loss of his beloved ship had eventually caught up with him and taken a terrible toll on that memorable macrocosm of a man.

★

The Naval Chaplain in *Hood* was the Very Reverend Tiarks, uncle of the beautiful Henrietta, Marchioness of Tavistock. 'Lofty', as he was known throughout the Navy, was a very popular man but his greatest companion, apart from God, was a pink-eyed, white bull terrier, who was very *un*popular. This dog he brought aboard from time to time and naturally the poor hound had to relieve itself. The fifteen-inch gun turrets were its surrogate lamp-posts, but for the more generous offerings, Lofty carried around his own 'pooper scooper'. In spite of Lofty's good intentions in cleaning up after Fido, the consensus was 'that it was a bleedin' liberty to 'ave a bleedin' mutt aboard a bleedin' ship in the first bleedin' place'.

So seconding a sympathetic Sparks to the 'anti-woofer' section of the crew responsible for the cleanliness of that part of the deck, a metal electrified plate was installed in the dog's favourite area for personal calls. So the next time the poor beast lifted his leg and had a squirt, he received up his stream such a severe whack in the winky, that it deterred him from ever repeating such indignities on that part of the ship again. He just went off to the stern and peed on someone else's gun-turret instead!

★

At just about the right time, for we all badly needed a rest, the ship was ordered into Rosyth near Edinburgh for a refit. This meant a long leave. I could go home, see some shows and try to forget the war for a week or two. A somewhat vain hope as the air-raids were still very heavy.

As a leave, it was a bitter disappointment: Carlotta had returned to Ceylon, my brothers were severally in the Army in Ireland and Burma, and my father was living in a small flat with his new wife, Kitty. After a fond greeting he seemed to find the prospect of my presence for more than 48 hours a source of irritation, so after going to the 'Olde Lanterne' and finding not one familiar face, apart from 'Ma', Nellie and the Misses Ione and Ella, I decided I would return to the relative peace and quiet of Edinburgh and continue the rest of my leave there. I arrived after dark and was mounting the Waverley Station steps leading from the railway station up to Princes Street, when a tremendous gust of wind blew me up the stairs. Gathering speed, I hit the guard-rail that had been put there for the express purpose of preventing people similarly out of control from being blown under the wheels of a passing bus. Coming to an abrupt and painful halt, my cap was whisked from my head and disappeared into the total darkness, God knows where.

This was a tragedy beyond all proportions, for seamen carry everything of import tucked into two pockets of their cap's lining. Leave-pass, watch card, identity card, money and pay-book.

I lay over the rail and nearly wept. What now? With my hard-saved money gone there would be no leave. All I could do was go back to the ship, where I would get into serious trouble for losing my cards and paybook, so I turned down Princes Street and in the pitch blackness started to shuffle my way down the gutter. This position off the pavement prevented you from banging into others in the dark and the feel of the edge of the curb against your foot greatly facilitated navigation. I had not walked more than a hundred yards or so when I felt my foot kick something soft and, bending down to ascertain what it was, I let out a wild cry of 'Eureka', for the article in my hands was my lost cap, complete with cards, pay-book and money. It had evidently been bowled down the gutter by the wind and had come to rest, quite unmolested, at the foot of the Robbie Burns memorial.

This called for a celebration. Retracing my steps, with cap back on and chin strap down, I made my way to the welcoming comfort of the Waverley Hotel. There, seated at the bar and deep into a gin and tonic, I made the acquaintance of a very desirable young American lady dressed in service uniform. It transpired that she was lonely and fed-up and would I like to join her for a drink? I would and I did. Then she joined me in one, then I her, until mellowed, she suggested that in her

162

considered opinion, it would be far more comfortable if we repaired to her room with a bottle and continued to build the foundations of our fast growing relationship in private. I heartily concurred and within minutes I was 'up and over', as the saying is.

Whilst I was enjoying a relaxing cigarette sometime later, the telephone rang by the bedside and out of habit I reached out to answer it. With an anguished cry of 'No!', my companion snatched the phone from my grasp.

'Hello, darling, you're back early. I didn't expect you till tomorrow morning. Where are you? Downstairs in the hall? Well give me a moment to make myself look pretty for you –'

That was enough, I was out of bed and grabbing for my clothes like an undercranked scene in a silent movie. Here I must explain that a sailor's 'tiddley' suit (his best) is cut so tight that it needs the assistance of one or more friends to pull you in or out of it. My present friend was not inclined to give me any assistance at all, other than screaming, 'Get out, get out' and flapping round the room like a headless chicken. So grabbing tunic, trousers, cap, collar, shirt, socks and vest, I made for the fire escape. I'd managed to get my underpants on, to afford me a modicum of dignity in the event of confrontation. Scrambling out of the window on to the iron grating of the fire escape, I felt the thwack of my boots hitting me between the shoulder blades, and as I turned to thank my ex-lover for a wonderful evening, the window slammed down, almost de-nosing me. It was a cold, wet night, so getting back into my clothes was of the utmost essence. To those males who haven't experienced trying to get into full sailor's rig in complete silence, standing on a grating a hundred feet in the air in freezing rain, and in abject fear of imminent discovery, let me assure you, you haven't missed much. I managed to get into everything but my tunic and boots, and with them slung over my arm was making ready to start down the fire escape, when I thought I'd peek in through the window to see how my erstwhile bedfellow was faring. She was faring splendidly, wrapped in the passionate embrace of her man, stretched out on the bed that I had so thoughtfully warmed for him. Looking at that serenely beautiful woman, I came to the conclusion that here before me was unfolding a classic example of quintessential *savoir vivre*.

The weather being too inclement for further voyeurism, I scrambled down the fire escape, the last section of which was counter-weighted, so that as soon as you put your weight on it, it sank slowly to the ground. Thus, descending backwards with boots in hand and tunic over shoulder, I stepped off the ladder straight into the arms of the Naval Patrol.

''Ullo 'ullo, and what exactly have we been up to, Jack? Doin' a bit of nickin' 'ave we?' asked a Regulating Chief Petty Officer.

'Of course not, Chief,' I replied indignantly.

'Then what exactly 'ave we been doin', lad?'

'It's not so much what, as who,' I said cryptically.

'Ah!' said the CPO, light beginning to dawn. 'Been doin' a bit o' visitin', 'ave we?'

'Well, yet you could put it like that,' I said, slowly regaining confidence.

'Then why, may one ask, are we leaving by the back door?'

This was going to be tricky, but working on the assumption that there is nothing a bored man likes better than a tale of salacious sex and passion, I started to regale him with the most exaggerated story of physical prowess and orgiastic delights that my imagination could summon up. By the time I came to the denouement, i.e. the entrance of the lady's true love, the poor cuckold had grown to six foot six inches, wore a black beard and tipped the scales at at least fifteen stone.

'My, my, we wouldn't want to get tangled up with a monster like that, now would we, son? So you'd better put on that tunic and them boots smartish and bugger off out of it, before I goes and rings the doorbell of the lady and gentleman concerned and ask 'em their version of the biggest pack of fuckin' lies I've heard in all me puff.'

Feet jammed hastily into boots and struggling frantically to get my tunic on I headed off down Princes Street from where this nightmare of a night had first started.

*

It was not long after that refit that *Hood* sailed on her last voyage. We were told that the *Bismarck* had come out of her hidey-hole at last and was on her way round the far north making for the Atlantic, where she would wreak havoc on the convoys from America. To circumvent this we were out of Scapa to hunt her down within a few hours of first getting the 'buzz'. From then on the Captain kept us informed of her every move. She would appear and disappear like a wraith and we knew that the time we had all either dreaded, or longed for, was upon us: the predestined sea battle to the death, of one or the other of us!

During one watch I was sent for, to go at once to Captain Irving Glennie's cabin. Now what? It was like being back at school again.

That awful feeling of apprehension I used to get when awaiting execution in the studies of those past Headmasters.

'Sit down, Pertwee,' said the Captain. 'I understand that you are an actor, and that you work on Radio Luxembourg?'

'That's right, sir.' Why on earth should he want to know that? I was perplexed.

'Tell me all about it. I've always wanted to know about commercial radio.'

It seemed an extraordinary time to be asking such a banal question, but he was the Captain, and who was I to deny him? So for half an hour he listened attentively as I told him everything I knew on the subject, plus a bit more. He thanked me profusely for my lucidity and I took my leave still puzzled as to the reasoning behind his strange request. It was not long in coming – the Master at Arms, Jimmy Green, informed me that I had just passed my 'Captain's Test' and was now a full-fledged CW candidate (Officer Cadet). I was to pack my kit and be over the side in twenty minutes, when a trawler would take me to the ship *Dunluce Castle* to await eventual transfer back to Pompey Barracks. What an extraordinary way to test a youngster's officer-like qualities. Still, I suppose when time is of the essence, you can learn a lot about a man by letting him talk about himself for half an hour. There were sixteen of us altogether who had been similarly tested, for the Captain, knowing he was sailing into action, decided rather than risk wasting potential Officer material, he would send us off the ship before the inevitable battle took place; thank God he did, for she sailed on into her disastrous battle with the *Bismarck*, that is now a part of Naval history.

After scoring the first strike *Hood* was herself hit, first on the bridge, putting her immediately out of control, second between the stacks, and thirdly just forward of the after fifteen-inch gun-turret.

With the first hit, Signalman Briggs and Midshipman Dundas were blown into the water; after the second, amidships, my messmate Bob Tilburn was removing his seaboots prior to jumping into the water, when the final shell went through two wooden decks, hit the armoured deck and the resulting blast, tearing through the thin hatchways of the magazine covers, blasted the ship into eternity. Of the 1415 men on board only those three men survived, plus the sixteen of us that were taken off before that final action.

It was a terrible, shocking thing, and I have never really got over it. To have had so many good friends die in the time it takes to snap your fingers. By the time I could get to a telephone to inform my family that

I was alive, their mail had been returned to them with a small sticker attached, which read 'Missing – presumed killed.' You can imagine their stunned disbelief, therefore, changing to great joy, when I walked in through the door.

Chapter Nine

After a short leave, I returned to Pompey Barracks and was about to start my CW (Officer Candidate's) course, when I was made quickly *hors de combat*. I was living in G Block, the CW's building, when the barracks was once again badly hit by enemy bombers. I had been detailed to go into the attic with three other candidates and firewatch. Around midnight, within a few minutes of the siren wailing out its warning, the enemy bombers were thumping their regular and instantly recognisable beat of 'waa-waa-waa' overhead. A shower of small incendiary bombs landed on the barracks, several punching holes in the roof and bursting into fiery blinding life around us. Remembering my fire drill, I grabbed a couple of sandbags and dropped them over the bomb, ostensibly to choke it into extinction. Unfortunately, although I had stopped the fire flame going upwards, I had, by jumping on the sandbags, encouraged the bloody thing to burn downwards. Within seconds the white-hot incendiary had burned through the floor, where, by falling into the hammock nettings below, it started a raging inferno. 'Everybody out,' I yelled, 'before we're all barbecued.' Suddenly, from a nearby rooftop-lookout, there was an urgent shout of 'Parachutists!' Oh God! They've come, I thought, what we'd been expecting for months. Before I could decide what to do and whether to collect my solid-barrelled rifle, pick-axe handle or pike, the cry of 'Belay parachutists, they're landmines.' These were enormous canisters, dropped by parachute into harbours and channels, that would explode magnetically when passed over by any steel or iron ship. Very sensibly, whilst I was busy doing my Indian war dance, my mates had already got down the iron escape ladder. But I was only half way down it when 'bang', the landmine made a direct hit on the block opposite, collapsing it like a pack of cards and taking off the end of G block at the same time. I don't quite know how, but the blast of the explosion sucked me out of the building instead of blowing me further *in*, and deposited me on top of the mountain of rubble exactly where the mine had gone off.

By landing heavily on my head I had received a six inch cut on my scalp which bled profusely and quickly formed a pointed haemotoma. Unconscious and covered in dust and rubble I was quickly taken on a stretcher across to the Officers' Mess, which, because of the considerable number of wounded, was being used as a temporary casualty clearing station. When I came to, I found I was lying on a marble slab in a larder. On the shelf above me was another, presumably wounded sailor, whose still arm hung down before my face. To get his attention and ask what the hell was going on, I gave his arm a firm tug, which, unfortunately, dislodged him from his narrow shelf and brought him crashing to the floor. One look at his poor pallid face told me that he was in no state to answer my question. In fact, he would never answer any question again.

Frightened, I looked around in the cold gloom of that black slate mausoleum and saw to my horror that every one of the shelves' occupants was already behind the veil in Abraham's bosom. That was enough. Had I been entombed aforetime? I started yelling blue bloody murder.

The door was flung open by an ashen-faced sick berth attendant. 'Hey! All these men are dead!' I cried in anguish.

'Blimey mate, I thought *you* fuckin' well was.'

'Well I'm fucking well not, so get me out of here, before I am,' I said, and promptly slipped off once again into a stupefied, sense-bereft state. With dozens of other unfortunates, I was eventually laid out on the floor of Haslar Naval Hospital in Gosport awaiting treatment. At one point, in a reverie, I saw a beautiful angel with a red cross on her breast fly down from the heavens to hover smilingly over me.

'What is your name?' she said looking down at the black-faced, bloody, pin-headed patient lying there on the stretcher beneath her. I could hardly hear a word she was saying as the blast had done my ear-drums no good at all –

'Wha'?' I said.

'Your name! What – is – your – name?' she repeated patiently.

'Oh, er, Pertwee, Jon, PJX 178358.'

With that the angel let off a cry like a factory whistle, and collapsed sobbing on to my chest. Hard to believe she was a girl-friend of mine, Aileen Anders, with whom I had just spent most of my last leave. I knew that she was training to be a nurse, but neither of us had had the slightest inkling that she was to be posted to Haslar. Unable to recognise me under all the blood and grime, she had had a nasty shock when she had heard my name. Quickly pulling herself together, she asked the MO in charge if she could be assigned to look after me as 'he is my fiancé,' she lied prettily.

Permission was given and for the rest of my sojourn in hospital, I had the private attention of a *very* personal nurse.

Still feeling a bit woozy, I returned to barracks to be put through the mangle of Chief Petty Officer Branch, now in charge of CW candidates' basic training. This was the Chief all the cadets feared but like 'Rebel Riley' at Wellington House, he made me laugh inordinately and I never resented his ways or obscene outspokenness. It wasn't long before he handed me my first good laugh.

Lined up on the parade ground for inspection, CPO Branch, took a turn along our rear ranks – coming to a sudden halt behind me he said,

'Ah, yes, it's Pestwit isn't it?'

'Yes, Chief – well near enough anyway.'

'Come to stay for a bit, 'ave we?'

'That's right, Chief.'

'Well it won't be for very long if you don't get your bleedin' 'air cut. You look like a bloody chrysanthemum.'

My father had a Staff Sergeant in charge of his cadet training in the First World War who must've been cast in the same mould as CPO Branch, for when marching his platoon up and down the parade ground had shouted, 'Get those shoulders back, Peewee. It's a case of me 'eads 'ere and me arse will be along in a minute.'

As prognosticated by the Chief, I wasn't long at the barracks before being drafted to an enormous tented camp not far from Fareham. This move was to get as many men as possible out of bombing danger, and was very much appreciated, as we were by now all a bit bomb-happy. Purloining a service bicycle, I successfully worked the 'messenger' trick throughout the month I was stationed there. This meant taking a large brown envelope with as many franked stamps on it as possible, all around the camp. When stopped and asked your destination, you replied urgently, 'I'm taking this important missive from the Captain to the First Lieutenant', at which point you trod smartly on the pedals and were away, before your interrogator could look too closely at your envelope. This ploy also enabled me, once I had the respect of the guards, to leave camp and head off to visit friends and pubs in the firm belief that I was delivering and collecting secret documents for the CO.

After that blissful rest, all new CW candidates were posted to *HMS King Alfred* ensconced in the old Roman Catholic public school of Lancing, for the first serious part of their training. My OLQs (Officer

Like Qualities) were all right, because that involved the physical more than the mental side, i.e. drilling, signalling, rope work, etc. It was in navigation that I fell down badly.

On the first day, the Lieutenant Commander Instructor said, 'Right, now you all understand the theorem of Pythagoras, don't you?'

My hand hesitatingly went up.

'I'm afraid not, sir.' Maths was my worst subject. Without fingers and toes I was finished. A day rarely goes by without my offering up a prayer of thanks to Mr Sinclair and his pocket calculator.

'Well, I'm sorry, but I cannot hold back the rest of the class by teaching you the fundamentals of geometry and trigonometry.'

'But, I thought that was the purpose of my presence here, sir,' I said politely, 'to learn such things.'

'Well you thought wrong,' replied the now irritated instructor. 'So in future, sit at the back of the room, pay attention and try to make as much sense of it as you possibly can.'

I did as I was bid, but as I could not make *any* sense of it, I drew pretty pictures of galleons on my exam papers instead, for which I obtained three marks out of 450 for neatness.

From that moment on I knew I was doomed. If I couldn't pass my navigation exam, I would never become an Executive Officer and would be relegated to the lower deck once again. This was a thought that filled me with fearful trepidation throughout the rest of my course.

Suddenly, one day in the middle of a class on pilotage, I developed a headache that literally blinded me, and necessitated my undergoing rigorous tests for eye damage. Evidently, my bang on the head had slightly displaced the retina in my right eye, causing me less than perfect vision – reason enough for not permitting me to continue my training as an Executive Officer. I was therefore brought before a selection committee to decide whether I should be returned to the lower deck or sent forward as a green-striper, or Officer of the Special Branch.

'What have you learned since you joined the Navy?' asked Captain Pelley – the panjandrum of HMS *King Alfred*.

'Apart from anything else, sir,' I replied jocularly, 'an entirely new vocabulary.' A remark that went down like a cup of cold mud with the good Captain. Like my performance at one of our ship's concerts in June 1941, when I very nearly blew my commission by: a) telling what was considered by the CO, Captain Pelly, to be a very tasteless joke;

and b) singing a vulgar song, that he thought suggestive in the extreme. It was written for me by Guy Morgan, a well known humorous writer who had been responsible for the wonderfully funny column 'Beachcomber', in the *Daily Express*. The song went down splendidly with the cognoscenti, and it was this point, I think, that saved me from expulsion, yet again. Sung by a bibulous, red-nosed seaman (me) the first two verses went something like:–

> They call me Seaman Harry
> I don't know why they do,
> For I'm full of hope
> When I pull my rope
> And the wind comes whistling through.
> They cannot do without me
> For the fact remains you see,
> If it was not for the seaman
> Where would the nation be?
> When Officers cry, 'Hi men!'
> The whole crew quickly rise,
> For we're keen to show
> We are not slow
> In answering such cries.
> No they can't get on without us
> It's plain as plain can be,
> That without some jolly Seaman
> Where would the nation be?

Pretty innocuous you would think, but take the two 'A's' out of Seaman and substitute an 'E' and you will see what the sensitive Captain was getting his knickers in a twist over.

However, despite this *faux pas*, my plea that it would be a shame to waste all the money that the Government had already spent on my training, and that I must be good for something, did not go unheeded, and I passed and became Sub-Lieutenant J. D. R. Pertwee, RNVR, Special Branch.

The proud day had arrived when I could go across the road to 'Gieves', the Naval tailor, and be fitted for my RNVR. Officer's uniforms. The tailor was a delightful Jewish gentleman whose command of the English tongue left a lot to be desired. There were two uniforms to be made, one in serge for everyday use and one in moleskin for 'best'.

Trying his utmost to please, Mr Jikster the tailor asked, 'For ziss soot, you should vant more pudding in the shoulders?''

From then on, whenever I wore that uniform, I had a vivid mental picture of my shoulders beginning to sag as the suet spotted-dog slowly subsided down my sleeves.

A few days later my commission was personally presented to me by Lord Louis Mountbatten, closely accompanied by Noel Coward, a good friend of his and his wife Edwina's, and who seemed to be always popping into my life at just the right time to give me his patronage and moral support.

'Congratulations dear boy,' said Noel, 'so you are going to sea to serve your King?'

'That's right, sir,' I replied, head up and lying through my teeth.

'Patriotic fool,' he said, *sotto voce*, 'best of luck and give my regards to your dear father, bless him.'

This dialogue had given a nice cosy feel to a proceeding that might otherwise have been somewhat overwhelming.

It was shortly after this, that I made a very grave error of judgement.

One fine morning a Senior Officer from Admiralty arrived, and stood importantly before us. 'Can any of you young Officers speak French?' he asked. Having been properly taught never to volunteer for anything, I remained silent. The Senior Officer now stood in front of me, having been pointed in that direction by my Divisional Officer. 'Is your name Pertwee?'

'Yes, sir.'

'But you speak French. It says so in your papers.'

Having horrid visions of being dropped behind enemy lines as a spy, I replied, 'Very little, sir, and that's pretty rusty, it wouldn't be good enough for what you had in mind, I'm sure, sir.'

'Pity,' said the SO moving down the line to another new Sub-Lieutenant. 'What about you then? Rankin isn't it? You're supposed to speak French aren't you?'

He, like me, pretended that his knowledge of the language was limited to just a few words. But the SO said, 'Never mind that'll have to do, come with me.'

'Poor fool,' I thought to myself, 'I wonder what dangerous mission *he'll* be sent on?'

You can imagine my feelings, therefore, when I found out that he had been made Resident Naval Officer in Tahiti, where he spent the rest of the war, lying in a hammock, sipping cold drinks from fresh green coconuts shells, and being fanned, rocked and loved by bevies of elderly Tahitian ladies of around seventeen.

Ten years later, when I was living in Tahiti, I asked the British

Consul Freddie Devenish, if he had ever heard of Tony Rankin – 'What, old "Randy" Rankin, I'll say! Mr Pertwee's asking if we have ever heard of "wham-bam" Rankin', he said turning to his own seraglio of dusky acolytes.

The hearty laughter and the twinkling in the eyes that followed his enquiry caused me intense and instantaneous jealousy, and I shall hate Tony Rankin until the day I die.

*

After a long leave, during which time I had continuously worn my uniform to show myself off, I returned to barracks to await my first draught. This time, though, I slept in a fine cabin on the third door of the Officers' Mess, not on a slate slab in the basement. Although I did go down there with some disbelieving friends, to see it once again for nostalgia's sake.

It wasn't long before I was posted to *HMS Valkyrie* in the Isle of Man as a Divisional Officer. The ship or stone frigate consisted of a collection of boarding houses and small hotels stretched along the front at Douglas, the largest, and centre one being the Officers' Mess, and the rest to right and left accommodating the Staff Chiefs, POs and men that were to undergo training as Radar Operators and technicians. There were four of these sections with an Officer in charge of each, and I was allocated the foretop division.

My Captain, a hero from Dunkirk, was a fey, elegant man called Mike Ellwood, who always looked as if his uniforms had been made for him by Hawes and Curtis, and his caps by Herbert Johnson. Thus impeccably dressed, with cap worn at a jaunty angle, he was a cross between Lord Beatty of Jutland and a nautical Jack Buchanan. His one great passion was German Lieder and, armed with song-book, he would frequently ask permission to enter our Mess, for the sole purpose of cajoling Sub-Lieutenant Ray Roberts (of whom more later) into accompanying him in a song – or twenty. Ever anxious to keep on the right side of the 'Skipper' we sat with faces fixed in false expressions of rapture, when in truth there wasn't one among us who didn't feel, as each reedy top 'C' was striven for, that a red hot centipede was crawling through his brain. One by one the Mess would empty, with every exit being accompanied by some banality or other such as 'Ah well, can't stop I'm afraid sir, got to get off and do me rounds, don't you know', or 'Damn, that's my favourite, but got to go, sir, the "Number One" wants to see me.' The fact that Number One was sitting uncomfortably in the corner of the room did little to aid the veracity of his excuse, but it seemed to be of no consequence, as the Skipper with eyes closed in rhapsody, was plainly transported to the very boards of La Scala, Milan itself.

The Commander of *HMS Valkyrie* was the ex-heavyweight boxing champion of the Navy, 'Ham' Darwin, a gruff man who walked with a limp and a stick, had tufts of hair growing from his cheeks and nostrils and went blind and deaf whenever it suited him. When informed by direct signal from Admiralty that he should leave the protective barbed wire fencing around the perimeter of the establishment where it was, he instantly had the lot torn down, sank it out at sea, and professed when confronted by the Captain that he hadn't had his monocle with him at the time and had completely misread the instructions. To me he had confided, 'What do those idiots up there expect me to do? Keep my ship looking like an infernal internment camp?'

'Ham' had an absolute thing about the internment camps on the island and the inefficient way in which he thought they were run. At a cocktail party one day, attended by all the local big-wigs and heads of the services, he proclaimed in a loud voice, when everyone was discussing the method of the most recent escape of a large group of Italians, 'Oh I should think they used the same tunnel as they used in 1915, only this time I expect they'll've got a turnstile at either end!'

Further up the front from us there were the many other boarding houses where hundreds of Italians, Austrians and Germans were interned and Commander Darwin had no intention of letting his ship look like *those* establishments with their towering barbed wire fences. So he drew immense stocks of canvas from stores and ran it round the perimeter painted in grey 'Pusser's Crabfat', in an attempt to make us look as much like a Naval vessel as possible. He even had constructed a canvas and iron railed area in front of the Officers' Mess, which was to be referred to in the future as the 'quarterdeck', and to be saluted every time anybody stepped into the sacrosanct enclosure. To remind all and sundry that this was indeed a ship of His Majesty's Navy, Ham had two white lifebelts hung to port and starboard of the 'quarterdeck's' entrance gap with *HMS Valkyrie* painted in bold lettering around them.

One day an elderly Paymaster who suffered badly from the staggers, tripped and prostrated himself on the road, right in front of the Commander's office. 'Ham', witnessing the episode, flung up his window, or as he would have had it, 'flung open his porthole', and yelled to the Quartermaster standing impassively on the front steps,

'Don't just stand there you fool, throw the Pusser a lifebelt!' On another occasion, standing at his window imagining he was once again back at sea on the bridge of his own ship, a rude boy on a bicycle rode up to deliver the Sunday meat, and temporarily leant his bike up against the quarterdeck's canvas jigger. Up went the window again and the stentorian voice of the Commander roared, 'That's no way to tie your dinghy alongside, boy. Take a line and tie up to that bollard over there', pointing a wagging finger at a newly grey painted lamp post.

The big laugh of the day was always the Commander's report, where culprits of various crimes were brought before Ham for umpirage. You could always be sure of a full house for these sessions as the office would be packed with Ham's fans. Normally loud, he was at his most dangerous when the volume of his voice lowered several decibels.

'What is your name, lad?' he asked softly of a seaman who had been four days adrift off leave.

'Smith, sir.'

'What Smith?'

'Zachariah Smith, sir.'

'Do you know who Zachariah was, lad?'

'No, sir.'

'Then I shall be happy to tell you, my boy,' he said at his most avuncular.

'Thank you, sir,' said Smith, rapidly regaining confidence from the soft tone of his Commander.

'Well, Smith,' he almost whispered, 'Zachariah was a man who walked with God. And for the next fourteen days,' here his voice rose to a roar, 'for the next fourteen days *you'll* walk with *me*! Fourteen days Number eleven. Next!'

And he was off on yet another case.

'Ordinary telegraphist Rugley, sir!' said the Regulating Petty Officer, 'was adrift from duty and found asleep in his bunk at 09.30, sir!'

'What have you got to say in defence of the charge, Rugley?' asked Ham.

'Well, sir, between you and me, I never heard the trumpet.'

'The *what*?' said Ham, his voice lowering a point.

'The trumpet, sir.'

'Bugle, man, you never heard the bugle.'

'Sorry, sir, the bugle, sir.'

'Well Rugley, all I can say is', his voice falling to its dangerous level, 'if you fail to hear bugles or trumpets' – there was a pause before the inevitable earsplitting payoff, – 'what the Hell will you do on Resurrection Day?'

Among Ham's many accomplishments was an astonishing capacity for alcohol and he would step up to the bar for his 'usuals' with great regularity.

'Scotch,' he demanded from the steward, 'J-J.'

'Yes sir! Large or small, sir?'

'Four fingers of it, boy,' he said 'with the fingers held wide apart!'

'Certainly, sir, any water?'

'Good God no! Neat, and give me a beer for a chaser.'

The steward promptly poured and passed him a frothy half pint of ale.

'What in the Lord's good name is that?' he said, looking scathingly down at the glass. 'Take it away until it grows up!'

Navy Day stands out in my memory, when Captain Ellwood invited a relative of our then Queen Elizabeth, Rear Admiral The Earl Granville RN Retd, the Governor of the Isle of Man, to make an official inspection of the ship. The old man was delighted to be asked, as, ever nostalgic for his Navy days, he would don his ancient uniform at the drop of a hat. So, giving his gold braid a bread polish – the best way to get it gleaming; brushing his suit and putting on his ridiculously minuscule cap (reminiscent of those worn by early Sea Captains sailing before the mast), he awaited the great day. Ham had everything possible painted, and a special dais constructed from which the Governor was to take the official salute. We four divisional officers were told to 'spit and polish' the ship up to a higher degree of brilliance than ever before, and to rehearse a march past of the ship's company with the Royal Marine band in white helmets leading, until we could pass Ham's eagle-eyed scrutiny. When the big day finally arrived, to make my division the smartest of the lot, I had executed a manoeuvre which resulted in my men being graded according to height, with the tallest on the right and left, sloping gradually down from either side to the shortest in the middle. A very pretty sight indeed.

I also summoned a very trendy Wren Officer and persuaded her to so arrange her girls that the most attractive would be displayed around the edges and the 'Plain Janes' hidden in the middle. They should also be very attentive to their make-up, wear the thin, not the thick black stockings, and have the tilt of their white-topped caps just so. The final result was excellent and Busby Berkeley couldn't have done better.

Standing at ease in front of the quarterdeck I was intensely proud of my shining, well-turned-out crew. At twelve noon exactly the Governor's vintage 'Roller' rolled up to the main gate. Captain Ellwood called the whole parade to attention and the Royal Marine band for some extraordinary reason struck up *All the Nice Girls Love a Sailor*.

'Oh God!' I thought, 'don't let me get an attack of the giggles, not today of all days.' The Officer of the Guard, a Lieutenant Pearman, with ceremonial sword resting on his right shoulder advanced towards the Governor, came to a stamping halt, saluted with his sword, brought it back to his shoulder, and executed a copy-book about-turn, at the precise moment that the Admiral proceeded to advance. The result was that the tip of Lieutenant Pearman's sword very nearly cut the Governor's throat from ear to ear. Uttering a cry of alarm the petrified Admiral stumbled and fell backwards, mercifully to be fielded by a phalanx of following officers close behind. It is just as well that they were there, otherwise I feel sure Commander Darwin would have thrown him a lifebelt.

After the Navy Day Parade was over, I was having a drink in the Mess when Captain Ellwood entered.

'Pertwee, a word in your ear if you don't mind.'

Taking me into a corner, he said quietly, 'I must congratulate you on the smartness and turnout of your Division, but there is one point upon which I would like to take you to task.'

'Yes, sir, and what is that, sir?' I asked.

'I realise that at heart you are an actor, but when issuing your terms of command, must you always play the part of a Cockney Sergeant Major from the Mile End Road?'

He must've been another Professor Higgins, for it was down the Mile End Road that I had learned to speak Cockney with other RADA students. I had been appearing in a play about François Villon at the new People's Palace Theatre in the East End. The play was produced by a sarcastic firebrand called Ronnie Kerr, who delighted in bringing his artists to tears and the point of suicide.

Backstage, the wings would be crowded with sobbing ingénues and white-faced juveniles, all bent on revenge for the indignities suffered at the hands of the venomous Mr Kerr.

I was walking across the stage in my capacity of a junior peasant, when a bellow rent the already purple air.

'Good God Almighty, Pertwee, you're walking across the stage as if you have piles!'

I stopped. Here was my chance for Lex Talionis, for retribution. A

Roland for my Oliver. Walking slowly, with simulated painful gait, I addressed my cruel taunter.

'Mr Kerr, I have, and God forbid that you should suffer so.'

This parcel of old crams seemed to have had the necessary effect, for we heard not one more derogatory peep out of him until the next day.

★

I remember when his Majesty King George VI came on an official visit to the island he was taken down to the southern tip, where the Manx language is most widely spoken. The King, anxious to hear some Gadhelic, asked if someone could be brought forward to give him a personal demonstration of the ancient tongue. 'Certainly, sir,' said the Governor, and seeing an elderly farmworker standing amongst the crowd, called him forward and said, 'My man, His Majesty is most anxious to hear the Gadhelic tongue, would you be so kind as to recite the Lord's Prayer for him in Manx?'

'Recite the Lord's Prayer in Manx?' said the elderly farmworker. 'I couldn't recite it in bloody English!'

Our Number One, Lieutenant-Commander Stewart, was a self-confessed worrier and a fuss-pot. Quite unlike me he held Commander Darwin in awe, whereas I looked upon him with esteem and not a little love. Ham would yell dreadful things at me that only succeeded in making me laugh, but when he yelled at Lieutenant-Commander Stewart the poor man fell apart at the seams.

He was a great one for signing things, was our Number One. According to his way of things, everything should be signed for, so his pockets were stuffed with pens and pencils for the signing of numerous passes, permits and forms that were permanently secreted about his person. Knowing how Ham insisted on *Valkyrie* being kept 'shipshape and Bristol fashion', he became quite beside himself if any litter was to be seen blowing about the ship and gave the crew hell if there were any lapses in this regard. One forenoon, a dustcart was chugging up the front when a gust of wind blew a screwed-up piece of paper into Ham's holy of holies, the quarterdeck. The Quartermaster on duty spied it and at once bade his sidesman to 'get that bit of paper PDQ'. But unfortunately another strong gust took it up the front steps and right into the Officers' Mess. The QM, knowing full well the Commander's paranoid hatred of litter, said sharply to the sidesman, 'Well, don't just stand there, lad, go in and get it.' At once the sidesman disappeared into the Mess to retrieve the offending piece of bumph. A moment later he reappeared with a resigned expression on his face. 'Too late,' he said. 'The First Lieutenant's signed it!'

There was also, aboard *HMS Valkyrie*, a funny little gnome of a man, Petty Officer Lacy who kept a permanent wad of chewing tobacco in his cheek and was able to hit a sedentary fly at five paces with the ejected juice with as much accuracy as that toothless cowboy star Gabby Hayes.

But there his talents ceased and he lived out his life in a welter of confusion. One morning, as I was going ashore, I found him on duty at the main gate and said, 'Petty Officer Lacy, I am expecting a Surgeon-Captain Critchley aboard in a minute, will you show him up to the Officers' Mess and say I'll be back in a moment?'

'Aye aye, sir,' said PO Lacy, smiling confidently. Knowing that he was inclined to get things wrong I asked him to repeat the message. With great pride he said, 'Certainly sir! You're expecting a certain chap called Ritchley aboard in a mini, and I'm to show him to the Officers till you come back from the Solent.'

As neither the skirt nor the car had as yet been invented, I never knew what the mini was to which he referred.

★

Rabbits were the scourge of the island and up on Douglas Head, the ground trembled with their passage. So my friend 'Yogi' Parkin and I obtained a ferret which we kept out at the back of the Mess and, armed with a big bag of nets and a crew of willing helpers, we worked the stone hedgerows and burrows where the rabbits were to be found in their thousands. I was quite an expert in the art of ferreting, having learned my trade at the hands of Mr Fred Pike, a master poacher down at Highleigh. After our first few Safaris, I had my ferret 'Schickelgruber' muzzled, so that he wouldn't kill in the burrow and lie-up, necessitating the spending of many hours digging him out. Previous to being muzzled, he was wont to kill, have a big rabbit dinner, go fast asleep and be found hours later with a seraphic smile on his face. In addition I put a small bell around his neck to signal which route he was taking on the underground. He also trailed a six foot length of string to facilitate our finding him should he get stuck behind a traffic jam of rabbits queuing up in front of him.

One day, we had lost touch with the ferret for ages and asked a local farmer who was watching from the other side of the hedgerow whether he had seen or heard him. 'Oh ay,' he said, 'not five minutes afore, he run up the hedge like a geese', a strange but memorable simile! After a long search we heard an almighty 'gerfuffle' going on inside the stone wall at least 300 feet from where 'Schickelgruber' had first gone in. Putting my ear to the wall I found the spot where all the noise was coming from and proceeded to remove two or three rocks. Suddenly as I broke through into the tunnel, I was overwhelmed by a stream of rabbits precipitating themselves out of the hole like bullets out of a Bren-gun. There must have been thirty or forty of them leaping, crashing and banging their way out of that tunnel of terror. I just lay there, head down, until the mass exodus taking place all over me eventually ceased. Assuring myself that the last tenant had left I looked up to see the cause of all that blind panic stroll casually into view, my nose not being more than a few inches from the furiously frustrated ferret proved too much of a temptation and with a leap at the speed of light he gave my rather prominent proboscis a deep scratch. The resulting blood flow, fear of septicaemia and the indignity of having a pink plaster stuck on the end of my nose, caused me to send Schickelgruber into permanent exile and turn to a .22 rifle instead. A gentleman from Derbyshire had informed me that his county was singularly short of rabbits and as this particular game was not listed as a 'rationed commodity' he would buy any rabbits I could send him for three shillings and sixpence (17½p) each. He would send the crates and pay the postage; all I had to do was shoot the rabbits, gut them, put them in the crates and send them COD to Derbyshire. This sounded to me like excellent business. So I formed a small company of good marksmen from my crew, drew six .22 rifles and a quantity of ammunition from the stores and took them with the complete approval of Commander Darwin, up to Douglas Head for 'rifle practice'.

'Thought it might be a good idea to have a number of crack-shots at hand just in case of invasion, you understand, sir.'

'Quite so, my dear boy, very perspicacious of you,' said Ham.

But our rifle practice was somewhat out of the ordinary in that it was done at night when the rabbits were out in force. Having dug and constructed various slit trenches and hides, we chalked our rifle sights to see them better in the dark and made for our individual hidey-holes. The top of the cliff at Douglas Head was our favourite area, for as I said before, the ground there was honeycombed with the burrows of literally thousands of rabbits. As dusk fell they started to come out to feed and for the next two or three hours we would shoot them as they were silhouetted against the night sky, never moving from our hides, for if we did, the jig was up and every rabbit would be gone. The crack of the rifles strangely enough did not seem to disturb them; only the sight of humans made them go to ground. After some hot tea we would gather up the rabbits, gut them, put them in sacks and take them back to *Valkyrie* to be crated and sent off to Derbyshire the next morning. With an agreed share-out of the takings, we all did splendidly and quite a few little nest eggs were banked for the days of peace to come. In fact one Safari member is still in the trade to this day.

★

The Isle of Man at this time went about its business as if there was no war on at all. In fact they had been at war with Germany since 1914 as the Tynwald, their own parliament, had inadvertently neglected to sign a peace treaty in 1918, making their little country's war with the enemy one of twenty-eight years' standing. But as I said, no-one would have known it, for food rationing hardly existed, there was an abundance of sugar, butter, cheese, tea, coffee, milk, meat, eggs and bacon, and as there was no petrol rationing either, I bought for twenty pounds a beautiful 500cc water-cooled Scott motorbike and for forty pounds, an immaculate one and a half litre blue 'Brescia' Bugatti sports-racing car, which later became a collectors' item and finished up in the 'Schlump' Museum worth over £30,000. But at the time the owner was most grateful for the forty quid and said, 'I'm glad to be rid of it, it takes up far too much room in the garage.' So these two perfect pieces of machinery were parked behind my office and kept in near mint condition by willing car and motorcycle buffs from my division. Sadly the Bugatti was temporarily immobile as it was in need of a new coil. I was hoping that one of the ship's artisans would, when he had the time, rewind the original for me, so until then I took to using the 'Scott' which buzzed over the island like an electric blender. With all the booze, birds, steaks, eggs, bacon and mobility I wanted, I was enjoying my time on that beautiful island more than at any other period of my life, and because Ham liked to wear 'civvies' when ashore, he allowed his brother officers to do likewise. So, once off the ship, the relaxing comfort of corduroy trousers and sweaters became the norm.

The Manx are a kind, hospitable and other-worldly race of people. The Tynwald in the House of Keys is the oldest parliament in the world and dates back to pre-history. There are many druidical sites of quite indeterminate age on this land, like the Tynwald Hill at St Johns where by tradition, every July 5th, all the laws are read out in Manx and English. Manx or Gadhelic is their own pure unadulterated language and they have strange indigenous names, rarely to be found off the island, such as Corteen, Cubbon, Kewley, Quaile, Clague, Qualtrough and Qwilliam, the Q before a name having the same derivation as Mac and Mc meaning the son of, hence Qwilliam – son of William, Qualtrough (MacWalter) – son of Walter.

And their tail-less cats are probably better known around the world than they are!

They run annually the best motorcycle race in the whole wide world, and in strange contrast firmly believe in the existence of fairies. There is a bridge situated in the middle of the island where it is traditionally advisable to bid 'good day' to the 'little people' as you cross. If you foolishly ignore this token of respect you are very likely to come across something nasty on the next bend, causing you to swerve headlong into a magic tree which has been awaiting with open branches such disbelievers as yourself. Wishing to continue my serene and happy life I quickly learned to show respect, and later allowed no expression of surprise to cloud my face when I observed the mother of a girlfriend putting out by the back door a saucer full of milk and honey for the little folks' delectation. 'It'll be gone by the morning, just you wait and see,' she said, instinctively aware of my disbelief. Maybe it showed a lack of fantasy in my nature, but I couldn't help but think that in the unlikely event of the hungry fairies being seen by a human being such as myself, they would've been more likely to appear in the disguise of dog, cat, fox or even hedgehog!

Although there was a preponderance of servicemen and their war-machines on the island with sailors from *HMS Valkyrie*, the *Port* and *HMS St George*, RAF from the fighter station at Ronaldsway and the Army from literally everywhere, in the two years I was there, I never saw a single enemy aircraft or ship. I am ashamed to admit, however, that once, soon after my arrival, in the early hours of the morning, I reported seeing the silhouette of a German submarine lying right in Douglas Harbour. After alerting the coastguard and a flotilla of MTBs in port, it was brought home to me very forcibly that my submarine was in fact an island, and had been sitting out there in the bay for several thousand years. For many nights following the event foreign cries were to be heard in the dark, of 'Achtung! Achtung! Leutnant Peevee zis is Deutsche U-boat RU12 speaking, surrender immediately or ve vill sink you!' The timbre of the voice sounded strangely similar to that of my friend Yogi's but I was never sufficiently certain to sink *him*.

Another incident I am not proud of involved my ramming Douglas

Pier with an Isle of Man Steam Packet boat. It is a long and complicated story with which I will not bore you!

There is a most beautiful late Victorian theatre in Douglas called the Gaiety. Designed by Frank Matcham and opened in 1900, it has just recently been restored to its original glory. The existence of such a theatre was too much of a temptation for me, so I decided to form a company of local amateurs and servicemen amongst whom were quite a few professionals. My first production for 'The Service Players', as the company came to be known, was *Night Must Fall* by Emlyn Williams, in April 1942, as I had always wanted to play Danny. But as my Welsh accent was not of the best quality, I decided to play it in Cockney and it seemed to work. The following 'critique' was to me no ordinary one, written as it was by the ex-editor of *The Yorkshire Post*, Mr George Brown. As such it gave me tremendous heart and encouragement at that time, and also during the ensuing years.

Of my performance as Danny, in *Night Must Fall*, Mr Brown said:–

Danny, played by a Sub-Lieutenant in the RNVR named Pertwee was really magnificent. Having seen the play in London, and having seen it on the films, we would give Mr Pertwee's portrayal of Danny as the best of them. He has before him a fine future on the English stage.

My co-producer was Sub-Lieutenant Jack Williams RNVR, now a most eminent television director. Among the cast was one professional opera singer, Norah Moore (no relation), and one professional actor, an old friend, Kenneth Henry, who played Inspector Bellsize. Mrs Bramson was played by Olga Cowell, the wife of a respected lawyer in Douglas, Robert Cowell, who was also the Steward of the Isle of Man TT. This magnificent *grande dame*, for she could only be so described, could wipe the floor with 95 per cent of all the professional character actresses I have seen. She was in the Dame May Whitty/ Margaret Rutherford mould, and with her grace and impeccable timing was a joy to work with. A tall, statuesque, bosomy lady, she carried herself with tremendous dignity and, like many large people, her feet positively twinkled. A turn around the dance floor with Olga was an experience not to be missed. She also played the piano with great flair and skill, a rare talent that I shamelessly tried to include into whatever play we were doing at the time. For many years I tried to persuade Olga Cowell to turn professional, but she would have none of it. 'Nonsense dear, I'm just a second rate amateur, no one would ever employ me,' she said. In every play we presented she received notices from the critics that should have convinced her otherwise, but she was adamant and stayed an amateur, delighting thousands of Manx theatregoers until she died, a great loss to me as a friend and to the theatre.

Another very talented member of the company was a young character actress called Vera Craine who with her husband Dick still helps to keep 'The Service Players' one of the finest amateur groups in Great Britain. I am very proud that the company I started 43 years ago is still going strong and one day before I retire, or, as is more likely in view of my past, 'am asked to leave', I should like to return to this idyllic isle and peform just one more play with them. In my second production *George and Margaret*, aged 22, I played with the aid of a very heavy make-up, Malcolm Garth-Bander, a man of some 65 summers. Now that I am 65, the character make-up being unnecessary, what better way to retire!

We once went in for a drama festival at the Villa Marina and having performed our entry, decided to go into the auditorium to watch the competition. 'Yogi' Parkin, Eileen Peters, Vera and Dick Craine and I found some seats in the middle of the stalls and settled down to enjoy ourselves. A country drama of great moment was unfolding on the stage, performed by an amateur group from Ramsey. Crouched in a chair before a pitiful fire, a rug around her shoulders, was a dying old woman. There was complete hush as she held everyone enthralled with her perspicacity and wisdom. Finally, leaning wearily back in her chair, she said, 'I'm slipping away, I can feel it.'

'No, No!' the loved ones cried. 'Don't go yet.'

'Yes, I'm going, the candles are burning low,' she croaked to the now quietly sobbing family. 'I can feel the draught blowing on me wick!!'

It was nothing to the draught those sitting in front of us received from the explosion of air and laughter that shot from us at the delivery of that classic line. Quite unable to control ourselves we crawled for the nearest exit and from there to the lawns of the Villa Marina, where we grunted and gasped the laughter out of our system. Vera, always thinking of others, kept repeating, 'The poor soul, fancy having to say a line like that! Tch! The poor soul.' The expression on her face was enough to send us off once again into still more agonising hoots of merriment.

As Divisional Officer of Foretop Division, I was allocated an office and a writer (office assistant) in the shape of Ordinary Seaman Claude Newman, the famous ballet dancer from Sadlers Wells. He was a life-saver for me, and although impossibly temperamental and disrespectful of my superior rank, an unending joy to have working with me. His being a pro, and therefore understanding my language was an unexpected bonus.

As a result, when not involved with 'The Service Players', it was not long before Claude and I had formed a concert party company to entertain the ship and anybody else on the island who wished to enjoy our multi-talents.

Another kindred soul was Sub-Lieutenant Raymond Roberts, a brilliant classical pianist who after the war made a considerable name for himself on the BBC talking in the intervals of concerts and operas about the life and times of the composers concerned. Ray was our permanent accompanist and musical arranger as well as being a most congenial companion. Another member of the Company was Sub-Lieutenant Tommy Thomas, a Welshman of good voice, who was married to the grand-daughter of the late great Marie Lloyd – sufficient theatrical connection there to guarantee *him* a place.

One of our most successful 'bits' was for Yogi and I methodically to take the ship's piano to pieces, while Ray Roberts played the *Warsaw Concerto* upon it. Our particular piano came into more pieces than most, and when the iron string section was finally apart from the wooden section, and lying on the floor like a piece of junk, Ray would continue playing the melody of the piece, by lying on the floor alongside it and banging on the strings with his pipe.

Why this desecration should be funny I don't know, but it is – very! If you have a piano to spare, try it out on your family and see for yourself.

It was producing and appearing in concerts and variety shows that gave me the incentive and experience to brave the music hall stage after the war as a stand-up comic. 'Yogi' Parkin, Ray, Claude and I put on shows of over two hours' duration that defied description. In the main we extemporised, starting with the thread of an idea and developing it as we went along. Yogi was the compere who continually referred to notes pinned all over the scenery and I was the comic and interrupter. Most of the monologues and sketches we performed were germane to the ship's company and the Navy, so were practically incomprehensible to the many outside visitors who also attended the shows. They would sit there with stony faces whilst the Sailors, POs and Officers split their sides with merriment and Ray Roberts with legs crossed and smoking a pipe gave the entire show a musical background as if he was a 1920s pit pianist accompanying a film on the silent screen. This astonishing accomplishment continued unabated for two hours or more of sketch, song, burlesque, dance, mime or even thought-reading. The latter item being performed by the famous Arabian Thought-Reader 'Alley-Ben-Alley-Cat' (me), turbaned (to conceal the earphones) voluminously trousered (to conceal the cables) and booted (to enable wires to be connected to metal plates on the heels). I, Alley-Ben-Alley-Cat, would walk on to the stage and, taking a chair, sit in such a position that my metal-plated heels made contact with two metal studs on the floor, under which two continuing wires led to a dressing-room off stage, where a wireless operator sat with a local telephone directory, a morse key and a pair of earphones that were connected to a hidden microphone in the auditorium. 'And now the sensation of the century, mind-reader extraordinaire, Alley-Ben-Alley-Cat,' announced Yogi to tumultuous applause. 'Would any lady or gentleman like to take this telephone directory and pick out a name, address, and telephone number?' he asked of the fascinated audience. 'Don't tell me what it is, just point it out to me.' This done, Yogi would shout 'Alley-Ben-Alley, the gentleman has chosen a name on page 33, first column, 28 names down. Can you give me the answer to this devilishly difficult question? Now concentrate hard, Alley, concentrate hard.' All this time while Yogi pattered on exhorting me to even deeper concentration, the wireless operator off stage would be frantically looking up the chosen name and number in his telephone directory. Once found he would hammer out the answer in morse, each piece of information being relayed by me to the by now riveted audience.

'I'm getting the name Firkenshaw, yes Firkenshaw,' I said slowly as if in a trance.

'Good, good,' said Yogi. 'Now the address please, Alley.' If the address was a long one Yogi's patter and exhortations for concentration were considerably extended and sometimes a trifle too loud for me to hear the morse-signals with clarity.

'Please meester, don'ta talka so much, you a-ruin my concentration.' This request had to be shouted loudly and angrily to let the operator off stage know that I wanted him to repeat the last piece of information.

'I have it, yes I think I have it now,' I cried eventually. 'The address is 16 The Drive, Onchan Head, Douglas.'

'Absolutely correct. And now the number, please, Alley? Tell the gentleman the telephone number.'

After a moment's more concentration the number was given and our devastating demonstration of thought-reading came to a cacophonous conclusion. To ring the changes, the same principle was applied to dictionaries, the Encyclopedia Britannica and even the Bible, when Alley-B-A-C was replaced by a 'turbaned archbishop' with holy regalia and accoutrements kindly supplied by our stage-struck Padre.

Alas, the famous thought-reader's career came to a shuddering standstill one night when Yogi, passing too close to Alley-Ben-Alley, inadvertently knocked off his turban to reveal to a shocked audience an embarrassed Sub-Lieutenant Pertwee sitting there with earphones on. The familiar sound of hoots, jeers and cat-calls followed the retiring ex-mind-reader as he hurriedly, and not for the first time, made for the hills.

Sydney 'Yogi' Parkin was short, plump as a partridge, taciturn and laconic with a dry sense of humour that I coveted and attempted unsuccessfully to emulate.

'You know your trouble my friend? You talk too much,' said Yogi. 'Why don't you try being more pauciloquent?' Even his choice of words caused me unstinted envy.

Another strange thing about Yogi Parkin was that when he ran, he travelled at the same speed as when he walked.

Calling Yogi my 'friend' once resulted in an extraordinary reaction and being brought very quickly to heel. This error of judgement was made in 1941 when giving him a rather vulgar tie for his birthday. My wording on the card had read 'To my good friend "Yogi" to make him sartorially more elegant'.

'But my dear chap, I've only known you six months. To be allowed the privilege of giving me gifts and calling me a friend, you will have to know me for at least five years. After that time I promise you, I will give the matter my complete consideration.' I have known him for just on 44 years and at our last meeting when I inadvertently called him a friend, it didn't seem to rankle unduly.

On and off the stage he was a fine exponent of that dry approach to humour that so long was the métier of the late Naunton Wayne. With his taciturnity and my brashness we made an excellent double act, and I would place our version of the classic Leslie Henson and Fred Emney sketch of *The Green Eye of the Little Yellow God* high up on the list. For this sketch we were admirably assisted by the ship's Padre, himself no slouch on stage nor in the pulpit. One special charity night to aid our poor Soviet Allies we performed at the local Palais an hour's cabaret of song and dance that was entirely Russian. For this function I enlisted the Russian-born wife of a local Manxman to teach me the words of several traditional Cossack songs phonetically, and I wrote them down the same way to facilitate the choir's learning of them. 'Chom chom neprichoff, ah ooh meenyah near zackoff, ah ooh meenyah tserlou coochkou yashka miltsa priddy baskoy.' We had no idea what it all meant but dressed in borrowed blouses, fur hats and seaboots we lustily sang our hearts out to the evident delight of all assembled. Yogi was an excellent bass and had seconded into the choir the most beautiful girl on the island, who possessed, as do so many Manx, a voice as glorious as her appearance. Her name, which I have previously mentioned, was Eileen Peters and she was obviously more than a little in love with Yogi, something for which I hated her, as I was more than a little in love with her myself. Ordinary Seaman Claude Newman caused a near riot that night when in the middle of a solo from *Petrushka*, a role for which he was much renowned, he unknowingly split his trousers from stem to stern, revealing his hirsute posterior, quite naked but for the straps of his athletic supporter. It was this revealing moment that brought the evening to a splendid sansculottic conclusion.

★

Inevitably, it had to come. Life was too good to last. The RAF in England, getting to hear that there was virtually no food rationing on our fruitful isle, sent over large empty planes, with small empty crews to Ronaldsway Aerodrome, to scour the island for meat, eggs, bacon, butter, cheese and drink. This booty, once properly bought and paid for, was then flown back to the mainland, to be heartily enjoyed by RAF Officers' Messes all over the country.

Naturally, this continuous drain on the island's produce could not go on for long, and soon after a raid of some dozen or so planes had left, laden like Christmas hampers, rationing came to the Manx for the first time in their long history. Sadly this also applied to petrol, which up until that time had been available just for the asking. It seemed as if my lovely Bugatti was doomed never to hit the open road.

Around this time I had a very nasty experience indeed. Admiralty were once again on the prowl for French-speaking Officers, to be involved, I suspected, in the forthcoming invasion. I had managed to avoid all such foolhardy participation up until then and was not too happy at the appearance of an Admiralty press-gang in our midst.

They arrived on *HMS Valkyrie* and after going minutely through my papers decided that this time, schoolboy French though it might be, it would have to suffice and that I was to report to the Admiralty in London quicker than forthwith.

A call was put through to the RAF and a ride was arranged leaving Ronaldsway for London within the hour. Hurriedly packing my green 'Pusser's' suitcase, I bade an emotional farewell to all my friends, convinced that my chances of ever seeing them again were slim. Yogi, who always had tremendous confidence in my ineptitude, shook my hand, and said with his normal laconism,

"Goodbye, old man, see you tomorrow no doubt.'

The plane I was to fly in was a clapped-out, patched-up Wellington Bomber. On entering it, I was told by the self-possessed, bum-fluffed pilot that to keep out of everybody else's way I should best lie down on a canvas stretcher just aft of the main wing spar. Naturally, there were no windows to look out of, so far from being a flight of interest, the journey looked like being a crashing bore. The Wellington was a noisy twin-engined aeroplane with a fuselage of a strange criss-cross design covered in a hard varnished canvas. It looked as if this 'doped' canvas had been sewn on to the frame by hand and by the time we were half way to London, it was very forcibly brought to my attention that it had been, and very badly sewn at that. For whilst I was lying on my stretcher, deafened by the noise, and sick from all the turbulence, there was an awe-inspiring rending noise and a six foot portion of canvas ripped off the fuselage right alongside where I was lying, and dis-appeared into limbo. If the plane had been pressurised I would have gone into limbo with it, but as it was, I lay strapped on to my stretcher, terrified out of my life whilst 10,000 feet beneath me the beauteous fields of England swept hurriedly by. There was no question of my moving to another part of the plane as I was paralysed not only with fear, but also from the intense cold. Not for me the warm fur-lined jackets and boots of the crew, just a thin Naval Officer's Burberry and sensible shoes from Gieves.

By the time we had got to Northolt, just outside London, I had turned a most interesting melange of blue and purple, from two hours icy blast upon my person. I was led stiff legged and zombie-like to the bar, where I inhaled several large rums, the quicker to facilitate the return of my senses.

The only good thing to come out of that hideous experience, was that presumably due to my frozen bodily state, my brain had become equally iced up. For once again the Admiralty passed me over in favour of another, brighter, more fluent linguist. I was back on the Isle of Man the next day, and was warmly welcomed by Yogi. 'Back already?' he said, eyebrow raised quizzically. 'It only seems like yesterday you left.'

Sad to relate there were only a few more peaceful weeks left to me on the island. I had just about reconciled myself to the fact that the loss of the Tahitian posting was not such a tragedy after all, when I was hurriedly drafted to the Security Staff of Naval Intelligence in Great Smith Street, Westminster.

Now I was faced with a dilemma. What was I to do with my two beautiful machines? After much consideration I decided that 'Scott' would have to be found foster parents and 'Bugatti' I would take to live with me, wheresoever I was going. But how in wartime does one transport a bright, azure blue, two-seater racing car across the Irish Sea unobtrusively? The answer is, one doesn't. In fact it seemed as if there was no way to transport it at all, until I did a favour to a bashful young skipper of a destroyer, by introducing him to a Manx girl that he had fancied from afar for some months. It didn't require much arranging, as she had been secretly nursing a passion for him, as well. Not that he was to know that until well after I had named my price. This was to transport my Bugatti across the sea to Liverpool Docks. Yes, he would be very happy to, he said. All I had to do, was get it alongside his ship by dawn the next day. So with the help of the 'Blue Beauty's' nannies I pushed her to Douglas harbour, where she was immediately slung aboard and deposited on the bow. I wish I had had a camera with me that wet and windy morning, for it was an extraordinary sight to see a Destroyer setting off into the teeth of a gale with a shiny blue racing-car sitting just forward of its gun turret. She arrived that evening and was duly left on the dock for me to collect at my leisure. When I was able to take delivery some weeks later she was in a most sorry condition. The salt water soaking she had received had done her no good at all, and it took quite a few weeks of work to restore her to her previous pristine state. To get her to London I enlisted the aid of an infamous con-man who increased his plausibility by adding a totally spurious 'MC, DSO' to his name. With his wife and small 'goo-gooing' son beside him he towed me by night the 210 miles to London with a three-litre Red Label Bentley. You must remember that there were few private cars on the road at that time and petrol was rationed and unobtainable except for very special people and purposes. I don't know what he said to the many Police who stopped us on that journey down but he must've convinced them that resplendent in our uni-forms, we were very special people and that our journey was of a very special purpose. His use of a distractingly beautiful child was a trick I was to put to good effect years later when transporting dutiable furniture across the border into Spain: my blonde baby daughter Dariel distracted the customs officials delightfully and we paid not a peseta.

The first thing to do before taking up my new appointment was to find somewhere to live, so naturally the first place I looked at was my old flat in St Martins Street. Arriving on the doorstep I rang all the bells, hoping that a helpful tenant would tell me who the present landlord was. The front door was opened by a tall, emaciated woman of unattractive mien, within the shadowy background, the eyes and teeth of several peering females.

'Good morning, I wonder if by any chance you know whether the first floor is occupied at the moment?'

'At the moment, no!' she said. 'Would you be interested in it?'

'Yes, very!'

'Then come upstairs and we will discuss the matter in greater detail. I am the Manageress,' she went on.

The 'peerers' faded back into the gloom as I mounted those familiar stairs for the first time in several years. Flinging open the door to what used to be my sitting room, I saw that the prominent feature was no longer the comfy Chesterfield suite, but an enormous brass bed and little else.

'There, will that be all right for you, dear?'

'No, I'm sorry to say, it won't, I don't want a bed in this room at all.'

'No bed?' She looked at me with grave suspicion.

'No bed, just bring the sofa back.' I unlocked and walked through the connecting door to my old bedroom. It too had a gigantic bed in it. 'If you'll remove this and put in a comfortable divan instead, I will take it,' I said with a broad sweeping gesture.

'You mean you want the *two* rooms, dear?'

'Of course I want the two rooms,' I replied.

'Well, I suppose I could arrange it, but it's going to be rather expensive, all that furniture moving you understand.'

'That's OK! If I'm going to stay, I shall want everything to be just right,' I said a trifle grandiosely, knowing full well that the Admiralty would be footing the bill.

'Will you be bringing a young lady with you, dear, or will you be looking for company?' she asked, through a plastic smile of evenly moulded teeth. I was momentarily speechless at the effrontery of her question. What the Hell had it got to do with her, anyway?

'How much will it be if I stay for six months?' I asked trying to ignore the impertinence of her question.

'Well, let me see, dear, if you were just taking the rooms for an hour or so, I would have to charge you five pounds, plus one pound for the maid, that's with you providing your own company of course. With one of my girls (and I heartily recommend young Doris), the charge would be twenty pounds a night plus the maid and any refreshments, but for six months, well, that is a different matter altogether, for a six month stay I'd be prepared to make you a very special price, throwing in young Doris whenever you are unaccompanied.' The horrifying truth dawned at last. I had blithely walked into a brothel. So that explained the sniggering in the shadows and the predominance of beds over other furniture. It also explained why the walls were covered in silver paper; for you could see yourself reflected in them. To think that I had lived in that gaudy but delightfully kitsch flat for all that time before the war, and had never once realised why it had been so decorated. Presumably, just prior to my first living there, it had been raided by the Vice Squad and closed, allowing myself and four other lucky young blades to occupy unknowingly the best little 'out-of-business' whore-house in London's WC2.

Suddenly, it seemed that the *second* thing to do was *also* to find myself somewhere to live, so mounting a Hercules bicycle that I had rescued from a bombsite, I set off in search of suitable accommodation within easy cycling distance of Westminster. Immediately behind Sloane Square Tube Station, there is, on the corner of Chester Row and Bourne Street, an extraordinary little beamed cottage. To its right in Chester Row was a three-house bombsite and to its left a burnt-out shell. The cottage itself was like a very old lady, badly in need of a face-lift and make-up, but even with its iron-studded front door hanging from its hinges, it still had an inviting air about it. So I went in. The top floor was empty, with its front door blown in and the ceiling on the floor. The middle floor was a deserted mess. The ground floor flat door was padlocked and when I peered through the windows it appeared to be occupied. I went down to the basement. There was a knocker on the door, so I knocked.

'Come in,' lilted a Scottish voice, so I did.

'Good morning,' I said. 'I was wondering if you knew if there were any flats to let in this house?'

'Oh aye,' said the voice from somewhere in the stygian gloom. 'This one will be, if you'll give me about fifteen minutes to get out, I'm having a babbie any minute.' She appeared from the shadows, enormously pregnant and glowing with the joy of it all. 'I'm just waiting for the ambulance, to take me the hospital,' she said. 'I'll no be comin' back, so here is the address of the house owner, a Miss Fenner' handing me a hand-etched card. 'She's awa' in the country at the moment so you must send the rent to her once a month, it's three pounds ten shillings a week. Ye can keep what's left of the furniture and kitchen utensils for five pounds, okay? The hot water comes from a geyser, so ye'll need some shillin's. Here's a couple to get.on with, and here's the key to the flat, the front door's nae too well and won't close.' She paused for a moment, cocked an ear and said, 'Ah, there's me ambulance, I hope ye'll be happy here, I was until my babbie's daddy pissed off.' And with that, this delightful balloon of a lady grabbed a suitcase and was off up the staircase and gone. I don't think I had spoken a word to her throughout the entire encounter. Nevertheless, I was now the possessor of a one sitting room, one bedroom, one bathroom flat in Chelsea for three pounds ten shillings a week, and there I lived for the next twenty years. Eventually I bought the house off Miss Fenner and restored it to its original glory. It still stands there today, with its black and white beamed walls, its oak-studded front door, its cobbled front and blue plates let into the walls. I sold it in 1965 for £8,500, but have just heard that it is about to be demolished, and a neo-terraced Georgian House is to be erected in its place, to resemble, I suppose, all the other houses in the street, and costing in excess of a quarter of a million pounds.

What a tragedy that uniformity is so often the only acceptable normality!

Once delivered to my flat, the Bugatti sat proudly outside 66 Chester Row where love was lavished upon it by a horde of small boys from Bourne Street. For a nominal sum they washed it, polished it and sat in it until I thought they would be through to the aluminium. But nowhere could I find another coil. I advertised, went to scrapyards, even tried having it rewound, but all to no avail. It had turned out to be nothing but a blue ornament, so stifling my sobs, I sold it to an enthusiast for £150, a veritable fortune in those days. If only I had had more patience, it would still be in my possession and not the subject of a legal dispute in the Schlump Museum, Switzerland.

*

For the life of me, I could not see the sense of my new appointment, for Intelligence Divisions of any service always smacked of codes and mathematics, two subjects at which I did not excel. So it was with great trepidation that I entered the office of my CO, an RNR Officer of great magnetism, who quickly allayed my fears that mathematics were an essential part of my job. What he wanted from me was my mouth he said, to utilise my abilities as an actor. A spy! My God! He wants me to become a spy!

'Come in and meet your brother Officers,' he said, leading me into another office where I was introduced to the most heterogeneous collection of men I had ever met. There was Lieutenant Bob Little RNVR, a prematurely balding, very camp dress designer. Lieutenant John Paddy Carstairs RNVR, the well-known film Director. Lieutenant R. S. Smith RNVR, a brilliant University Don of twenty-four who died two years later with the hardened arties of a man of ninety. Lieutenant Harold Warrender RNVR, the eminent stage and film actor, and a tall, good-looking, round-faced Able Seaman, later to become the Prime Minister of England, James Callaghan.

We were all connected in different ways with the better security of the Kingdom. My particular brief was to travel this country and others, to lecture and browbeat those members of the men's and women's branches of the service most closely connected with secrets of national importance, into watching their wagging tongues. I was, for example, to visit establishments of WRN Signallers and Coders and after showing a most harrowing documentary film, involving great loss of life due to careless talk, I was to give them a psychologically designed lecture that punched home between laughter and tears the tremendous importance they must attach to Security. It was an acting job, pure and simple, and the reason for my appointment was now clear.

Another day would be spent instructing Commandos prior to a raid in the use of escapology equipment, e.g. hidden compasses in brass buttons on right-hand threads (a simple twist that confused the methodical mind of the enemy for many years); magnetised fly-buttons, the biggest hole of which, when one was balanced on the upturned other, pointed to north; magnetised sewing-needles, which when suspended on a piece of cotton, swung northwards; white cotton handkerchiefs, which when soaked in urine turned into full colour maps; wire files sewn down the creases of trousers which when clipped to two signet rings could cut through steel bars like butter; a pipe that you could smoke but was also capable, by a twist of the bowl, of firing one .22 bullet in a case of extreme emergency.

But most important of all was the teaching to a few chosen members of a raid the special intricate code which enabled Intelligence to receive vital information from prisoners of war via seemingly innocuous letters to lovers and loved ones. Intelligence Divisions were also able to reply, by having the writers inculcate seemingly innocent additions to their letters. The job necessitated continuous travel by train, plane and internal combustion engine, and was made all the more exacting and fraught by having to carry, as well as my personal luggage, a large padlocked canvas sack of secret films and books. As this additional encumbrance had to be carried quite unaided, I was soon as fit and strong as a yak.

The one good thing about carrying secret documents was being locked into railway compartments by myself, which, for the first time since the outbreak of war gave me plenty of room to stretch out and sleep. The bad thing was that on several occasions the guard failed to release me on arrival at my destination, resulting in my having to alight at some God-forsaken spot with a suitcase and a sack, and not a snowball's chance in Hell of getting to my port-of-call in time.

If a train was too crowded to allow me a private compartment, then I resorted to being locked in the cage of the guard's van, where I would crash out on an old pre-war lilo airbed that I carried with an inner tube repair outfit for such emergencies. I once had to travel all the way from London to Lincoln sitting in a first class lavatory, sleep being made impossible by a continual hammering on the door and accompanying cries of 'Good God, have you died in there?'

I had to visit on quite a few occasions, the top secret midget submarine base in north-west Scotland and, being situated in the outlandish place it was, to go out for a drink, a meal, or pay a visit to the cinema necessitated quite a long trip in a Naval picket-boat. On my previous visit I had been introduced to a delightfully decorous young Wren of style and extreme naughtiness. Her name was Kitty and she always managed to look in her Naval Issue like a front cover of *La Vie Parisienne*. After due acquaintance I found that beneath the blue serge, she continued the 'Oh La La!!' impression with lingerie that would have put Janet Reger's eyes out.

On the liberty-boat one evening, returning from a run-ashore, to get out of the cold and spray, Kitty and I crawled right up into the bow under a six foot covering of deck where, as we had an hour to while away, we made merry as if in a haystack.

On arriving back at the ship, composed and now under perfect control, we alighted, and walked down the jetty towards our various quarters. At that moment the full moon came out from under the clouds bathing us in its light. The sound of raucous laughter came from immediately behind us.

'What are they laughing at?' asked a perplexed Kitty.

'I have no idea,' I replied vainly looking around in search of a clue.

The laughter got louder and louder and from the accompanying whispered sniggerings, it was plain that we were the butt of their unseemly mirth. The reason why, I could not fathom.

'Goodnight, thanks for a lovely evening,' I said, as Kitty turned sheepishly into the Wrens' quarters. It was only then that everything became clear. Some seaman had done a stirling job of freshly painting the ribs of the picket-boat white. Kitty, striated like a zebra, had white horizontal stripes all down the back of her jacket and skirt. A most compromising collection of marks – but no more than those to be seen on me when I myself turned hurriedly towards the Officers' Mess. In the still bright light of the moon, Lieutenant J. D. R. Pertwee RNVR NID, stood before the snickering, smirking sailors, with two pure white kneecaps, and two forearms of similar colouration.

As you can imagine, my lecture on 'Security' the next day went down a storm, and during one momentary hiatus, a straight-faced, three-badge Stoker complained that there was a distinct smell of wet paint emanating from the platform, and that I should be well advised to avoid getting any on my nice new uniform.

★

After some months I found that giving the same lecture over and over again stultified the mind and impaired the concentration. So much so, that one day in the middle of such a lecture, I gave myself a very nasty turn. I had just spent a very pretty weekend with a very pretty girl, who must've been a High Priestess among sexual innovators, and was halfway through my powerful lecture on Security to a large audience of both sexes, when my concentration slipped and I allowed myself to be transported back to the loving arms of the afore-mentioned sex-goddess. For unknown moments erotic thoughts flooded my mind until suddenly a warning bell rang in my head and I was jerked back to the present, with the audience coming into instant focus and looking thoroughly shaken. My God, what had I been saying? I knew that I had been talking all the time, but what words had been issuing from my mouth? Had I suddenly gone into a running commentary on that heavenly sexual encounter? Had I been giving a blow-by-blow description of fornicating gymnastics? From the open-mouthed expressions on the faces of the audience it certainly looked as if I had. Politely requesting them to excuse me for a moment, I rushed into the wings, where I grabbed at a young Seaman-Electrician and asked him what I had been saying. His face suffused into scarlet as he said, 'I'm very sorry sir, I'm afraid I don't know. I must've dropped off.'

The only other person backstage was a behemoth of a Wren Chief Petty Officer. I approached her with caution and again asked if she had heard what I had been saying. 'Oh yes sir, thank you very much!' she simpered. 'Every word, and most edifying it's been I can assure you.'

With that ambiguous reply she excused herself, leaving me to return to the platform, not knowing until the lecture was over, whether I had been holding my audience in thrall by the power of my oratory or with my highly original approach to sex instruction.

I discovered later over a pink gin that my lecture had in fact continued unabated, with no stories of a similar colour to the drink I was holding, which proves once and for all that it *is* possible to think of one thing and do another at the same time.

★

About this time I was staying the weekend with Uncle Guy in Caterham when the Germans sent over their first flying bombs. Our house 'Torcross' was, you may remember, at the top of a long ridge of hills and therefore very vulnerable. I was helping myself to some breakfast bangers, when with an almighty earth-shattering roar a black monoplane with stubby wings and spouting fire shot over the house. So low was the plane and so intense the vibration of its engine that seconds after its disappearance, the roof tiles began to fall to the ground like rain. Uncle Guy and I rushed out to the cross-roads, from where we could see in both directions. Within ten minutes another of the noisome machines was upon us. But this time before it clipped the top of a big beech tree and careered on its way to London, we were able to get a good look at it. It was small compared to a normal fighter plane, with short square-tipped wings and a long tube mounted high up on its fuselage. From this tube came a noise that was a fluttering cacophony of mind-bending volume, causing anyone within its vicinity to clap his hands over his ears to avoid having his drums shattered.

'What the Hell kind of plane is that?' I asked a trifle anxiously.

'That,' said Uncle Guy as if he had an ear to Hermann Goering himself, 'that, my boy is Hitler's new secret weapon.'

For months Hitler had been hinting that the war would take an abrupt swing in his favour once his devastating secret weapon had been put into operation. Thank Heavens, due to the accuracy of our coastal batteries, the skill of our pilots and the inaccuracy of the information supplied to German intelligence by the famous double agent 'Garbo', the effect of the V1s was nullified. But as a 'terror' weapon it succeeded admirably. When the 'fluttering' stopped, if you had any sense, so did you, and made for ground as quickly as possible, although once the engine had stopped the ungodly machine became completely unpredictable and glided every which way and that. Once, when I was walking up Regent Street with the great Australian comic actor Dick Bentley, a flying bomb stopped its engine over Piccadilly Circus and headed in a fast glide up the street we were on.

'It's only a suggestion, mind,' Dick said. 'But why don't we take a left here and make our way with all speed to Bond Street?'

'A good idea,' I said as we turned and hurried up Vigo Street.

We had just got to the back entrance of the Albany when Dick looked over his shoulder to find to his dismay that the bomb had banked sharply to the left and was heading down towards us.

'Jesus H. Christ,' said Dick, upping the tempo of his steps, 'the bloody bomb's following us.'

We were showing a remarkable interest in a string of pearls in a Burlington Arcade jewellers when the bomb burst a quarter of a mile away in Bruton Street.

Within a few weeks the nerves of the city were jangling from the incessant stream of flying bombs raining down on us, and by now the even more alarming V2 rockets were landing on London. This was the only bomb that you heard coming down *after* it had exploded. If you didn't hear it, you were probably dead. At the time of these raids I was sharing the flat with a Captain in the South African Army, painter D'Oyly-John, who like me was very anxious to survive the war, whose end at last seemed to be just over the horizon. My bathroom in Chester Row was constructed out of a coal cellar and made a perfect air-raid shelter. As soon as we heard the devilish fluttering of an approaching V1 we would cry out simultaneously, 'I think I'm going to have a bath' and would both rush headlong into the bathroom. Whosoever was first, jumped into the bath fully clothed while the other sat on the laundry basket until the bomb had gone on over or exploded. When we had friends in, the small cellar became somewhat reminiscent of the famous Marx Brothers scene in the ship's cabin, and resulted in much hilarity. But behind all the laughter there lurked the desperate wish that by going to ground in this seemingly cowardly way one was in fact building up the odds against death, and improving the chance of surviving the six year war after all.

★

Over a drink one evening, a brother Naval Officer and I got involved in an argument concerning the British trait of letting extraordinary things unfold before them without batting an eyelid. I had, I told him, some months before, met a man in a pub who looked a dead ringer for Adolf Hitler, so I had asked the gentleman if I might take a photograph of him, as an evil idea was germinating in my mind. Taking the resulting photo to an expert in the field, I had an official Naval pass made out, in the name of the Fuhrer himself, to which the aforementioned photo was neatly affixed.

Arriving at *HMS Vernon*, Portsmouth, the following week, in my capacity as a Security Officer of NID, I was challenged at the main gate by a sentry.

'Can I see your pass please, sir?'

'Mein Pass? Ja, Ja, natürlich,' I said in an appalling cod German accent.

The sentry took the fake pass, studied it carefully, handed it back to me, and said, 'Thank you very much, sir, do you know your way?'

'Nein, but I'm sure zat if I vanted a guided tour of ze most secret parts of zis establishment, you vood be ze best man for ze job.' It was only then that he began to look apprehensive. In retrospect, he must've looked a lot worse after the Commander's report the next morning.

My Naval friend found the story hard to believe.

'Oh come on! He must've seen that the photograph wasn't you and would've recognised the name and Adolf's picture as soon as he gave it a second look.'

So to prove the veracity of my belief that people can go temporarily blind, I dared him to join me in a little experiment, albeit one with a modicum of danger. The next morning saw the two of us walking slowly up Regent Street immaculately dressed by Monty Berman's Theatrical Costumiers as two German Army Officers, with appropriate decorations, high leather boots, belts, side-arms, correctly badged caps, and in my case monocled à la Conrad Veidt. My point was proved to his complete satisfaction when we arrived at the top of Regent Street without once being stopped and questioned. Not only did we walk the whole street unmolested, but we had the honour of being smartly saluted by several members of His Majesty's Forces, including a Junior Officer in the RAF, who did, I admit, give me a pretty funny look when I returned his salute by raising my palm backwards and upwards. In retrospect it was not a very good joke, for if we had been physically roughed up, we would've had no recourse whatsoever. But it had proved conclusively that if you are bold enough, you can play with impunity on the national characteristic of 'not getting involved', whether it be conscious or unconscious.

Years later when I first stepped into the street of Hampshire's Braishfield village dressed and made-up as the scarecrow Worzel Gummidge with his carrot nose, corn eyebrows, warts, twigs, straw and cocky robin peeking from a hole in his pullover, several female villagers standing outside the general store answered my greeting (in Worzel's quirky nasal voice) of 'Good mornin' ladies, lovely day fer scarin' rooks', by momentarily ceasing their tittle-tattle, turning towards me and saying, without any reaction whatsoever to the uniquely ugly figure standing before them, 'Yes it is, isn't it?' And with that, they turned from me and continued with their gossiping, seemingly unaware anything out of the ordinary had occurred.

During my time with NID I had to attend many official cocktail parties and receptions. Standing in the line with my invitation card was frequently embarrassing, as somehow I always seemed to follow the nobs.

'The Duke and Duchess of Sunderland,' the Redcoat would announce, 'Lord and Lady Anthill!'

'The Prime Minister of Uganda, Mr Limpopo, RSC, DOF!'

'Brigadier General Sir Harold Farnsbarnes, VC, DSO.'

And then as if a nasty smell was synonymous with my name, he would announce with distaste, 'Lieutenant Pertwit!'

On one wonderful occasion, a most eminent member of the Royal Air Force preceded me, and was desperately fumbling in his pockets for something.

'I'm so sorry, but I seem to have mislaid my invitation card,' he said to the Master of Ceremonies.

'That's quate all right, sir. Can I have your name, please?'

'Of course, it's Air Chief Marshall Henry Robert Moore Brooke-Popham, GCVO, CB, KCB, CMG, DSO, AFC.'

The MC looked stunned.

'I beg your pardon, sir. Would you mind repeating that?'

'Certainly. Air Chief Marshall Henry Robert Moore Brooke-Popham, GCVO, CB, KCB, CMG, DSO, AFC.'

The MC's jaw dropped fractionally, and he seemed to have suddenly contracted Bright's Disease, for his eyes were popping out of his head. Taking a deep breath and raising his eyes to Heaven, he bellowed,

'*Air Popham!*'

The net result of this diminution of the Air Chief Marshall's name and title was my hurried dash from the room to avoid a vulgar display of hysteria being seen in public!

★

Harold Warrender was a big brown bear of a man whose small round mouth when angry would emit air as if from a blow-hole. When our CO was away, Harold, being the next Senior Officer, took over and instantly assumed the mantle of Captain Bligh. For some reason I became his Fletcher Christian. It was 'Pertwee do this' and 'Pertwee do that', as if I was still on the lower deck and not a brother Officer of almost equal rank. One day I entered the office and said, 'Oh Harold, I wonder –' His withering glance stopped me dead in my tracks. 'I am your Commanding Officer, Pertwee. You will kindly address me correctly and call me "sir"!'

He must be jesting, I thought. He was a Lieutenant and I a Sub-Lieutenant, not enough seniority to warrant addressing him as 'sir', except perhaps when on duty and within the hearing of ratings.

'You are joking aren't you?' I said. 'You can't possibly be serious.' If he was, our future Prime Minister had better look to his laurels and stop calling me 'mate'.

'I am *very* serious' he replied.

'But why only me?' I noticed his ruling did not seem to apply to others in the section, including Able Seaman Jim Callaghan.

'Because, Pertwee,' 'Sir' went on, 'you strike me as being the type of young man, that if I gave you an inch, you would take a mile.'

It was a strange quirk of fate that nine months later brought Lieutenant Warrender before me as my possible assistant, when I was also a Lieutenant and Number Two in the Naval Broadcasting Section.

'My dear old Jon,' he said. 'How are you?'

He was a sitting duck – 'I'm very well, thank you, Warrender, but if we are to have any sort of rapport in the future, as your Senior Officer I shall expect you to address me correctly by calling me "sir".'

He had a short memory for an actor and didn't seem to get the irony of my remark.

'Why on earth should I call you "Sir"?' he asked, falling right into the trap.

'Because,' I said with schoolboy glee, 'apart from anything else, you strike me as being the type of young man, that is so slow off the mark that if I gave you a mile you'd only take an inch!'

It was only then that the penny dropped, and with an embarrassed grin of his little O, he slunk his six foot plus frame out of my office. From then on we had a very good working relationship and continued working happily together on the radio for several years after the war.

★

It was my six years on both the lower and the upper decks of the Navy that gave me the background experience of Navy life and humour that was to prove so invaluable to me years later, when, on being offered a radio series by the BBC, I persuaded them to allow me to do one about the Navy.

My experience, in turn, became a priceless asset to Lawrie Wyman, and later George Evans, who used me as a 'sounding board' for information, ideas and anecdotes when they wrote what was to become the highly successful radio show, *The Navy Lark*.

Chapter Ten

In 1958, Michael Standing, who was then Head of Programmes for BBC Radio, sent for me and intimated that the BBC would like me to do a new radio series for them.

'Splendid,' I said. 'What ideas have you got?'

He told me and I was frankly unimpressed, but being the perspicacious man he was, he said, 'All right, Jon. What ideas have *you* got?'

I had been thinking for quite sometime that the war had been over long enough, now, for a new Services show on radio. After all, *The Army Game* was doing very well on ITV and *Sergeant Bilko* was getting enormous figures on BBC Television. It was surely time for radio to jump on the band wagon, I said.

'I agree,' he replied. 'What service had you in mind?'

'The Royal Navy,' I said promptly, and the Royal Navy it was!

The next step was to find a producer for the show, and Michael introduced me to Alastair Scott-Johnston, with whom I had already worked on such successful 'one-off' radio spot shows as *Vic Oliver's Variety Playhouse* and *London Lights*. Alastair was an excellent choice, for he knew his comedy backwards, and how he handled our extremely self-willed cast, seemingly without any undue effort, for the next eighteen years is still beyond my comprehension.

Alastair was the author of the 'W' Plan, an original theory on how situation comedy writing should be constructively tackled. You aimed for certain 'peaks', and it worked like this. First, you started at the top, the first peak of the 'W' with a very funny scene to grab your audience and get them hooked. Then you slackened off a little to get the point of the story over, then back should come your laughs to take you to the peak of the middle of the 'W'.

With your audience now thoroughly 'with' the show, you could afford to let them simmer down a little, because unless you are careful an audience can laugh itself out. Then penultimately, back you come to the final peak of the 'W' where, if you've done your job properly, the audience should be hysterical with laughter and falling out of their seats. The denouement should be short and to the point, to let the audience come down to earth, and, you hope, leave the studio saying what a thundering good show it was and could they come back next week!

Alastair suggested a writer by the name of Lawrie Wyman. Lawrie was highly experienced, and at the time was writing for various shows in one of many small offices in Light Entertainment's Aeolian Hall, which were known in the trade as 'horse-boxes'. Lawrie's first job, therefore, was to write a pilot of the show to 'sell' to Michael Standing, so I just sat back and awaited results.

Now the curious thing was, that if it had been left up to Lawrie *The Navy Lark* would never have seen the dust and death-watch beetles of the BBC archives. For some unknown reason, after his meeting with Alastair and me, Lawrie sat reluctantly at his typewriter and proceeded to write a script with about as much humour in it as Tolstoy's *War and Peace*. This done, he sent it off and forgot all about it. The redoubtable Alastair, casting his experienced eye over the uninspired script, completely re-wrote it. That done, he popped it into Michael Standing's 'In' tray, and then he, too, sat back and waited.

Like the late Sir Noel Coward and many others in our precarious and insecure profession, I have what Sir Noel calls in his Diaries 'An unworthy and sordid preoccupation with money'. So a few weeks later, having heard nothing from the BBC, I was to be found sitting in my flat in Chester Row, totting up how much I had to cosset me from starvation from my Insurance Policies, and looking back over my shoulder to see if the Ghost of Unemployment Past was chasing me, once again.

I remember it was around 3.15 when a cock-a-hoop Alastair Scott-Johnston rang me. Most BBC radio producers rang before one o'clock and after three o'clock, because in the great days of steam radio, during those two intervening hours, they could almost always be found taking a glass in the Grosvenor Arms pub, just round the corner from the Aeolian Hall.

The Grosvenor in those days was the focal point of radio. Writers, producers, agents and artists met there to discuss new ideas and formats for shows. Many of the legendary successes were born or developed there, like *Life With The Lyons* with Bebe Daniels and Ben Lyon, *Take It From Here* with June Whitfield, Jimmy Edwards and Dick Bentley, *'Ancock's 'Arf-hour*, *The Arthur Haynes Show*, *ITMA* and many more.

I picked up the phone.

'Yes?'

'Is that you, Jon?'

'Yes, Alastair.'

'It's on! Auntie has commissioned a pilot script! Isn't that marvellous?'

It was indeed marvellous, for that pilot script of *The Navy Lark* gave rise to radio's longest-ever running situation comedy show, either side of the Atlantic. Destined to sail over the BBC's sound waves for more than eighteen years!

'Congratulations, Alastair,' I said, 'that's great! Does Lawrie know?'

'I'm going to phone him now,' he said, and rang off.

Apparently the Scott Johnston–Lawrie Wyman telephone conversation went something like this . . .

'Hello, is that you, Lawrie?'

'Yes, Alastair.'

'Great news! The Beeb have commissioned "The Navy Lark!"'

(*Sotto*) 'Sod it!'

'I *beg* your pardon!'

'I said great! Great!'

'I'll send you a copy of the script straight away.'

'Funnily enough, Alastair, I've already got one!'

'That's what *you* think,' said Alastair, a trifle smugly.

When it came to casting, I told Alastair that I would like at least two names comparable with mine, because anything I'd ever done before that was a 'Team Show', had always succeeded. A lot of actors make the mistake of trying to do everything themselves. And there were certain stars who refused to have actors of equal stature anywhere near them. Sir Donald Wolfit was one of those utterly averse to any competition whatsoever.

Alastair agreed and suggested stage and filmstar Leslie Phillips to play the idiotic Sub-Lieutenant, and Dennis Price, comedy star of British films as the superior and suave Captain of *HMS Troutbridge*.

Our fictitious *HMS Troutbridge*, as a mark of esteem was later officially made a sister ship to *HMS Troubridge*, an actual frigate in the Royal Navy, and once captained by my cousin James Pertwee who provided us with endless factual material.

The supporting character actors in the show, who played all the extra male parts, were not then as well-known then as we three, but all future stars in their own right.

They were Ronnie Barker, the late Michael Bates, and Tenniel

Evans, and they each turned in memorable cameo performances with an incredible and bewildering display of voice variation.

Richard Caldicot played the bullying, blustering dockyard Superintendant, Captain Henry Povey, at work a tyrant, at home a quivering, obedient, hen-pecked wreck who 'had the honour' to be married to the awesome and formidable Mrs Ramona Povey of the off-key singing voice and incredibly dreadful parties, played by 'Wren' Heather Chasen, who also played anything from voluptuous Mata Haris to sex-starved spinsters.

And from time to time, there was the added bonus of an appearance by my favourite comedy actress, the incomparable June Whitfield, with whom I later made a very successful album called *Wonderful Children's Songs*.

Of the three leads, there was me, Chief Petty Officer Pertwee conning the hell out of all and sundry, and thinking I knew all the answers; Leslie as the naive Sub-Lieutenant Phillips who didn't know any of the *questions*, let alone the answers, and Lieutenant-Commander Dennis Price who was always one jump ahead, and knew all the questions as well as the answers!

An interesting point, is the number of times that people have said to me, 'Oh, I never missed *The Navy Lark*, never! Marvellous show! What part did you play in it?'

'Well, it wouldn't have been Sub-Lieutenant Phillips, would it?' I'd say.

'Nooooo, I don't think so . . .'

'And it wouldn't have been Lieutenant-Commander Dennis Price (or, later, Lieutenant-Commander Stephen Murray) . . . ?'

'Nooooo . . .'

'Then how about Chief Petty Officer Pertwee . . . would that be a possibility?'

With a sheepish smile, they would then say, 'Oh, yes, of coooourse!'

It is astonishing how often I have been asked that damn' footling question!

Dennis Price had his own extraordinary and unique way of delivering comedy lines. He would inflect every one of them arse about face. So before the first show I approached Ronnie and Leslie and said, 'Do you think we ought to tell Dennis that he's inflecting his lines completely arsy-tarsy? He'll never get a laugh saying them like that!'

But to our complete astonishment, Dennis went out in front of the audience that night and wowed them, putting stress on words in the most unlikely of places and getting every laugh in the book! This was the art of Dennis Price. It was his unique way of doing things!

Thank God, the show was a success from the start, which was shown by the astonishing number of repeat programmes we were given.

By the end of the second series it was an established favourite, and rivalled even Tony Hancock, *Take It From Here* and *Beyond Our Ken*.

When the third series began, the original was transmitted on the Wednesday, we had our 'built-in' repeat on the following Sunday lunchtime, General Overseas Service repeats on the Thursday, Friday and Saturday, a delayed repeat in four months time! And London transcription put it out all over the world.

Every Sunday, we would arrive in the Paris Studios in Lower Regent Street for afternoon rehearsals and the show in the evening. The Paris was an old stamping ground for me, because I used to record *Mediterranean Merry-Go-Round* there with Eric Barker, and later *Waterlogged Spa* (also with Eric), *Puffney Post Office* (the Postman's first show of his own) and *Pertwee Goes Round The Bend*.

We would meet in the canteen where we would have endless cups of tea and sandwiches, Ronnie Barker would tell the week's latest joke, and we would exchange all the current gossip of the 'business'. Then Alastair and his wonderfully phlegmatic secretary, Evelyn Wells would appear, and after a few minutes we would adjourn into the studio where we would take our places in the stalls for the 'read-through'.

We all had our favourite and individual seats, and for eighteen years we sat in the same ones, a habit we just fell into and never broke.

I used to sit in the front row of the stalls, three in from the centre of the aisle; Richard Caldicot sat on my left and on my right – when he took over after Dennis – sat Stephen Murray. Immediately behind me sat 'Tweedle-dum and Tweedle-dee', as we dubbed Michael Bates and Tenniel Evans, and Ronnie Barker sat alongside them but with an empty seat in between them and him. (He needed that bit of extra room, he said.)

Four rows up on the left side of the aisle sat Leslie Phillips, by himself, with Heather Chasen sitting about five rows behind everyone else, wearing dark glasses. The glasses were a vain attempt to disguise a Sunday hangover, for she was inclined to 'indulge' a modicum on Saturday nights after a teetotal week of starring in the West End.

The writers, when George Evans joined Lawrie, always sat three rows behind us on the left hand side of the aisle, Lawrie in the seat nearest the aisle and George, one seat in in the row behind him.

Alastair, as Producer, sat on the stage facing us.

Before the first read-through of a new series, I suggested to the cast as a gag that everybody should sit in everybody else's seat, so I sat where Leslie sat, Leslie sat where Richard Caldicot sat and so on, until although all the same seats were occupied, they were occupied by different people. Alastair, having finished his cup of tea, came in, sat down and said, 'Well, ladies and gentlemen, it's lovely to see you all again, looking so . . . it's – er – well . . . er . . . it's great to . . . er . . . to see . . . to . . . er . . . um . . .'

'What's the matter, Alastair?' I said.

'I don't know. I – er – something's wrong . . .'

'Wrong? Are you sure you're feeling all right?'

'Yes . . . er, no.' He looked puzzled. 'I'm just feeling . . . a bit disorientated, that's all.'

'That's probably because we've been away,' I suggested.

'Yes, yes. I expect that's it,' he agreed. Then suddenly his eyes sparked and his head flicked from side to side. 'Why, you bastards!' he said. 'I knew something was different, but for the life of me I couldn't tell what it was!'

An excellent practical joke, and perfectly orchestrated!

*

It was at the end of series two that Dennis Price, committed to a play in New York, had to leave the show. Alastair, with a fine stroke of inspirational casting, rang that splendid classical actor Stephen Murray to ask him if he would like to take over the Captaincy of HMS *Troutbridge*.

Stephen, noted for his delivery of such lines as 'What bloody man is this?' and 'Is this a dagger that I see before me?' rendered the hot line between him and Alastair extremely silent, so Alastair asked him the reason for his reticence.

'It's just that nobody's ever asked me to play comedy before.'

'Well,' said Alastair, 'your luck's changed because I'm asking you now!'

Stephen took over the part so successfully that poor Dennis Price, on his return from a shatteringly brief run in New York, couldn't get his job back!

The Navy Lark was also the favourite radio programme of Queen Elizabeth the Queen Mother, who once asked us to appear in a big

WRNS reunion at the Festival Hall. We all turned up in uniform, and afterwards talked with the Queen Mother, who gave us each a beautiful silver ashtray inscribed with the words, 'WRNS Reunion, 5th November 1960. Presented by HM Queen Elizabeth, the Queen Mother to . . .' and finished with our names.

The Admiralty vetted our scripts for detail and accuracy, through a very brave man called Commander Mervyn Ellis. Not meaning that Mervyn was brave because he had to read the scripts, but because of his war record, fighting with the French Resistance; yet to look at this smiling, modest little man over his large pink gin, you would think that he wouldn't have stepped on a wood-louse.

One particular Sunday afternoon, taking our usual seats, we noticed something unusual. A somewhat serious Mervyn had turned up with an even more serious and saturnine-looking companion. Apparently Lawrie Wyman had dreamed up a story involving an anti-submarine device, and when he read the script, Mervyn Ellis almost had a coronary. It seemed that the Admiralty already *had* an anti-submarine device that was identical to the one Lawrie had written about. Naturally, the Admiralty thought there had been a leak in the Department that had allowed Lawrie to find out all about it . . .

Once the show had been put in the 'can', we went home in the belief that everything was all right.

And so it was – until the Monday morning when Alastair went to his office in the Aeolian Hall in New Bond Street to find two men dressed as he later described them in 'dirty raincoats'. After showing him their badges of authority, they proceeded to go through his office with minute detail. This DR Brigade remained with Alastair for nearly three weeks. Everywhere Alastair went, they went! Until one day, feeling suddenly lonely, he realised that his shadows had gone. They had evidently decided that Scott-Johnston really *was* only a BBC Producer after all, and not a Man from Moscow, as suspected.

Lawrie Wyman had experienced exactly the same thing, except that in his case they didn't enter his house. They merely followed him wherever he went.

It was in the early stages of the tremendous success of *The Navy Lark*, that the late Herbert Wilcox decided to make a *Navy Lark* film, and a monumental disaster it turned out to be!

First of all, Wilcox objected to Dennis Price being in the film on the grounds that he was too 'camp'! In an interview with Mr Wilcox I tried to set him straight. After all, Dennis was one of our finest light-comedy actors, a big draw at the box office, and after thirty odd shows in the role, closely associated with the project. Wilcox wouldn't have this, saying again that Dennis was too 'swish' for the role of a Naval Officer, and that he was going to recast him.

Leslie was very hot in films at the time, so naturally Wilcox chose him to play his original part of Sub-Lieutenant Phillips.

Ronald Shiner was chosen to play my part as he had recently made a couple of very successful films, including *Seagulls Over Sorrento*. I was naturally very put out over this as it would have been quite a 'break' for me. Although I'd made a reasonably large number of films since the war, this would have been my first major role in an 'A' picture.

Wilcox was of the opinion that Ronald Shiner would be a big draw at the box office, which, judging by the receipts was an incorrect prognostication. Not only was Ronnie considerably more expensive than me, he also had great difficulty in remembering his lines, which made them run many days over schedule and cost Wilcox a great deal of money.

To my mind, the film would've stood a much better chance of success if we had all played our original parts, as then *The Navy Lark* would've been as the public knew it.

★

Alastair gave the same introductory welcome speech before recordings for eighteen and a half years, and the fact that he got the same laughs in the same places from virtually the same audience completely mystified us. Even now, some of his 'bon-mots' stick in the mind. Such as when he told them how important it was for the show that they should laugh, because 'If you laugh, we eat!' Everytime he said this, he sounded as if he was producing a pearl of originality. Another of his treasures during the hot weather was 'Those of you who so wish, may divest yourselves of any garment you may with decency remove,' and he always beseeched the audience not to feed the man in the fish tank at the back – referring to the Sound Engineer in the Producer's Box in the rear of the studio.

The late Michael Bates, a wonderful comedy actor and later to become a star of *The Last of the Summer Wine* and *It Ain't 'Arf 'Ot, Mum* also contributed to the informality of the evening, albeit unconsciously, during the performance. Michael would invent the most marvellous characters which would absolutely slay us, one of the most popular being the Padre, with his canting chant.

During the rehearsals, Michael would do the character perfectly, but when it came to actual performance, more often than not he would have forgotten it! This gave us the chance to throw our scripts at Michael, chant the words for him, shout, 'Get it right, Batesey,' and so on, which added immensely to the general entertainment.

I remember Michael, not for all the laughs he gave us over the years, but for his immense courage. At our final 'Jubilee Show,' Michael was very, very ill. He could hardly walk, let alone stand, and should never have done the show, but to him *The Navy Lark* was just as much his show as it was ours and he insisted on being present. We had to help him up on to the stage, and for the first time in his broadcasting career he used a stool, laughing and joking his way through the show, when every movement must have been agony for him. Anyone who saw his brilliantly original performance in *Loot* will realise what a loss he is to the British theatre.

One thing we discovered was that the sound of somebody breaking wind was enough to render Tenniel Evans almost unconscious with mirth, so if we wanted to get Tenniel going, all we had to do was to walk behind him, let go a quiet raspberry as an assimilation, and that would be it! Tenniel would be off! On one occasion when he was making one of his long speeches as Sir Willoughby Todhunter-Brown, from behind my script I sounded off a little 'Freep!' After struggling with his self-control for a few convulsed seconds, he was away and gone. Tenniel's laughter was horribly infectious, and within a minute the whole cast were speechless and crying with laughter! The audience were soon to join him, causing Alastair to stop the show until we had all regained some sort of control.

From the very beginning, *The Navy Lark* gained an obsessive audience of loyal fans who loved the show so much that they attended every one of our recordings, actually sitting in the same places each week for years.

There was a certain blind gentleman who liked to sit in a particular seat in the front row of the stalls. One night, another member of the audience all unknowingly sat in his seat. The blind man coming in found his way to his seat, and without preamble, sat in the usurper's lap.

'What on earth are you doing, sir?' asked the squashed gentleman.

'Sitting in *my* seat,' said the blind man.

'This is not *your* seat,' replied the gentleman.

'Oh yes it is,' said the blind man, 'I've been sitting in this seat for fifteen years, and if *that* doesn't make it mine, I don't know what *does!*'

When Ronnie Barker left the show after the sixth series, Alastair asked me, 'Who shall we get as our new "voice-man". Any suggestions?'

'Yes,' I said. 'Me! I'm tired of just playing the Chief Petty Officer!' Alastair agreed. After all, I'd been a 'voice-man' for Eric Barker and Jewell and Wariss for years, but up to now, in *The Navy Lark*, I hadn't had a chance to put that ability to use.

So the Chief was now joined by Commander Wetherby, the stuttering officer from Naval Intelligence, who could never quite finish what it was he had intended to say; Admiral Buttonshaw, who repeated the last syllable of certain words such as . . . 'And as far as I'm concerned you can go to the bottom of the class – arse-arse-arse . . .' Or, 'And for the moment, that's it-tit-tit-tit-tit . . .'

A favourite character of mine was Vice Admiral 'Burbly' Burwasher. Burwasher was a 'Thinking Man'. He would turn up at a meeting with a problem on his mind which would take precedence over everything else, and while the others were waiting for him to tell them why he was there, we would hear Burwasher's thoughts working out his dilemma. I used to play him with two voices – a slightly higher one which was his 'Conscience' voice, and a deeper one which was himself answering.

My old friend Commander High Price, Chief of MI5, turned up occasionally, but George and Lawrie's favourite was the self-styled Master Criminal, 'The Master', whom I played as a slightly camp, nasal impression of my father's impression of Sir Beerbohm Tree. The part of 'The Mistress' was played by June Whitfield, who had her Headquarters in Hong Kong, in a 'front' she called her '. . . h'almost h'undetectable Wig Centre!'

After two hundred and forty shows, I only ever met one man who had the courage to say that why people laughed at *The Navy Lark* was beyond him. That gentleman was John Simmonds, now retired, but then Deputy Head of Light Entertainment. He also admitted that he knew what it felt like to be in the minority! John was present at our memorable two hundredth show, which was memorable for two reasons, one, because it was the two hundredth show, and the other, I am coming to.

After the show, attended by the Head of Light Entertainment, Con Mahoney, Douglas Muggeridge the Controller, and others of the hierarchy, the BBC threw a celebration party on the stage of the Paris Studio for us. Wives, husbands, children, friends and lovers of the cast were all invited to come along and partake of the BBC's renowned hospitality.

When it became speech time, Alastair surveyed us all with a proud smile, before he began to recap on the shining record of the show. Fascinating though *The Navy Lark* may have been to all of us who sailed in her, fascinating it most certainly was not to an alcoholically-flushed, red-headed lady sitting in the front row of the stalls. This was plain to see from the look of utter boredom she was affording her empty glass!

It took only about four or five minutes of Alastair's rhetoric to release the inhibitions that had been bubbling away inside her, and when they burst forth, their timing for shock value could not have been bettered by Alfred Hitchcock himself. Alastair had just reached the end of a sentence, and was pausing for effect, when she was in! Irish in lilt, mellifluous in tone, and bell-like in clarity, her voice split the silence.

'Hey! Alastair! What about a fuck?'

To our great disappointment Alastair majestically ignored her invitation and continued his speech without cessation or reply.

The Navy Lark was a team show. It was *our* show, and we were immensely proud of it. As I have said, it was the longest, and in all probability will remain the longest running situation comedy on radio for all time.

But this was all years ahead, and might never have happened if the Admiralty had not posted me to a new section with far-reaching personal effects. Our section of Naval Intelligence was deemed to have served its usefulness and was purposefully run down, with all of its members scattered to the winds. My new appointment was to the previously mentioned Naval Broadcasting section which necessitated a move of some 500 yards from Great Smith Street, Westminster, to Queen Anne's Mansions, overlooking St James Park. My new Commanding Officer was an actor of repute, 'Paul Temple' himself, Lieutenant Commander Kim Peacock, RNVR, and our job was to produce and record programmes of every kind for the pleasure and edification of men and women in all three services. These programmes were recorded on acetate and distributed to ships and service radio stations all over the world.

The name of the multi-service section we worked with was 'ORBS' – 'the Overseas Recorded Broadcasting Service' – and was headed by a brilliant young Flight Lieutenant in the RAF called Harry Alan Towers, later to make a considerable name for himself in more ways than one. On the committee were Regimental Sergeant Major George Melachrino, Flying Officer Sydney Torch, Flight Lieutenant Peter

Yorke, and Sergeant Eric Robinson, all very well known musicians in their own field, while Kim Peacock and I tagged along to look after the Navy's interests. We had the use of Drury Lane and the Fortune Theatre to record our programmes and after my previous appointment the whole thing was a delightful doddle. I would spend hours sitting in the stalls auditioning prospective artistes and then put together the kind of programmes that we thought the servicemen and women would like. Singers, music-hall comedians, instrumentalists, and a Welsh counter-tenor called Ivor Pye who had the most beautiful voice I have ever heard. Though it was more like the voice of a woman his programmes were, strangely enough, immensely popular with the troops; in truth, I had expected little but derision.

One day I was asked to go down and listen to the swing choir of the Royal Army Pay Corps Choir under the leadership of a Sergeant George Mitchell. They were magnificent and I'm proud to be able to say that I gave this now world-famous choir their very first broadcast.

Into my office one morning came a very, very young Ordinary Seaman called David Jacobs. He had been seconded to our section for training as a radio announcer and once trained was to join MacDonald Hobley in Ceylon (Sri-Lanka) as an announcer on radio SEAC (South East Asia Command).

He looked very frail and slight in his tight fitting blue-jacket's uniform and with his dark Semitic looks was strikingly good looking. Now, not to put too fine a point on it, Kim Peacock was of gay persuasion. So the arrival of a handsome young teenage sailor in our midst gave me cause of suspicion that O/S Jacobs was the 'friend' of our Lt/Comdr Peacock. I became all the more convinced when O/S Jacobs was continually addressed as 'David' and I, by now a full Lieutenant, as nothing else but 'Pertwee'. Naturally, I took an instant dislike to the young man. I later discovered his feelings for me were much the same, as I worked him to death at every opportunity.

One morning, travelling on the underground to a recording session, I heard issuing from the side of the mouth of O/S Jacobs a muffled 'Cor! will you look at that.' So I looked. Directly in front of us with a short black skirt pulled well up over her knees and wearing a tight white sweater that looked as if it had been moulded to her mamilla, sat a very attractive girl indeed. I was puzzled. Nubile young ladies were surely not in O/S Jacobs line, so I said as much.

'Sorry, sir, I don't know what you mean, sir,' said Jacobs.

'Well, I thought that perhaps you were more likely to be stirred at the sight of a pretty gentleman?'

'Sorry, sir, I still don't know what you mean, sir.'

'Well, bearing in mind your "friendship" with Uncle Kim, I didn't think you were much interested in females of the species.'

Light began to dawn, and O/S Jacobs' face turned bright scarlet.

'Oh my God! You don't mean he's one of those?'

For the next twenty minutes I enlightened the completely innocent young man with the facts of homosexual life. By the time we alighted from the train we had a whole new respect for one another, and had each learned a lesson – he to understand better the pitfalls that lay in store for such handsome young innocents as himself, and I to be more careful in future before jumping to completely unjustified conclusions.

So to cement our new relationship and to further his heterosexual future, I invited him to take tea backstage in the Windmill Theatre canteen, where pert and barely clothed young ladies were to be found in abundance. I was a regular visitor to the 'Mill' through my friendship with a most exotic black-haired, long-legged beauty called Pat Raphael. Pat was one of the 'Revuedevilles' principal show girls and a great favourite of her boss 'VD' (a singularly unfortunate abbreviation of his name, which was Van Damm). She was not only loved, admired and secretly desired by her audience, but with her wonderful body was also the pin-up to end all pin-ups. I felt most honoured to be one of her principal suitors, and showed her off to David with tremendous pride. Pat and her husband Vic Sephton are still two of my and Ingeborg's greatest friends and no-one who considers himself to be anyone (including James Bond), passes through Hong Kong without calling in for a drink with Pat at her world famous bar 'The Bottoms-Up'.

David took to the nudist camp atmosphere backstage like a fried fish takes to chips and with our new found friendship firmly based on a common interest in the female sex we proceeded to enjoy life to the full.

I have always found listening in on other people's conversations absolutely fascinating. None more so than one we heard on the top of a London bus. Two young girls were talking and each seemed to find the other unutterably boring. Their conversation seemed to dry up. Suddenly, after some minutes of silent travel, girl number one said, 'I'm going to ve fearter on Fursday.'

'Oh yeh,' said the other, 'Wot 'yer goin to see then?'

'I fink it's called *Sealions in Toronto*.' (She meant of course *Seagulls over Sorrento*.)

'Oh yeh? Sounds nice!' There was another long pause, followed by girl number two asking, 'Is that the one with the Chinaman in it?'

'Nah!' said girl number one. 'I don't fink so.'

'Pity,' opined girl number two, 'I like a Chinaman in a play.'

If you wrote dialogue like that for the theatre, critics would castigate you for a complete lack of human understanding.

My friend James Hill, Producer/Director of *Worzel Gummidge*, heard this mystifying conversation between two women on a crossed telephone line.

'So I stood there 'till my vest was wringin' wet.'

'Yes, well you would, wouldn't you.'

'I said to myself, could it have been a horse?'

'No, dear, it couldn't've been a horse.'

'A rabbit then?'

'No, couldn't have been a rabbit.'

'Why not? They've got big teeth.'

'Yes, but rabbits can't reach hanging baskets.'

How about that for a perfect non-sequitur?

To keep myself in trim for character parts after the war, David and I invented an excellent game. Whenever we were out on the town or at a party where the other was not likely to be known, one would introduce the other as a character that he would have to stay in throughout the evening, be it a Hungarian Lion-Tamer, a Yugoslav Teeter-Board Champion, a Komodo Dragon Breeder or on one occasion, at the Hammersmith Palais de Danse, the Youngest Colonel in the Russian Army, Colonel Ivan Nastikov. According to David's autobiography, *Jacobs Ladder* this was positively my finest hour, as it appeared I was quite unfazed when David assured the gaggle of giggling girls sitting at our table that although the Colonel's English was heavily accented, he possessed a remarkable ability to speak in any British dialect. Cockney, Cornish, Welsh, Scottish, you name it, the Colonel could speak it. So for the rest of the evening I regaled the enthralled young ladies with light-hearted anecdotes of my travels through Britain, switching from thick Russian into broad Cockney or the soft lilt of Inverness at the drop of a Cossack's hat. The 'pulling' power of the Colonel was so evident that it was a long time before David was unwise enough to introduce me as Colonel Ivan Nastikov again. For a change it had been he, and not me, that was the gooseberry.

Douglas 'Cardew the Cad' Robinson threw excellent parties and at one he gave in the 50s I introduced David as the celebrated French actor Gérard Philipe, to whom he bore a striking resemblance. David's French was not of the best, but he had a great ear for impersonation and after a momentary pause to get over the shock of hearing his set task for the evening, was off into an excellent impression of the great French heart-throb and drove the girls wild with excitement. There was a young man present who, just starting his career as a film Director, spent the entire evening trying to talk David into making a film for him. It was a most frustrating exercise for both of them. Years later, by now one of England's most eminent Directors Lewis Gilbert (for it was he) and I were reminiscing, when he reminded me of the time I had introduced him to Gérard Philipe, and how he had tried so hard to sign him up for a film. 'Then you can try again,' I said, 'for funnily enough he's here with me tonight', and with that I introduced him to the by then famous-in-his-own-right David Jacobs.

'Do you know what you've done, Jon?' he said frostily, when all became clear. 'You've ruined an illusion of years.'

Perhaps that joke was a misfire, for strangely enough I have never been cast in one of his films.

Another bus game was carried out on the top deck in mufti, and played on the public's natural inclination to interfere. David would sit directly in front of me, and, on the bus passing Nelson's column, for example, would turn and in the thick accent of whatever country he had chosen for the day, enquire,

'Pliss am visiting zis country and no knowing much, could you be telling me what zis big post is?'

'Certainly, mate,' I replied in loud, rich, 'The Cut' Waterloo Road Cockney. 'You've asked just the right geezer. I was born and bred ahrand 'ere, an knows it like the back of me 'and. That there pillar is wot's called "The Monument". It was put there to celebrate the great fire of Puddin' Lane, which started right there,' I said, pointing down Northumberland Avenue.

Passengers looked at each other aghast not believing their ears at this clap-trap.

'An' that there,' I said, pointing to the Horse Guards Parade 'is Buckinghampshire Palace, where the Queen hangs aht.'

'Zank you, you are most kindly,' said David seemingly unaware of the whispering around him.

'The man's mad, he knows as much about London as my Aunt Letitia.'

'Fancy tellin' the poor soul all them lies.'

'The berk don't know his arse from his bleedin elbow.' But the high spot came when we got to Downing Street and I pointed up to Number Ten and said, 'Now up there, mate, is the flashiest 'ouse in Lunnon , Number Ten Downin' Street!!'

'Is zat so, very interesting, an 'oo is living zere zen?'

'George Formby,' I replied.

That was it!! The 'interfering passenger' was found. We knew he would be eventually.

'Excuse me, sir,' said the IP, rising to his feet and facing David, 'but I could not help but overhear the tissue of untruths that this so-called Londoner has been telling you. The man, sir, is a lunatic, and is filling your head with utter balderdash. He is a veritable mine of misinformation and should be ignored. As for you, sir,' he said, turning to rail at me, 'you are a charlatan, a mountebank, a disgrace to your race, for two pins if I were not a gentleman I would take a horsewhip to you.' Snapping his thumb and middle finger in my face he expostulated, 'A fig for your London ancestry and birth. You are more likely to have been found under a stone.'

So saying, he collapsed on to his seat puce and perspiring.

I would then slowly rise and say to David, 'Come along Montmorency, I'm not stopping here to be insulted.' David would get up and with a toss of his head, he and I would walk arm in arm off the bus, leaving the passengers completely non-plussed. When on a long train or bus journey do try it – you'll get some wonderfully funny results, I promise you. Though I would advise that you drop the camp exit.

David and I had a very severe lesson in sexual tolerance towards the end of our time in ORBS. We were sitting in the canteen in Queen Anne's Mansions laughing it up over a male colleague's predilection towards his own sex, when a Lieutenant Commander RNR sitting at the same table brought us horrifyingly to heel.

'Can I tell you two ignorant and intolerant young men something that might perhaps help you to understand the agonising of a homosexual such as myself?'

We were virtually speechless, but managed a swallowed, 'Yes, of course sir.'

'I am a 46-year-old married man with three children but from my early youth I always felt "different" and dissatisfied with the way I was living. I felt as if my body did not belong to me at all.' It was like being at a confessional. 'Then about five years ago on holiday, I met up with a psychiatrist who persuaded me after days of private discussion and deliberation that my problem was a simple one. It was that I was a latent homosexual and the quicker I admitted the fact and faced up to it, the quicker I could begin living at peace with myself. Most of what he said was absolutely true, but there was one thing that I didn't tell him and that was my terrible underlying fear, and it is because of this fear that I get down on my knees every day of my life and thank God that I have three daughters and not three sons.'

With that devastating statement he rose from the table and said, 'So in future, instead of subjecting people like myself to your intolerance and ridicule why not try a little compassion?'

Never in my life had I felt so humbled and ashamed and we slunk away to think, lick our wounds and vow to never again be so wretchedly inconsiderate.

*

Early on the morning of 6th June 1944, having just returned from the north west of Scotland, I was having breakfast in the Dutch Oven restaurant in Baker Street, when a young airman flew in through the door and dropped a bomb.

'It's started,' he yelled. 'The invasion has started.' I straightaway rushed back to the Admiralty where I followed the first few hours of that historic event on the radio. Once the Bridgehead had been established and the Cherbourg Peninsula was in our hands, it was decided that a small unit of French-speaking Army and Navy broadcasters and engineers should be flown in to the recently liberated island of Jersey, to interview locals about their treatment under the German occupation. From there we were to proceed by Tank Landing Craft to Cherbourg and drive down the Peninsula, recording similar interviews on acetate.

Now this is a job where I'll find my French is not all that bad, I thought, and heartily looked forward to the trip. We took off from Southampton in a much dented DC3 and within the hour were circling the Jersey Airfield prior to landing. Sitting up front near the pilot, I observed with mounting horror that as we were making our final approach, dozens of German soldiers were pouring on to the airfield. 'Keep going, keep going,' I yelled into the pilot's ear, 'it's a mistake, we haven't taken the bloody island after all, look at all those damn soldiers!!' Quite unconcerned, the pilot put the plane gently down, as the Germans continued their forward-rush towards us. 'You fool', I said to the grinning pilot, 'now we'll all be taken prisoner.'

The door of the plane was opened and we scrambled out, filled with trepidation. The emaciated German soldiery immediately grabbed our luggage and equipment and smilingly bore them across the airfield watched over by a lone Army squaddie with a Sten gun. Far from us becoming their prisoners, they had become ours, and turned out to be the last German soldiers remaining on the island. Disarmed, they were hanging around the airfield prior to being shipped out to POW camps in the United Kingdom.

★

From Jersey, having recorded a few hurried interviews (in English, naturally, after all the explicit instructions that they should be conducted in French) we embarked for Cherbourg, where we boarded two ten-hundredweight lorries. From my old kit-bag I produced two Union Jacks with which we draped our bonnets and set off down the Peninsula in hot pursuit of our duties and the rapidly advancing Army. We hadn't gone but a few miles along a country road from Cherbourg when we arrived at a badly shot-up farmhouse.

'We won't be very popular here,' said our leader, an Army Captain called Ronnie, 'so let's move it on out.'

As he spoke, French persons of every age and gender began to appear out of the woodwork. They had seen the Union Jacks and came pouring into the farmyard.

'Vous êtes anglais?' they cried.

'Oui nous sommes anglais. Ça va bien?' we answered.

'Oui, maintenant que vous êtes arrivés. Venez prendre un petit coup avec nous.'

At that, we were whisked into a barn where, as if by magic, several bottles of excellent calvados were produced and the party began. It was not long before cries of 'Vivent les Anglais et merde à la Boche' echoed into the night.

Calvados is a very potent drink made from apples and could best be described as a stamping fluid. Toss a small glassful down the gullet and one's immediate reaction is to breath out hard like a dragon belching fire and stamp the right foot on the ground several times until the burning sensation in the windpipe begins to ease. After an hour or so of merrymaking, it was unanimously decided that we should take full advantage of our hosts' hospitality and partake of a fine young goat that they would be roasting in our honour. Then again the sturdy young farm lassies were beginning to get more beautiful by the minute and were becoming more 'laid back' as the party progressed.

Un bon jeu de mots there, n'est-ce pas?

I remembered little after the generous helpings of goat and calvados, and by midnight had passed gently out on a pile of straw where I snored away until morning, much to the chagrin of lusty, busty Louise who said, when I awoke, that I was certainly no gentleman. I defy anyone to be much of a gentleman after a skinful of calvados!

So the caravan moved on, laden with cadeaux of cheese, wine, a bottle of cognac, and of course a litre of stamping fluid to keep us going. It didn't have to keep us going for long, as after travelling for just under an hour, we came across a badly shot-up farm house.

'Let's move it on out,' said Ronnie, our now dead-eyed, green-faced leader.

'Vous êtes anglais?' cried French persons crawling out of the woodwork. 'Venez prendre un petit coup.'

At that we were whisked into a barn, where as if by magic several bottles of calvados appeared and the party began. If you think I've said all that before, you're right, and I'll say it again and again and again. For as soon as our Union Jack was sighted that is precisely what happened at practically every farm house we stopped at. The only difference being that this time, most of us were careful not to insult the young ladies by lack of 'gentlemanly' attention.

Early one morning a Major in the field security police and a Commander from NID ran us to earth. They wanted to know how we were getting on and if we were gleaning anything of interest from the French.

'Oh yes, indeed sir, yes indeed,' said a bleary-eyed Captain Ronnie, the previous murrain of pustules upon his face now miraculously gone. 'But we've been having terrible trouble with the recording equipment. Practically every interview to date is US so we'll have to start all over again.' It was just as well that our visitors never heard what little we *had* recorded, for I'm certain the background of the interviews would've been liberally interspersed with shouts of 'Vive les Anglais. Prenez un autre, mon cher, servez-vous! servez-vous!! All we have is yours.' Followed quickly by Gallic cries of 'Stop that, you naughty boy', or conversely, 'Don't stop, you naughty boy.' It was a riotous trip, utterly useless, of course, but *wonderful* for public relations. We returned home, laden with gifts for our loved ones, and modestly prepared to receive their plaudits, for our valiance and bravery in the face of overwhelming odds.

My father was a great lover of cheese, so my gift to him was a two-foot high Brie, packed between two sheets of straw and two pieces of three-ply wood. He and my step-mother Kitty were out when I delivered it to their flat in Cottesmore Court, Kensington, so I put it in a narrow gun-cupboard in the hall and told the cleaning lady, who had let me in, to be sure to tell my father, that there was a two-foot high cheese in there. It was about six weeks before I got a chance to go there again and when I did it was to make a startling discovery.

'Hello, Dad, etc. etc. How did you enjoy the cheese I left for you?'

'What cheese?'

'The cheese I put in the gun-cupboard, the Brie.'

'My God! So *that's* what the smell was,' said my father. We advanced to the cupboard filled with dread at what we might discover. There it wasn't. The two pieces of wood were, so also was the straw, but of the cheese there was no sign. Like any ripe Brie is wont to do, it had moved irrevocably on. For when a Brie gets over ripe, it melts, and left on its side will run completely away leaving only two pieces of wood, two sheets of straw and a crusty rind. Mine had behaved true to form and had, on its onward march, found its way through the cracks in the floor boards.

'The smell has been diabolical,' said my father. 'But it didn't seem to come from that cupboard at all, rather from under the sitting-room floor.'

He was probably right, as the cheese would've passed through that area on its stinking peregrination.

'We even called in the ARP wardens to inspect the roof' (their flat was on the top floor) 'in case there was a decomposing corpse up there.'

It seems that the cleaning lady had also moved irrevocably on, and had neglected to tell my father of the cheese's existence, let alone its whereabouts, before she left for doorsteps new.

One day in 1945 Kim Peacock sent me to the Criterion Theatre in Piccadilly where a certain Lieutenant Eric Barker RNVR was to record his Naval version of *Mediterranean Merry-Go-Round*, the other two versions being performed by Army and RAF casts. Stationed in Lowestoft, Lieutenant Barker would come down to London with his wife, WRN Pearl Hackney, and Petty Officer George Crow and his Blue Mariners Dance Band, which featured one of the world's greatest saxophonists, Petty Officer Freddie Gardiner. Now it seemed that Lieutenant Barker was going a bit over the top with some of his political jibes and jokes, so in order to get an official report on his verbal shenanigans, my CO duly dispatched me to find out if there was any truth in the allegations.

Sitting in the gloom at the back of the pit, I heard Eric Barker ask,

'Where's Lieutenant Nelson-Burton?' (now a successful Director of television and films in the USA.)

'Sorry but he can't get here today, Eric, he's on duty.'

'Can't get here? Then who's going to shout out the lines from the audience?'

My hand shot up. 'I will,' I cried.

'Who said that?' said Eric, shielding his eyes from the spotlights' glare as he peered into the darkness.

'Me, Mr Barker.'

'Who is me?'

'Er – Lieutenant Pertwee.'

'What are you doing here, Lieutenant?'

'Oh, I'm a spy,' I said.

'And very nice too,' said Eric. 'But who exactly are you spying on?'

'You, sir, I've been sent down from Admiralty to check on the veracity of several complaints made against you.'

'Me? What am I supposed to have done?'

'Upset members of His Majesty's Government by your insensitive barbs,' I replied. 'But I'll tell you what, if you let *me* shout out those lines from the audience, my report about you will be as pure white as snowdrops from a Mother Superior's garden.'

'OK, Lieutenant you're on,' said Eric. 'Incidentally are you related to Roland Pertwee?'

'Yes, sir, son.'

'Then you better be good, son, because your father is a man of real talent.'

Eric and Pearl were arguing and Pearl was definitely getting the best of it. This was where I came in. Leaping to my feet from my place in the stalls I delivered the first comedy line of a career on radio that was to span forty years.

'Why don't you leave 'im alone?' I shouted to Pearl in raucous cockney. 'You're always pickin' on the poor perisher.'

'Who on earth is that?' asked a bewildered Pearl Hackney, after my first laugh on radio had died down.

'That?' said Eric. 'Oh, that's the Minister of Education.'

This was precisely the type of joke that I had been sent down to report on and prevent, for the incumbent Minister of Education was a badly disguised cockney to the core. But I was as good as my word and reported Lieutenant Barker's script as smelling only of violets.

'Can you come back in three weeks?' asked Eric. 'I think we can find a place for you on our team!'

Every actor throughout history has waited for his break and this really was mine. Three weeks later I joined the cast and remained with Eric for the next five years, playing dozens of characters in both *Merry-Go-Round* and later in the top-rated civilian spin-off *Waterlogged Spa*.

Some that you may remember were Svenson the Norwegian seaman, who only ever said, 'Er-yaydon yowdon yaydon, neggerdi-crop dibombit.'

This was a regularly repeated line I had taken from the world news at nine o'clock. 'And here,' the announcer used to say, 'is the news in Norwegian, 'Er yaydon yowdon yaydow neggerdicrop dibombit . . .' etc. etc.

Which, as I understood it, had something to do with bombing and air raids. But no Norwegian I ever encountered, even though I will swear to its accuracy, could make any sense of it.

The years of '44 and '45 heard the beginning of the radio catch-phrase, and all over the UK people were repeating my characters' phrases. Like the bugler from Plymouth Barracks with his 'Buglin' buglin' the 'ole time buglin'.' The nervous and stuttering Mr Cook and his 'Dabra-dabra-dabra, that's right, yes!' The schizophrenic efficiency expert Robin Fly, who on hearing music immediately changed from a hard ultra-efficient machine, to a fey, musing fairy, eulogising about his Nanny with his 'Ah, music.'

Lord Waterlogged's daughter, the honourable Phoeb's 'affianced', Mr Wetherby Wett. The security-conscious Commander High-Price, late of the secret service: 'Hush, keep it dark!'

And the best known of the lot 'The Postman' of Waterlogged Spa, who always finished up saying, 'Well, what does it matter what you do, as long as you tear 'em up?'

They were great days, those early days of steam radio, and were my stepping stone to bigger and better things. For this I thank most sincerely my mentor Eric Barker. He was a brilliant writer, broadcaster and film actor with an immense future before him. Tragically, he was incapacitated by a stroke and forced into an early retirement.

If it was not for him and the 'break' that he gave me, I would in all probability still be a jobbing actor.

*

When I first began to write this book, I felt apprehensive, for although I have done many things in my life, writing about them, with the hopeful prospect of entertaining you, was something entirely new to me and seemed an awesome task. Memory is notoriously unreliable and I was convinced that sooner or later it would let me down. The early years of my life seemed vague and blurry and apart from a few fading photographs and some old scrapbooks I had little to connect me with the past. So, after due deliberation, I decided to skim through my childhood and adolescence and embark as quickly as possible on the far safer subject of my 47 year career in the theatre. I would tell of my extensive and adventurous travels around the world; of my encounters with the famous, the infamous and the eccentric; of love and marriage; of sport, motor-racing, hydroplane racing, sub-aqua diving, the starting of water skiing; my days in Ibiza before it became the Fourth Reich.

But to my surprise, as I forced my memory back over my early life, I discovered that one recollection sparked off another and yet another long forgotten incident. It was like splitting the atom of memory. Suddenly back came people, places and events that I had buried long, long ago among the jumble of my mind. Self-indulgently I travelled back through time and rediscovered my early years. And I found that I had written 200 pages about the period I had intended to skim through. Before I reached the stage of being 'full of wise saws and modern instances' (for those of you who haven't been paying attention, that's the Seven Ages of Man again), I stopped – for how could I pack the experiences of 65 active and lively years into a manageable book without leaving yawning gaps in the intricate pattern that shaped the life of

Yours sincerely